PENGUIN BOOKS

I DON'T KNOW WHAT IT IS BUT I LOVE IT

'A superbly paced book. Full of riveting anecdotes about possibly Liverpool's finest campaign, the Treble in 1983–84. The book is worth the admission price alone for Evans's retelling of Souey's jaw-busting encounter with Dinamo Bucharest's Lică Movilă, followed by the Reds' triumph in Rome. This is how a football book should read'
Daily Mirror (Book of the Month)

'An engrossing, sharply observed, very funny read [and] a stark reminder of how different football used to be . . . Evans, who saw most of the sixty-seven games that season, mixes his memories with access to the players to provide real insight into the scrapes and controversies, the crises and the triumphs that made up what many Reds still call the team's greatest ever season . . . Liverpool fans will love it, of course, but anyone with an interest not only in football but in what it can mean to people will find this hugely entertaining'
Martin Cloake, *Sabotage Times*

Tony Evans has been football editor of *The Times* for five years and was born a Liverpool fan. He writes a weekly column for *The Game*, *The Times*'s weekly football supplement. He came to journalism at the age of twenty-nine and spent his twenties following Liverpool and playing in bands, including a stint in The Farm. In 1983–84, he saw all forty-two league games and most of the matches in other competitions.

I Don't Know What It Is But I Love It

Liverpool's Unforgettable 1983–84 Season

TONY EVANS

PENGUIN BOOKS

PENGUIN BOOKS

UK | USA | Canada | Ireland | Australia
India | New Zealand | South Africa

Penguin Books is part of the Penguin Random House group of companies whose addresses
can be found at global.penguinrandomhouse.com.

First published by Viking 2014
Published in Penguin Books 2015
001

Copyright © Tony Evans, 2014

The moral right of the author has been asserted

Set in Dante MT Std
Typeset by Palimpsest Book Production Ltd, Falkirk, Stirlingshire
Printed and bound in Great Britain by Clays Ltd, St Ives plc

A CIP catalogue record for this book is available from the British Library

ISBN: 978-0-241-96654-9

For Minnie, Annie and Mum:
three women who made sure I had money for the match

Contents

Contents

Dramatis Personae

Joe Fagan	'Smokin' Joe'. Long-time back-room man. Now first-year manager, aged sixty-two.
Bruce Grobbelaar	Talented but erratic goalkeeper. Unpredictable.
Phil Neal	Steady, experienced full back. Ironically nicknamed 'Zico'.
Alan Hansen	Stylish centre back. Barely raises a sweat on pitch.
Mark Lawrenson	Brilliant but junior partner in central defence.
Alan Kennedy	Left back prone to mistakes and scoring outrageous goals. Known as 'Barney Rubble'.
Sammy Lee	Combative little midfielder. Only Scouser in team.
Graeme Souness	Captain and leader. Silky skills and brute force. Gloried in 'Champagne Charlie' moniker.
Craig Johnston	Australian overachiever with strange taste in music. In and out of team.
Ronnie Whelan	Irish midfielder with game-changing skills.
Steve Nicol	Goofy young Scot on periphery of side. Butt of dressing-room jokes. Nicknamed 'Chico'.
Kenny Dalglish	Greatest player in club's history. Nearing end of glorious career.
Ian Rush	Goalscoring predator. Emerged from cocoon of shyness to be best in Europe.
Michael Robinson	Boyhood fan; recently joined the club. Big striker whose signing was a surprise.
Roy Evans	Coach. Confidant to players. Good cop.
Ronnie Moran	Coach. Taskmaster. Bad cop.
Bob Paisley	Recently retired manager. Father-figure of club.

Prologue

May 1984

Tel Aviv

The sound of raucous young men drifted across the square, a gut-tural, alien and dangerous sound. The clink of glasses, which earlier in the afternoon had sounded like an invitation to a party, was now a warning siren. Testosterone and menace were in the air.

The mood was turning. It had been happy at first but a tipping point had been reached; too much alcohol had begun to sour the atmosphere. The locals had stopped smiling and concern clouded their faces. Things could spiral out of control quickly.

The scene had been played out in plazas and squares across Europe over the past decade. One of football's less attractive by-products was the crews of young men who travelled with the teams from country to country. When they swilled too much beer, any-thing could happen. Violence piggybacked the sport and was rampant.

Now, on a warm spring night, tension was building. Liverpool were in town. The club did not have a reputation for hooliganism but isolated incidents were always likely. The men had been singing pop songs and banging on the tables, chanting the words 'I don't know what it is but I love it' repeatedly. Now they were moving on to a drinking game.

Suddenly it kicked off. No one seemed quite sure of the spark but a scuffle started between members of the group. Punches were thrown. Shouting, shoving, finger-pointing. Word spread rapidly: there's trouble in the square.

The news reached the Liverpool team hotel quickly. One of the club's directors, Syd Moss, was angry. 'Lock them up, lock them up!'

he shouted. Like most people in the boardrooms of the game, he was sick of hooliganism. He headed for the entrance to see what was happening and as he reached the street he was made aware of how shocking the incident was.

'Don't call for the police,' someone told him. 'It's not fans. It's the players.'

Moss was stunned. In little more than a week, Liverpool were to play AS Roma in the European Cup final. In the Italian capital. In the opposition's home stadium.

Their opponents were sequestered in a boot camp in the Dolomites, away from temptation and prying eyes. Here in Israel, the majority of the Liverpool squad had been involved in an all too public drunken brawl. The most sought-after striker in Europe had blood streaming from his nose and one first-team player was sprawled on the pavement, too drunk to walk.

Now Moss, rather than the police, began rounding up the miscreants. At the hotel he packed them into a lift in an attempt to get them back to their rooms. On its short journey between floors, the antiquated elevator broke down. Despite the anger and confusion, a form of team spirit kicked in at this new crisis. The drunks began to sing the theme from *M*A*S*H*: 'Suicide is painless . . .'

The Italian journalists sent to cover Liverpool's preparations listened in shock in the lobby. How could this group of thugs hope to match the mighty Roma?

This would be less suicide, they imagined, than the public execution of a football dynasty witnessed by a global audience. Liverpool FC were a club in crisis. How could they bounce back from this?

1.

The Party's Over?

1981–82

It seemed that an era had come to an end. From 1976 until 1981, Liverpool FC had dominated football in both England and Europe. Over that period, Anfield's trophy room had been home to four League Championships, three European Cups, a Uefa Cup and a League Cup. It was an unprecedented haul, earned under the stewardship of Bob Paisley.

The 1980–81 season had continued to bring success, but there were worrying undertones. Liverpool won the League Cup for the first time, beating West Ham United 2–1 in a replay at Villa Park after the final at Wembley was drawn 1–1. May brought more glory when a 1–0 victory over Real Madrid in Paris delivered the European Cup to Anfield for the third time. Yet amid the celebrations there were deep concerns for Paisley. Liverpool finished fifth in the league, a shockingly low position for the club. And things were about to get worse.

Being champions of Europe kept the gloom at bay during the summer but the new season opened with more negativity. It was clear that a period of transition had begun. What was not clear was where it would end.

The heroes of the previous years were gradually being eased out of the club. Ray Clemence, still an England goalkeeper, left for Tottenham Hotspur. The four-man midfield that had evoked fear across Europe was dismantled as Ray Kennedy, Jimmy Case and Terry McDermott departed, leaving only Graeme Souness to harness a new cast across the middle of the park.

The replacements struggled to gel. By Christmas, the team had already lost four games. On Boxing Day, when Manchester City came to Anfield, a full-on meltdown seemed to be under way. The match was not even close. City won 3–1 and, to increase the shame even further, a bottle thrown from the Kop hit Joe Corrigan, the City goalkeeper.

The famous terrace was the epicentre of football culture. Its reputation for fairness and goodwill – especially to opposition goalkeepers – was legendary. Now, the mood turned nasty as Liverpool's hegemony appeared to be slipping away.

At the other end Bruce Grobbelaar, Liverpool's new goalkeeper, looked as though *he* had hit the bottle. The former Rhodesian soldier had been bought from Vancouver Whitecaps with the intention of schooling him in the reserve side for a year or two. Instead, Clemence's departure meant the new boy needed to learn on the job.

Grobbelaar had a rash tendency to try to catch balls that were beyond his range. He fumbled like a drunk and gifted City two goals. He was undergoing the harshest education.

The team were booed off. They would start 1982 in twelfth place in the league, having lost three games out of nine at Anfield since the start of the season. To put this in context, Liverpool had lost only eleven games at home during the entire 1970s.

Worse indignities loomed. On the next Friday, *Kick Off*, the football preview show on Granada Television, focused on Liverpool's problems. There was little positivity from the pundits. The team had lost its core of quality players and it was known that Paisley, at sixty-one, was beginning to entertain thoughts of retirement.

The show finished with images of defeated and despairing Liverpool players and the soundtrack was Frank Sinatra singing 'The Party's Over'. Few football analysts disputed the programme's verdict. But a man nicknamed 'Champagne Charlie' was boiling with anger. No one was going to stop the good times at Anfield. Not if he had anything to do with it.

Graeme Souness liked the high life. Not everyone liked him. Archie Gemmill, a team-mate for Scotland at the 1978 World Cup in Argentina, said: 'If he was a chocolate drop, he'd eat himself.'

Opponents liked him even less. As well as being supremely skilled, he had a mean streak a hit man would kill for. England forward Frank Worthington summed up much of football's view of Souness: 'He's the nastiest, most ruthless man in soccer,' Worthington said. 'Don Revie's assassins at Leeds were bad enough, but there is a streak in Souness that puts him top of the list.'

Paisley spoke for Liverpool, though, when he listed the Scot's qualities: 'Most midfields are made up of a buzzer, a cruncher and a spreader,' the man who brought Souness to Anfield said. 'This boy is all three.'

Even in training, Souness exuded attrition. He craved it, drew it to himself and relished its results. It was an attitude that rubbed off on the younger players. 'He was tough,' said Steve Nicol, another Scot. 'When I first came to Liverpool, I used to try and get in about him at training. I bounced off him. He used to laugh when I tried. But he liked it that I was trying.'

It was Paisley who gave the Scot his nickname. After a poor performance, he criticized 'playboys and champagne Charlies'. The cap fitted Souness perfectly.

Souness was born in Edinburgh in 1953 and spent time at Tottenham Hotspur as a youngster. Those who played against him in those early years remember his ability and his brilliance in playing one-twos. They recall with awe the inability of opponents to thwart this tactic even though they knew what was in Souness's mind. They talk of an elegant teenager who assumed a superior smirk when he was on top.

He was homesick in London and eventually made his name at Middlesbrough in the north-east. There, under Jack Charlton, he added a more physical edge to his game. Top-flight midfields were no place for the meek and Souness would not be bullied by anyone.

He arrived at Anfield in January 1978 to bolster a team that had won the league title and the European Cup the previous season and quickly became a regular. Within four months of joining the club he was playing in a European Cup final and creating the winning goal for Kenny Dalglish in a 1–0 victory over Bruges. The sublime pass that unlocked a determined Belgian defence illustrated Souness's delicacy of touch. He would never be out of his depth, even on the biggest stage. That he would reach the heights so quickly did not surprise the Scot. His swagger indicated genuine fearlessness and ambition.

Paisley, with characteristic astuteness, knew where to turn for a quick fix during the rancorous holiday season of 1981. He removed the captain's armband from Phil Thompson and handed it to Souness. The Scot initially had second thoughts, fearing that he lacked seniority in the team.

'I'd twisted my ankle and was leaning against the post in training,' Souness said. 'It was shooting practice and I was saying to Bruce, "That one's going over, you'll never save this one."

'Bob came up and said, "Do you want to be captain?" I said I'd love to but there were people in front of me, like Phil Neal and Kenny. Bob told me not to worry about it. So I said yes.'

The manager knew exactly what he was getting. The new captain would, Paisley cracked, probably toss up with a gold American Express card instead of a coin.

Thompson, a boyhood Kopite from Kirkby and the proudest of Scousers, took it badly but it did not matter. 'Results proved Bob right,' Souness said. 'There was never any bad feeling towards Thommo from my side.'

During the late 1970s, the big characters in the dressing room were all Merseysiders: Tommy Smith, Terry McDermott, Jimmy Case and Thompson. The centre of power at the Melwood training ground and on the pitch had now moved north.

Scottish influence had been growing at Anfield since the arrival of Kenny Dalglish in 1977. With Souness in the midfield and Alan Hansen emerging as the best centre half in the game, Scots already formed the spine of the team. The elevation of Souness to captain now confirmed their dominance.

'The Scots set the tone,' said midfielder Craig Johnston – an Australian, despite his name. 'They decided what was funny, what was acceptable, who played well, who played badly. They were like strict schoolmasters. They understood how you had to behave if you were a group of men who wanted to win things.'

There was no place for shirkers in the dressing room. 'They were warriors,' Johnston added. 'There was a bit of the Braveheart culture about them. They were clansmen. If you were tired, not contributing or slacking, they didn't want to know you. The Jocks kept everyone in line. They kept the rest professional. They were savage about getting the job done in the most direct way.'

Nobody embodied this warrior culture more than Souness. Giving him the armband was a master stroke.

The effect was immediate. The next match was an FA Cup tie away to high-flying Swansea City. It appeared to be the sort of game that a struggling Liverpool would dread: John Toshack, a former Kop hero, had overseen a remarkable period of rapid success at Vetch Field. Swansea were third in the table, just a point off the lead, and it looked as if Toshack had transplanted Paisley's methods to south Wales while freshening them up with youthful ideas. Few predicted anything other than a home victory. Liverpool won 4–0.

Paisley judged it perfectly. 'A dressing room full of footballers from tough backgrounds is like a pack of wolves,' Johnston said. 'They smell blood. There's an animal instinct at work. They hunt the ball down like a pack, get it and then want to show off when they've got it. And Souness was an alpha male.

'A manager's job is to sense when the pack are on top and working together and promote that feeling. Or realize when it isn't and make a change to get it back. Bob was a master.'

It was a turning point. The team went on a stunning run. In the league they racked up twenty wins, lost just twice and drew only three more games. Along the way they picked up a second League Cup with a 3–1 victory over Spurs at Wembley.

In the penultimate game of the season they defeated Tottenham at Anfield by the same scoreline as at Wembley. The Kop celebrated wildly but the most symbolic moment came after the final whistle when the Championship trophy was presented. Souness jogged back on to the pitch holding the venerable piece of silverware by its stem, one-handed. Most players cradled the old cup like a baby but the Liverpool captain waved it as if it were a bottle of champagne. He ran towards Ronnie Whelan, one of the young midfielders now blossoming in the restyled team, and threw the trophy towards the Irishman. The entire crowd gasped. Fear and shock filled Whelan's face as he reached two-handed for the priceless artefact. He caught it with relief and hugged it in the traditional manner. It was over in a blink of the eye and the celebrations moved on. Everyone on the Kop cracked the same joke: 'Thank God he didn't throw it to Grobbelaar!'

It was a message from Souness. The trophy – and the team – were his. He could do what he liked. It was a breathtakingly arrogant act. The party was back on. Souness was its life and soul.

Just to underline the point, hours before the last game of the campaign, a midweek game away to Middlesbrough, Champagne Charlie gathered the team and suggested it was time for an end-of-season drink. Like a number of other players, he had been annoyed that the club had not organized a shindig to celebrate winning the title. So Liverpool, the champions of England, went for an afternoon session and warmed up for a league match by downing pint after pint. By late afternoon they were back in the hotel sleeping off the drink ready for a 7.30 p.m. kick-off.

If Paisley and his staff knew about the boozing, they turned a blind eye. It is hard to imagine that the manager and his Bootroom team of Joe Fagan, Ronnie Moran, Reuben Bennett and Roy Evans failed to notice the stink of stale beer. The Middlesbrough players could smell the alcohol on the breath of their opponents. No matter. The match was a 0–0 draw.

What did matter was that Souness had further cemented his leading role in the dressing room. Where he led, the rest would follow.

2.

Retiring Types

1982–83

It was a strange decision. Bob Paisley announced his retirement before the start of the 1982–83 season, ten months before it was to take effect. The question of succession at Anfield hung over the campaign.

There were plenty of names thrown into the hat. John Toshack's feats at Swansea made him a popular choice, even if the managerial momentum was stalling for the former Liverpool striker. Paisley wanted his chair filled by an internal candidate. 'I envisaged my successor being one of these three: Joe Fagan, Ronnie Moran or Roy Evans,' he wrote in his autobiography. It was always the likeliest scenario. It was the way things were done at Anfield.

On 1 December 1959, Bill Shankly was given the job of rebuilding Liverpool, a team struggling in the Second Division. Most managers arrive at a new club bringing a set of fresh ideas and an urge to sweep away the past. Shankly brought something different: he brought a philosophy for life.

Instead of clearing out the coaching staff and bringing in a core of acolytes, the Scot took a long look at the coaches he had inherited and assessed their abilities. Paisley, Fagan and Reuben Bennett might have expected to lose their jobs. Instead, they became part of a brains trust that was to become known as the Bootroom, for it was in the unprepossessing oversized closet filled with players' footwear that Shankly's football cabinet gathered to discuss the game over tea, brown ale and Guinness.

Shankly reigned for fifteen years. By then Anfield had been transformed from a ramshackle provincial ground to one of Europe's most famous stadiums. Nobody expected his sudden resignation in

1974, but fifty-five-year-old Paisley stepped into the role and, after a trophyless first season, went on to achieve unparalleled success.

Fagan was next in line for the job, but that would mean replacing the sixty-four-year-old incumbent with a man just two years his junior. 'When Bob decided to retire, it frightened me that they might ask me to take over,' Fagan said. 'I said years ago that I'd never take on a manager's job, that coaching was my game.'

It was the vacancy almost everyone in football would have killed to fill. Yet the man poised to inherit the job did not want it.

Joe Fagan was born in Walton Hospital in 1921 and brought up in Smith Street, a rugged part of Kirkdale, two miles from Liverpool city centre, squeezed in between Scotland Road and Bootle. His father was a bookie's runner and young Joe was about as streetwise as they come. As might be expected from this background, he was tough. At a travelling fair he took on the challenge of fighting the troupe's resident boxer. Young Fagan knocked him out and then proceeded to take on all comers, leaving opponents sprawled on the canvas.

In time he would earn a boxer's nickname, 'Smokin' Joe', but that was for his constant dragging on cigarettes. The habit never harmed his sporting career, though. Fagan excelled at most games but football was his first love. At seventeen, he signed for Manchester City. A year later war broke out and gouged seven years out of a promising career. He joined the navy, which turned out to be a spectacularly bad choice. Fagan was a victim to seasickness in even the slightest swell. Later, he would say, 'I throw up on the Seacombe ferry. I'm the world's worst sailor!'

He patrolled the waters of Egypt aboard a minesweeper for much of the war, a period that had a huge impact on his life. He was reluctant to talk about the experience. The mental scars of those years were rarely visible. The war left him with physical scars, too, but they were not the result of enemy action: a bout of boxing and a surgeon's strange decision altered his appearance for ever.

In *Joe Fagan: Reluctant Champion* by Andrew Fagan and Mark Platt,

Michael, his youngest son, explained: 'He was a hard man. A really hard man. He was a good bare-knuckle fighter and used to earn money from it. He was wiping the floor with everyone, winning all this cash until some officer got wind of it, went into the ring with him and pasted him everywhere, breaking his nose. The surgeon was supposed to fix his broken nose but instead took the bone out. That's how he got his flat nose.'

When the war finished he returned to football, but the prime years of his career had been taken away by Hitler. He left Manchester City in 1951 and spent three years as a player-manager for Nelson, a non-league club playing in the Lancashire Combination. In his first year, Nelson won their title and were unlucky not to be voted into the Football League, which comprised the top four divisions of English football. After that, he became an assistant manager at Rochdale to Harry Catterick – who would go on to great success with Everton. In 1958 he joined Liverpool's coaching staff, lured back to the city by the promise of a club house in Anfield. He could not have imagined he would still be at the club a quarter of a century later and living in a humble semi-detached property within walking distance of the ground.

By 1983 he looked like a caricature of an old-time trainer, the sort of man who carried an iron bucket filled with iced water and a 'magic' sponge. Certainly, he appeared anachronistic in the age of the suave, telegenic and articulate manager. The likes of Brian Clough, Malcolm Allison and John Bond were 'personalities' in their own right, media-friendly and famous. Fagan was the opposite. He was, like the avuncular Paisley, easy to under-estimate. Those who failed to take either man seriously almost always lived to regret it.

Twenty-five years after joining Liverpool and less than half a decade away from retirement, Fagan had a dilemma on his hands. Should he take Paisley's job? None of the former Liverpool players making a career in management had the sort of convincing CV that would make the board look outside L4.

The other internal candidates had question marks alongside their names, too. Roy Evans, just thirty-five, was too young and there were worries at boardroom level whether this affable and talented coach had developed the authority to fill the void left by the most successful manager in English history. There were hopes that Kenny Dalglish, the club's talisman and greatest player, would develop into a Bootroom leader but, at thirty-two, the Scot was still massively influential on the pitch and some way off hanging up his boots. Fagan was the board's choice and, before Christmas 1982, the local press were suggesting an agreement had been reached. The *Liverpool Echo* trumpeted 'Fagan Ready for Anfield Hot Seat' in mid-December. The newspaper was more certain than its headline's subject.

'My first reaction at the time was that I wouldn't take it,' Fagan said. 'But I thought about it carefully and realized that someone else might come in and upset the whole rhythm. I finally decided to take it and keep the continuity going for a little longer.'

Roy Evans is blunt about Fagan's rationale. 'He basically did it to keep us in our jobs,' Evans said. Dalglish agrees: 'He didn't want to take over. But he knew if someone else came in everything would change. It didn't need to change. It was the measure of the man that he did take it. He could have been selfish and said no. Credit to him.'

Had a new manager arrived with a belief he could do things better than the traditional way, it might have been a recipe for disaster. Fagan's simple and straightforward way of dealing with things appealed to the side. They also knew how tough he could be. During the crisis of 1981, as Paisley made the switch of captaincy, Smokin' Joe had decided to make an intervention of his own.

Unexpectedly, Fagan gathered the players and gave them a glimpse of his fiery side. 'He could tear you apart if he wanted to,' Phil Neal said. He did just that in the dying days of 1981 when he placed the blame for Liverpool's sliding standards at the feet of the players.

Each individual in the team was given a devastating critique of his shortcomings. Fagan let loose with both barrels and put the onus to improve on the senior members of the squad. Added to the change in team leadership, it made a massive difference to performances. 'We were stunned,' Neal said. 'We got on the bus to Melwood and he said, as if nothing had happened: "Now let's have a high tempo at training." No one was going to slack off then and risk another blast.'

'Managerial magic is largely a myth,' Craig Johnston said. 'The key to it is understanding team spirit. Knowing when it's strong and when it's weak. And knowing how to recover it.'

Smokin' Joe was no revolutionary but he knew how to harness a group of players. He also knew that it was important not to over-manage.

From the Bootroom to the dressing room, everybody knew that it was unlikely any outsider would have Shankly's perceptivity and a clear-out of staff and players would probably have followed the appointment of a new man. Fagan was set to take the job. For just about all the wrong reasons.

After the reaction to the crisis of Boxing Day 1981, no one was going to write Liverpool off again. However, Paisley's final season, a campaign that once again brought the League Championship and League Cup to Anfield, waned horribly in its final six weeks. Liverpool lost five of the last six league games and drew the other one. They were so far ahead that they could afford to slip up so badly but Paisley was enraged. The title was confirmed by results elsewhere on the day the team were beaten 2–0 by Tottenham at White Hart Lane. There were three games to spare but the manner of winning gave the retiring manager no pleasure. 'It is pitiful,' Paisley said. 'Needing a point to win the title, we didn't even look like getting it. We are struggling along with eight players and three also-rans. Not good enough.'

It seemed that Shankly's classic recipe for a great side had been subverted. 'Good teams are like a piano,' he said. 'You need three to play it and seven to carry it.' Liverpool were severely out of tune now.

Nine days after the season ended and a month after the Tottenham debacle, on 23 May 1983, Fagan was confirmed as the next manager of Liverpool. 'Bootroom boys still rule OK!' said the *Echo*. As usual at Anfield, there was no contract, just a verbal agreement and a handshake.

The man who was so comfortable in the privacy of the Bootroom or the training ground swapped his tracksuit for a tailored one. He appeared vaguely ill at ease in shirt and tie when he was introduced as manager – but it was the limelight rather than the clothes that chafed. The first questions he fielded were inevitably about his age. He admitted that it was an issue. 'When the chairman and the board asked me, I wasn't too happy at first,' he said. 'It was really a question of my age but they decided I was not too old.'

He felt sprightly enough to do the job properly. The players believed this, too. 'Joe Fagan was a magnificent beast,' Phil Neal said. 'He could charm you. He was a great person. We all wanted him. Age didn't matter.'

'He'd been running around every day in training,' Dalglish said. 'He had plenty of energy.'

For Fagan, the age of some of the squad was a bigger worry. The faltering finish to the previous season had thrown up a number of questions for the new man. Who were Paisley's three 'also-rans' at Tottenham? If the squad was running out of steam at the rate its previous six games suggested, it needed to be strengthened over the summer.

Phil Thompson, the captain displaced by Souness, was now beginning to creak. He was only twenty-nine but injuries were taking a toll and Alan Hansen and Mark Lawrenson were developing into a formidable centre-back pairing. The loss of the captaincy still smarted with Thompson. His role in the team would come under scrutiny very quickly.

There had always been question marks over Alan Kennedy. The wholehearted left back was a fan favourite. No one could fault his effort and his run-through-the-wall style had earned him the nickname 'Barney Rubble' after the *Flintstones* character. There was a cartoonish, comic aspect to his play, though, and he lacked concentration. Despite him scoring the winning goal against Real Madrid in the 1981 European Cup final, the Bootroom staff were always looking for another option on the left of the defence.

Craig Johnston, in the midfield, had a similar all-action style to Kennedy. He also shared the tendency to make bad decisions. He had more ability but he could infuriate his manager. Up front, David Hodgson was a support striker to Ian Rush and Kenny Dalglish. Fagan was praying his first-choice pairing stayed fit.

If the new manager had qualms about his playing staff, the squad were delighted almost to a man that the coach they knew and admired was now in charge. The core of influential players lent their support to Fagan. 'We all thought it was a brilliant appointment,' Dalglish said. 'It was what we all wanted. Everyone respected and believed in Joe.'

Outsiders might have raised questions about Fagan but those inside the club were certain that things were being done the right way. 'We knew what we were getting,' Dalglish said. 'But most of the world didn't know about Joe's qualities because he had always been behind the scenes and that's why they questioned the appointment. They didn't need to. He was good.'

There were no sceptics in the dressing room. 'Joe was a genuine, honest, plain fella,' Neal said. 'But he knew about football.'

'A hundred per cent of the Liverpool players wanted Joe to be the manager,' Hansen said. 'Sometimes it can be a bad thing if the board appoints the man the players want. But everybody knew Joe was hugely respected. He knew all the ins and outs and what the players wanted was continuity.'

Souness was a particular advocate and a strident voice in support of the manager. The change of regime seemed natural to the captain. 'I was a huge supporter of Bob Paisley,' he said. 'He stuck his neck on the line to sign me. Bob and Joe were the same. They were quiet until you upset them. I didn't upset them.

'Both were incredibly wise men when it came to football. They kept things brief. They kept things simple. They were direct.'

The goodwill towards Paisley was transferred organically to his replacement. 'We were desperate to do well for Joe,' Souness said. 'He did most of the talking and day-to-day communication with the players during the years Bob Paisley was in charge. We all recognized Bob for the manager he was – a genius. But we had a tremendous respect for Joe as well.'

However, even he admits to a few lurking doubts. 'The only possible thing you could have worried about was the decision making, picking the team and being ruthless.'

This trio of Scots, Dalglish, Hansen and Souness, were the backbone of the side. They were world-class. They backed the appointment and went on holiday in the summer of 1983 happy. Would the mood be so upbeat once the regime got up and running in July?

New Dire

Summer 198

Preparations for the 1983–84 season began ~~~~~~~~~~~~~~~ ~~en
Fagan reported for his first day in his new r~~~~~~~~~~~~ was still available as a sounding board for his old friend but now the buck stopped
with a new man. 'Suddenly, I became the man who had to make the
final decisions regarding team affairs,' Fagan told the *Liverpool Year-
book* some months later. 'And I must admit that inside the first few
weeks of taking over I had my eyes opened regarding the way the
club was run from a management point of view.'

Administrative and boardroom issues would change the nature
of Fagan's working day and mean he was less involved in training,
but his support staff meant the team were in good hands. The men
of the Bootroom were imbued with the ethics that Bill Shankly had
brought to the club and there was little need for innovation at the
Melwood training ground. Ronnie Moran, Reuben Bennett, Roy
Evans and Chris Lawler had mastered the Liverpool way.

'You wanted to be in the company of Joe, Reuben, Ronnie and
Roy,' Johnston said. 'It was an era when it was about men. You
enjoyed being with them. They were a group – a council of football
men – who knew what they were doing. There was no scientific
formula they had written down. But they married Shankly's philosophy with hard work.'

The first day back after winning the title the previous season
meant that an Anfield ritual needed to take place: the presentation
of the medals. 'Ronnie would go round from player to player and
ask you how many appearances you'd made in the league in the
previous season,' Neal said. 'He'd say: "How many, Nealy?" I'd say
forty-two and he'd give me a medal and move on. There was no

...atulations. No ceremony. That was all last year
...ng.'

...as straight back to work.

...ing was simple. It was predominantly one-touch games to
...prove passing and awareness. There was also the legendary 'sweat
box' – four wooden walls each divided into squares with numbers
on them. Balls were thrown in and the player inside had to aim for
whatever number was specified.

Moran was the most hands-on. 'Ronnie knew the secret of not
getting caught in possession and taught it relentlessly,' Johnston
said. 'Pass and move. He had been an average player but I used to
watch training and be amazed by how good it was and he was.'

Johnston, raised in Australia in a non-football environment, was
fascinated by the way the coaching staff operated. Moran was the
voice of the group.

'Ronnie would be shouting at us, calling us big-headed bastards,
making sure we did the right things,' Johnston said. 'He insisted on
simplicity. In one-touch games you need to know what you are going
to do with the ball when it arrives, otherwise you don't want it. Training was all about getting the ball, giving it and getting into space in
support of the next man with the ball. If you did well, Ronnie would
reward you with an all-in game, with as many touches as you liked.'

In the background, the rest of the staff looked on.

'They'd sit talking and drinking coffee,' Johnston said. 'Watching.
Always watching.'

Moran was the voice of the Bootroom but advice from any of the
group needed to be heeded. 'Ronnie Moran was like their appren-
tice,' Souness said. 'They were incredibly wise in football terms.
There never had been, nor ever will be, people who understood the
game more. They knew you had to keep the ball moving and move
yourself. They always said if a target stayed still, it was easier to hit.
So keep moving. They would tell you the important stuff and then
say, "You can work the rest out for yourself."'

Those who failed to apply the instructions did not last long. And
any shirking was spotted immediately.

'They didn't spend sessions shouting instructions at you,' Steve Nicol said. 'But they knew what you were doing. If you were feeling it and not putting in a hundred per cent one day, Ronnie or Roy would just come up and whisper in your ear: "We're watching you." You'd shit yourself.'

Even being the best did not satisfy the Bootroom. 'They always made you feel the players they'd had before were superior,' Souness said. 'You could win the European Cup but it was "well, you could do this a bit better, or that a bit better". They made you think you could still improve.'

This was one of the great positive aspects of Fagan's appointment. The system was working and it needed little micro-management. Simplicity and hard work were the ethos and Moran was the sergeant-major who ensured the group were disciplined. 'There was no big tactical plan,' Dalglish said. 'It was always find space, be available, get the ball, keep it moving, find a shirt. Don't dare idle and work hard.'

The spirit that Shankly had imbued ran through the club and infected players who came from as far away from Liverpool as it was possible to travel. 'It was such a great learning curve for me,' the Australian Johnston said about life at Melwood. 'I was like a sponge, sucking it all up.'

From all the days spent watching the players on the training ground, Fagan was wholly familiar with the strengths of the squad. Now he was focused on the weaknesses. He knew where it needed reinforcement and where it was strong.

The first-choice goalkeeper, Grobbelaar, was massively talented but erratic. He was worth the risk. His deputy, Bob Boulder, had just signed for the club after playing almost 200 games for Sheffield Wednesday. Boulder was a good man to have in reserve but was never a viable candidate to replace the Zimbabwean. He would leave Anfield after two years without playing a game for the first team.

The defenders were a mixed bag. The back four, Phil Neal, Alan Hansen, Mark Lawrenson and Alan Kennedy, were an impressive unit. Neal, at thirty-two, had been a high-class England full back for seven years. He had benefited from good midfield protection during his Liverpool career but was solid defensively and position-ally. He took both penalties and responsibility in his stride. 'People never gave him the credit he deserved,' Dalglish said. 'He scored goals. Not only penalties, but in free play. He was so consistent. Unbelievable.'

Hansen was the finest centre half seen at Anfield. His elegance caught the eye, as did his awareness of opposition tactics. He could bring the ball out of defence in a style that evoked comparisons with the great Franz Beckenbauer. 'The washerwomen must have loved him,' Nicol said. 'He never got his shorts dirty, never mind his shirt. He saved them a job. Didn't need to wash it, just hang it back on the peg. He knew what was happening so would never need to get off his feet and go sliding in like other centre backs. He'd just casually take the ball away.'

As part of the ruling class in the dressing room the defender had a golden aura about him. It had not always been this way.

When the youngster came down from Partick Thistle in 1978, he had gone into digs close to Anfield. The local teenagers would play football nightly on the tarmac car park which comprised the corner of Stanley Park between Anfield Road and Utting Avenue. Hansen would come out and join in the ad hoc matches that would con-tinue until the light faded or the pub beckoned. The local boys were not overly impressed. One of the more talented youths used to make a point of nutmegging the young Scotsman, pushing the ball between Hansen's static legs and collecting it on the other side. The teenagers of Anfield – mostly home and away Liverpool fans – expected little from the centre half.

When he made the first team, they were forced to admit that playing on a car park was very different from facing the best players in England and Europe. If young Hansen looked uncomfortable on concrete, he looked absolutely at home on the turf of the world's finest stadiums.

That made Lawrenson the unluckiest man in football. Without Hansen, he might have been the best central defender in Liverpool history. He was quick, a master of the impossible, last-gasp tackle and rivalled his partner for grace on the ball. But Hansen did everything better. Lawrenson wore a bushy moustache and it was easy to suspect that if the handsome Scot would have grown his own facial hair, it would have been more lustrous, attractive and masculine than his colleague's.

Alan Kennedy played on the left. There was a constant hope that someone better would come along, but they never did. Lawrenson was tried at left back when he arrived from Brighton and Hove Albion in 1981 but both Paisley and Fagan kept returning to the irritating force of nature that was Barney Rubble.

With the intention of reinforcing this unit, Fagan quickly dipped into the transfer market and bought Gary Gillespie from Coventry City a week after taking control officially. Gillespie was another stylish centre half but his price tag of £325,000 reflected his status compared to the two mainstays of the central defence – Lawrenson had cost £900,000. But the new boy would have a role to play.

Gillespie's arrival was a further blow to Phil Thompson. The man from Kirkby was the prototype centre half that Liverpool's success was built upon. In 1974, after being knocked out of the European Cup by Red Star Belgrade, Shankly had an epiphany. He realized he could not win the Continent's premier trophy with a hulking, traditional British bruiser of a stopper like Larry Lloyd. The twenty-year-old Thompson was ushered into the first team and Lloyd was shipped out to Coventry. Thompson went on to win three European Cups, captaining the side in Paris. Ironically, Lloyd won two European Cup winner's medals with Nottingham Forest, but Shankly's instinct was right.

Now, Thompson was nearing the end. His anger with Souness over the captaincy switch in 1981 lingered. Dealing with the former captain presented a real problem for Fagan. Before long they were barely on speaking terms.

There were youngsters on the playing staff but they were not ready to take their place in the team. John McGregor, a twenty-year-old Scot, was on the periphery of the squad but way down the pecking order. His countryman Steve Nicol had been a fixture in the reserves for two years, making a handful of appearances at senior level. At twenty-one, it was time for him to make a breakthrough to the first team. Reserve life was beginning to chafe. This would be a crucial season for Nicol. He was expected to replace Phil Neal but the veteran full back just kept on going.

The midfield was built around Souness. He was the most influential midfielder in the First Division and world-class. He was not quick but he used space beautifully and had a delicate touch that delighted those who appreciated supreme technical ability. He glided around the pitch, his arrogant gait infuriating the opposition and their fans. His tendency to brute force enraged them even more. 'If they come to play, we'll outplay them,' was Souness's refrain. 'And if they come for a fight . . .' He did not need to articulate the rest.

Few who challenged him physically came out on top. As a driving force, only a handful of players in the history of the game could match Souness.

If the captain was characterized by his strutting economy of movement, he had the perfect foil in Sammy Lee. At 5ft 2ins, Lee looked a pushover. But he was from St Andrew's Gardens – better known as the Bullring – a complex of arc-shaped tenements on the fringe of Liverpool city centre. Many overlooked his ability because of his size and pumping-dynamo, perpetual-motion style of play. No one settled on the ball when Lee was around. His man-marking job on Paul Breitner in the 1981 European Cup semi-final against Bayern Munich was a masterpiece of harassment. Bayern had drawn 0–0 at Anfield and gloated afterwards. The team believed they would be in the final and Breitner believed he could dominate any midfield in the world. Wrong on both counts. Lee smothered the German playmaker and Liverpool drew 1–1 in Bavaria to advance to Paris on the away-goals rule. They were never in trouble.

Ronnie Whelan played on the left. He was right-footed but worked hard on his weaker foot and most people were fooled because his left foot was so deadly. The Irishman could adapt his role to suit the circumstances. As a thrusting, attacking midfielder he was a threat no defence could ignore. His shooting was accurate and canny. Yet he also had the ability to use space when the opposition had the ball, a rare quality. He gave the side balance and, along with Souness and Lee, was a mainstay of the team.

Craig Johnston was making a claim to be the fourth member of the group. His parents had sold their house in Australia to pay his fare to England when, aged fifteen, he was offered a trial with Middlesbrough. Jack Charlton, the manager of the Teesside club, told the young Aussie that he was the worst player he had ever seen and to 'fuck off and don't come back'. It was the first day of what was supposed to be a six-week trial. His flight home was more than forty days distant. The emotional teenager phoned his parents, told them Charlton loved him and Middlesbrough was wonderful. 'Then I put the phone down and cried for two days,' Johnston said.

With nowhere else to go, he hung around the training ground and hid from the manager while he worked on his game. Souness was one of the senior Middlesbrough players who helped protect the young Australian from Charlton's ire. 'The thing is,' Johnston said, 'Charlton was right.' So he set about improving. Two years of hard work won him a place in the team at Ayresome Park. At the age of twenty he had developed his skills enough to earn a move to Anfield.

Johnston had a remarkable engine but – perhaps due to growing up in a non-footballing country – suffered from tactical naivety and a tendency to make poor decisions on the ball. And was he an attacker or a more deep-lying player? Two years at Liverpool had not answered these questions. Now Fagan needed to make a definitive verdict.

Up front, Liverpool were the envy of Europe, if not the world. In Kenny Dalglish, Fagan was able to call upon the most complete attacker in football. Dalglish is – by far – the best player ever to wear a Liver bird on his chest. Even at the age of thirty-two, he was more important to the team than Souness. Their relationship was crucial. Champagne Charlie was not known for humility but he understood that even with his prodigious gifts he was second fiddle in terms of talent to Dalglish. It was a marvellous and mutually beneficial relationship. They made each other look better. They were friends and room-mates, too.

Although countrymen, the pair were very different types of Scot. Souness was from a comfortable Edinburgh background and was more refined. Dalglish was Glaswegian and earthier. In his autobiography Souness claimed his room-mate initially questioned his sexuality because of his groomed moustache and use of eau de cologne. 'He thought I was a poof,' he wrote.

There was a streak of competition between them. Often, a session at Melwood would finish with a challenge that would pit the two Scots against each other. 'At the end of training Souness would challenge Kenny,' Johnston said. 'They'd line up five balls on the eighteen-yard line and try to hit the bar. Souness would go first and then we'd all bet money on whether Kenny would beat him. It was a great, fun way to end training. Everything they did had a competitive edge.'

Dalglish had the perfect foil in Ian Rush. The twenty-one-year-old had blossomed into the most dangerous striker in Europe. His on-pitch relationship with Dalglish appeared telepathic. Off the pitch, the age difference meant they were not quite so close.

Rush had the benefit of playing with a genius but there is no doubt he would have been an impressive goalscorer anywhere. The worry for Fagan was that an injury to either of the front men would cause a significant drop-off. David Hodgson, the back-up in place, was hard-working but ordinary. The manager knew he needed another quality striker.

For all the questions about individual ability and weak areas in the squad, this was a tight-knit group with its own pecking order. At the top were Dalglish, Souness and Hansen. They were quick-witted and unforgiving in their humour. Weaknesses were seized upon and exploited relentlessly. 'The Scots lived for the opportunity to take the piss,' Johnston said. 'If you made a rick, they would slaughter you. You had to take it. These were the days before political correctness. If you were precious, it wouldn't have worked.'

Being a first-team regular brought status and respect, as did exceptional talent. Rush and Lawrenson came high in the pecking order, as did the veteran Neal. Fringe players came lowest on the list but Grobbelaar and Kennedy, automatic choices in the side, were frequently on the sharp end of the dressing-room jokes. 'The Scots were clever with a caustic sense of humour,' Johnston said. 'They were never the butt of the jokes. They were always having a laugh at someone else's expense. The group dynamic needs leaders and butts.'

Those who were made of the right stuff relished the culture of the squad. 'They were halcyon days,' Kennedy said. 'We got the job done. It doesn't mean we didn't have differences. When you've got fifteen to twenty guys working together, tackling each other, taking the piss out of each other, day to day, you're bound to have differences. It could kick off. But on the pitch we left all the disagreements aside and worked for each other.'

Getting the right sort of player to complement this mix of personalities was crucial. The main target of the summer of 1983 was Charlie Nicholas, the Celtic forward, whose skills evoked comparisons with Dalglish. Liverpool, Manchester United and Arsenal all offered the same fee: £750,000. Paisley, after his tenure ended, and Fagan, before his had begun, attempted to convince Nicholas to come to Anfield. Instead, he chose Arsenal. The decision raised eyebrows and questions about the new manager. Nicholas went on record saying that he had been more impressed by Terry Neill, the Arsenal manager, and his assistant, Don Howe, than the Liverpool delegation. Fans and pundits saw this transfer as sending out a message: the Scot had chosen the club of the future rather than the club of the past.

Dalglish suggests there was another reason for the young man's decision. 'He told us a different story when we were with the Scotland squad,' Dalglish said. 'He told us he was worried he wouldn't get a game at Anfield.' The man who most people believed that

Nicholas had been targeted to replace was disappointed to see the striker sign for Arsenal. 'It was a shame,' Dalglish said. 'He would have been an asset.'

Liverpool also made a serious attempt to sign Michael Laudrup, the brilliant Danish forward. Instead, he chose Lazio. The board were not prepared to meet his contractual demands. There was more money in Serie A.

More disturbing was that Swindon Town's Paul Rideout chose Aston Villa over Anfield, as did Steve McMahon. Were Liverpool losing their attractiveness?

At Anfield, there was widespread awareness that the squad was short-handed. Peter Robinson, the club secretary and de facto chief executive, admitted: 'Our present squad is dangerously small.'

Fagan needed reinforcements. Fast.

4

Drinking It In

Late summer 1983

Continuity came as a relief for the players. They liked the way things were done at Anfield. Individuals were not micro-managed on the training fields at Melwood nor in their private lives. Fagan, like his predecessors, trusted his men on and off the pitch.

One successful modern Premier League manager learned a big lesson from the new Liverpool boss in the early part of the 1983–84 season. The young coach, not long retired as a player, saw the Liverpool manager enter the directors' box at an away game. Just as Fagan was about to sit down, another man caught Smokin' Joe's attention and the pair embraced warmly. They started an animated conversation.

The game kicked off, with Fagan seemingly more interested in his friend than the match. Afterwards, the ambitious coach was eager to learn and began talking with Fagan. He asked the Liverpool manager about the man he had been chatting with. Ah, Fagan said, he was an old navy friend. They had not seen each other for years and had enjoyed the catch-up. 'But you didn't seem to be watching the game,' the younger man said. Fagan laughed. 'When you've got players like mine,' he said, 'they manage themselves.' Liverpool, of course, had won the match.

There were times when a good manager didn't even need to watch. There were also times when he turned a blind eye.

Liverpool gave their players plenty of leeway. After training, there were few restrictions. Certain pastimes were frowned upon, although the attitude to extra-curricular activities confounds modern expectations. 'As soon as training was finished, it was time to go boozing,' Alan Kennedy said. 'I think the club were happier I was drinking rather than risking getting injured doing something else.'

That something else was golf. 'They hated golf,' Nicol said. 'They thought it was a strain on the legs, walking seven miles or so.

'If you were a drinker, they were happy. Joe and the rest would enjoy the tales of drunkenness and have a laugh about it. If you were a golfer, you'd have to keep it quiet or you were in trouble.'

The likes of Dalglish and Hansen – who had been a champion golfer in his youth – had to be furtive about their exploits on the fine links courses around the city. 'It went back to Shankly,' Dalglish said. 'He thought it tired the legs. They would rather you were pissed than golfing. The boys tried their best to do both.'

'When training was done, about one o'clock, you could go off and do almost anything you wanted,' Kennedy said. 'Just nothing that could risk injury. They would rather you were shagging and drinking. An afternoon on the ale was perfectly acceptable.'

Playing other sports brought disapproval. The boozers rarely got into trouble.

'Once the work was done, Joe liked a beer and a good time,' Neal said.

The long drinking sessions were used to foster team spirit and the single players, stuck in club accommodation far from home, embraced the boozing culture with gusto. 'You didn't want to go back to your digs and sit there all day,' Nicol said. 'So you went to the pub. Any excuse. There was one rule: when we go out, we do it together. Just the team. No mates. No outsiders. As long as you took your medicine in training the next day, you were fine.'

It could get rowdy. 'We were always playing drinking games,' Kennedy said. 'It could get boring in the pub and we had to find a way to liven things up.'

For local landlords, the sight of Liverpool stars arriving in the pub was a mixed blessing. They were good customers but things could get out of control. A group of players – including Hansen, Kennedy and Thompson – were banned from the Hen and Chickens pub in Kirkby after getting too boisterous on a drunken afternoon.

The sessions often dragged on into the night. Regulars in the city's clubland were used to the sight of an internationally renowned football player leaning with his elbow on the bar in even the seedier sort of nightclubs.

'It was easy to go off the rails and we all had our moments,' Grobbelaar said. 'A friend of mine said to me if I stayed in Liverpool I would become like George Best. He said to me: "You must have a goal, in getting home after games and not staying in Liverpool." So I bought a house in Wales and had to travel, which took me fifty-five minutes every day in the morning to get to Liverpool and then back home.'

It did not last long. The goalkeeper was soon back residing in the city, living on one of the new estates in West Derby, similar to the setting of the TV soap opera *Brookside*. It was not just the lure of team-bonding sessions. The club preferred players to live in the city, close to the fleshpots, rather than in distant suburbia. Being late for training was a bigger transgression than turning up with a hangover.

'The nights out were great,' Nicol said. 'We'd meet in the Holiday Inn on Paradise Street and go to the Beehive across the road or the Crocodile.' Places like this had a rugged clientele, many of whom were fans of either Liverpool or Everton. Trouble was rare but, in a city where everyone has a view on football, robust exchanges of opinion often took place.

'People would let you know what they thought,' Nicol said. 'And we'd give as good as we got.'

For less visible sessions, the players would go to Southport, with Toad Hall being a favoured venue, or to one of the leafy pubs on the Wirral.

Rumours frequently swept the city: a fight here, an unconscious drunken player there. 'Most of them were true,' Johnston laughs.

The Bootroom boys had an unsophisticated attitude to alcohol. 'They thought it was fine to drink beer,' Kennedy said. 'Most of it is water and you can run that out of your system or piss it away. At least, that was their thinking.' Lager was the tipple of choice for most of the team but as they drifted further away from sobriety they were not shy of turning to harder liquor. Drinking spirits would raise eyebrows at Melwood. 'They thought vodka or brandy was harder to get out of your system,' Kennedy said. 'There was always the smell of alcohol at training. We thought you could run it off, burn it out of your system with a good session. You'd work hard to get rid of the effects. Then go for a beer when you were finished.'

Disapproval of spirits made little difference once the drinking started. 'It was mainly beer but we'd drink anything,' Nicol said. '"Charlie" liked a glass of champagne. The spirits would start flowing with the drinking games. It was competitive here, too. No one wanted to be the first to crash out.'

Much of the time they made no attempt to disguise their sessions. Society's attitude to football and the men who played it was very different then. It was still a working-class game and those who played it had not been elevated to the giddy heights of international stardom. They were still accessible to the general public. One woman who socialized with the players at the time puts it into context. Naomi Jacobs met the team when they were in Spain, preparing for the season. She came from a wealthy, middle-class background and soccer stars meant little to her. 'Football wasn't glamorous then,' she says. 'It's not like now. It was very different. Normal people shied away from it. No one talked about football at dinner parties.

'The players were wealthier than most people but they weren't rich. They were just well off. They weren't like film stars.'

In an age where players are multimillionaires and WAGs are as famous as their partners, it is hard to get a sense of how the biggest stars in football were perceived in 1983. Jacobs, a Londoner, who shared some wild nights out with some of the younger players in the 1980s, is able to supply some perspective.

'We met them in southern Spain,' she said. 'They were there training. My friend's parents had a holiday flat so we spent time there. Hull had been there the year before and we'd had fun with them. They were a group of young, fit boys having a good time. We used to laugh after we met the Liverpool lot and say to each other: "We've been promoted!"

'They didn't marry supermodels or get followed around by legions of women. No girls I knew wanted to marry a footballer. They were a bit ordinary, a bit gauche, not glamorous. A friend of mine was having an affair with Omar Sharif! That was glamorous!'

She found the most striking thing about the players' social life was the amount they drank. 'They were a good laugh. They liked a drink and, boy, could they put it away,' she said. 'We went out with the young ones. They were fit, single and great fun. They behaved like gentlemen, mostly. I could never believe how much they drank, though.

'I started paying a bit of attention to football because I knew them. It was hard to imagine they were the best in Europe. I thought, "How much must the other teams be drinking for this lot to win?" Then you'd watch them play and the daft lads we knew turned into something else. I didn't know much, but you could see they were good.

'They knew how to have fun but they knew how to win. Even when they were out having a good time, you knew that winning was the most important thing. They were terrified of Kenny and Souness. They didn't want to upset them.'

Likewise Fagan. The players enjoyed the freedom. Part of their support for the new manager came from concerns about how an outsider might affect the Anfield routine. Some of the gossip from other teams around the league was worrying. 'We were being treated as men at Liverpool whereas at other clubs we heard that players were treated like kids,' Kennedy said.

The trophies were proof the system was working. If Fagan failed, the culture of the club might change. No one was keen to let that happen. They liked the new manager and they liked things as they were.

Souness set the tone early. He gathered the team together and gave a short pep talk. 'I just said that we all thought the world of Joe and to make sure we don't let him down,' Souness said with more than a hint of understatement. There were no dissenters. That it needed to be said showed that the captain had some concerns, though. 'Graeme knew the pressure would be on Joe and that's why he gave his little speech,' Mark Lawrenson said. 'Just to ensure every player was one hundred per cent behind the new boss.'

This was a group of winners who believed that they were doing things the correct way. 'Everyone could remember Brian Clough going to Leeds ten years before and the whole thing falling apart because he didn't get on with the players,' Dalglish said. 'We were winning the league and cups. It would have been mad to change things around. Joe was the right man.'

Fagan was concerned. The job was about to start in earnest and there were high expectations to live up to.

5.

First-Year Jitters

Pre-season, 1983

Manchester United, Testimonial, Windsor Park; Hamburg SV and
Feyenoord, Rotterdam Tournament, Rotterdam; WAC Morocco,
Testimonial, Stade Mohamed V; Atlético Madrid and
Dinamo Bucharest, La Linea Tournament, Estadio Municipal

A year earlier, when Paisley announced his decision to step down, Stuart Jones in *The Times* had articulated the thoughts of many about the task confronting the next man in succession to the chair of Shankly. 'To follow one Anfield legend is far from easy,' Jones wrote of Paisley's tenure. 'To follow two is a challenge for any mortal.'

In his diary, Fagan reflected on this, recalling his predecessor's first, trophyless season. 'Everything seemed to go wrong then, including the results,' he wrote. 'Since I took over there are similarities. The storm clouds are gathering – so I must keep a clear head and not panic.'

Paisley's first year overshadowed the pre-season. 'You couldn't help thinking about 1974–75,' Roy Evans said. 'It was in the back of your mind. We didn't want the trophies to dry up.'

The depth of the squad took a further blow when Ronnie Whelan was ruled out with a hip injury that required an operation. The Irishman's loss was a blow. Without him, the midfield looked unbalanced and, even with the presence of Souness and Sammy Lee, a touch lightweight.

The first match was in Belfast on 3 August, a testimonial for Billy Drennan, an Irish FA official. Normally, this sort of friendly would be against a local side, someone like Linfield; a bunch of semi-professionals that would allow the English champions to ease back into match fitness with the minimum of fuss. This game was not normal. It was against Manchester United.

Even warm-up games between these clubs had an edge. They were due to meet in the Charity Shield seventeen days later and these early skirmishes were the prelude to what most people thought would be a season-long tussle for the title. United had won the FA Cup in May, beating Brighton after a replay, and appeared to be a side growing in stature.

The first forty-five minutes of the Fagan reign seemed to blow away the worries that had clouded the summer. Liverpool swept to a 3–1 lead and provided a footballing lesson for their great rivals. Aside from Whelan, the new manager picked the side that finished the previous season for Paisley. At half-time, the job looked easy. Three-quarters of an hour later, Fagan's fears had been underlined.

Ron Atkinson, the United manager, made six changes at the break, using his bigger squad to great effect, and the fresh legs made the difference. United scored three goals to win 4–3, Lou Macari scoring the winner in the last minute.

Four days earlier, Fagan had predicted this weakness in a diary entry, writing: 'Looking through the pro staff (we have twenty-seven), we have numbers but not quality. Maybe there are thirteen players who are pretty good but after that we could do with a good player in midfield and up front. The temptation is to go out and buy now, but that could be fatal to the rest of the season if we signed the wrong ones.'

The lesson of Belfast was that Fagan needed to take a risk and dip into the transfer market as soon as possible.

Things were not going to get any easier. The next game, the first of a pre-season tournament in Rotterdam, was against Hamburg, the European champions. After a 0–0 draw, the game went to a penalty shoot-out, which Liverpool lost. Fagan did not care. 'I told them not to worry about the missed penalties,' he said. 'Funny that the year should start like that,' Kennedy said. 'On the spot right from the beginning.'

Fagan was concerned about injuries to Ian Rush and Gary Gillespie. The severity of Rush's groin problem meant the hunt for a back-up striker could no longer be postponed. The man earmarked by Fagan to add strength to the side raised eyebrows when the news came out. Even the player was shocked by the news he was a Liverpool target.

Michael Robinson was a boyhood Liverpool fan. He had travelled to Anfield to stand on the Kop as a boy and dreamt of wearing a red shirt. The forward had begun his career at Preston North End and became the most expensive teenager in football when he moved to Manchester City. His time at Maine Road was unsuccessful and he moved to Brighton, where he scored goals in a team that reached the FA Cup final but was also relegated. Now they were out of the top flight, Brighton needed to sell. Robinson expected to go abroad to a Spanish club but the summons to Schiphol airport outside Amsterdam came out of the blue. 'I would have swum across the Channel for Liverpool,' he said.

For a player like Robinson who, by his own admission, was more workhorse than world-class, the £250,000 deal offered him an opportunity beyond his wildest dreams.

He was quickly introduced to the Liverpool way. After signing, Fagan asked whether he wanted a drink. Hoping to impress his new employers with his professionalism, Robinson requested a coffee or sparkling water. He was told in no uncertain terms to have a beer.

His next lesson in Anfield's philosophy was even more surprising. The newcomer asked Fagan and Paisley how they wanted him to play. The question surprised the men from the Bootroom. They hoped, they told Robinson, that *he* knew how to play or they'd wasted a lot of money.

The striker persisted. What about the system? Fagan explained how things were done with the patience of a schoolteacher instructing an infant. When Liverpool had the ball in midfield, they passed to another man wearing the same-coloured shirt, the manager told him. When he was close to the opposition's goal, he had to kick the ball into the net. If he couldn't do that, he had to kick it to someone who could. Liverpool's strength was simplicity.

There was little subtlety about Robinson's game. He was strong in the air but lacked the style of Dalglish and Rush. Yet he had a touch of sophistication about him – at least off the pitch. 'He always looked like he should have a butler,' Nicol laughs. In a dressing room that contained too many 1970s-style perms and moustaches for the changing era, Robinson was different. 'He liked the fancy stuff, the high life, his clothes perfectly pressed,' Nicol said.

The man from Blackpool was not the average footballer. He read broadsheet newspapers and had refined habits. He was politically aware and was, like the majority of the fan base, out of step with the prevailing mood of Thatcherism. With a different personality he might have been a dressing-room outsider but most of the squad immediately took to the new recruit. He formed a particularly good relationship with Souness.

While the new arrival would not send waves of fear through the division or Europe in a way the sight of Charlie Nicholas in a Liverpool shirt might have, Dalglish appreciated the commitment and work rate that Robinson brought to the team. 'Robbo made a huge contribution over the season,' he said. 'He gave us another option.'

The trip to Rotterdam ended with a 3–3 draw against Feyenoord and another losing penalty shoot-out. Yet again, no one attached much importance to the missed spot-kicks. It was a friendly tournament. No one expected to end a game this way for the rest of the season. 'It was something that happened in friendlies,' Kennedy said. 'Shoot-outs didn't happen in real matches.'

Still, things were not firing for the team. It was a deep concern for Fagan. Whelan's absence left a huge hole in midfield and there was still a lack of class up front when Rush was unavailable. There was little time to dwell on this. The squad returned from Rotterdam, had a day off, and were then back on a plane, this time on a tour of Morocco and Spain. In Casablanca, Fagan recorded his first win as a Liverpool manager as his side strolled to a 3–0 victory over WAC, a local team. Robinson scored on his debut – albeit against very weak opposition – but Roy Evans felt the mood was improved by the win. 'No matter how important a game is, it's always a relief to get the first win under your belt,' he said. 'The longer you go without a win, the press pick up on it and it can start affecting the players psychologically.'

In Spain, friendly games at La Linea against Atlético Madrid and Dinamo Bucharest produced mixed results. A 2–1 defeat to the Spanish side was followed by a 3–2 win over the Romanians. The pre-season was over and Fagan was far from happy. The loss of Rush and Whelan put the spotlight squarely on the problem areas. 'The disappointments were Hodgson, who will not try more shots, and Nicol at left midfield,' Fagan wrote in his diary. 'I wasn't too happy at the last two games he played. We must tighten up in midfield. All our midfield players are more concerned with attacking rather than defending. Got to get a happy balance.'

One game remained before the league campaign started: the Charity Shield. This game was often referred to as 'the showpiece opener to the season'. For once, the cliché was valid. Liverpool would play Manchester United inside a packed Wembley Stadium. United had not won the league since 1967 but there was a confidence about the self-styled 'biggest club in the world' that persuaded many that this would be the year when they would break the hoodoo. What is usually no more than a glorified friendly became rather more important in August 1983.

6.

Giving It Away

August 1983

Manchester United, Charity Shield, Wembley

The phoney war was over. And it was clear to Fagan that he did not have the weaponry to fight a real one. Ronnie Whelan was a long-term absentee but the focus was on Ian Rush. The striker did not feel confident that the groin injury he had picked up in the first pre-season match was sufficiently healed to play. However, his manager and Ronnie Moran were applying heavy pressure on the Welshman to turn out against Manchester United at Wembley.

'I wasn't happy about facing United,' Rush said. The coaching staff had watched hundreds of players over the years and were convinced that the injury was minor. Fagan thought the problem was in the striker's mind and managed to get Rush to play by using some Paisley-style psychology: 'The way he put it was: "Why not give it a go? It's not worth messing about with. If it's gone, it's gone. Give it a try and find out." He told me that if I couldn't get through the game, he'd just leave me to rest the injury until Christmas.'

Rush agreed to take part. 'Joe's motivational powers were so good,' Neal said. 'He could lift you even when your instincts went the other way.'

It was a massive risk but the Charity Shield was taking on significance beyond its usual status.

The void up front was filled but Fagan was still worried about the midfield. Neutralizing Bryan Robson, United's 'Captain Marvel', would be key to winning the match.

To compensate for Whelan's absence, the versatile Mark Lawrenson was moved from the back four to the middle of the park. An increasingly marginalized Phil Thompson was recalled to partner Alan Hansen after being left at home for the pre-season tour. Liverpool were worrying about United rather than the other way round.

In the preview to the game, *The Times* suggested 'the psychological advantage lies with United'. All the indications were that this was true.

Fagan's first big day in the national stadium turned into a grim afternoon. Liverpool started well but United soon asserted themselves and scored first. Robson, the man Liverpool had set out to stop, ran wild. Yet it was the manner of the second goal that caused everyone to question the new Liverpool manager, even himself.

With just under half an hour left, Fagan decided to inject some pace into the midfield and fresh legs up front. Craig Johnston and David Hodgson replaced Thompson and Michael Robinson. The tactical gamble of playing Lawrenson in the midfield had failed and the switch allowed him to drop into his normal centre-back position.

The logic was impeccable. The timing was gruesome. Fagan made the substitutions at a United corner kick. As at most football clubs, one of the basic rules at Anfield was never to make a substitution at a defensive set piece. A single change is a mistake. A newcomer needs to be certain of which position he needs to take up and which man he needs to mark. A double switch amplifies the confusion. Especially one that changes a midfielder into a defender.

Liverpool's marking was shocking. Amid a chaotic penalty box, Robson popped up to poke the ball into the net. The substitutions were rendered useless within seconds. United were well on top for the rest of the game.

It was easy to write off poor performances in friendly matches. It was a different thing to lose to your greatest rivals and the biggest threats to your hegemony as the result of a schoolboy error. Liverpool, the fabled Red Machine, had seized up. The *Echo* called the double switch 'the howler of the afternoon'. It was a chastening experience for Smokin' Joe.

'It was a bit of inexperience,' the sixty-two-year-old Fagan said later. 'All right, I should have known better after twenty-five years, but in the early stages of command you tend to do these things. It amazes me now but I won't make the same mistake again.'

But the manager had already made another mistake by speaking his mind in public: 'We are not hard enough or enthusiastic enough to win anything. At the back of my mind I have this feeling that certain players are going through the motions. They have lost the spark to win more things.'

The blast did not go down too well in the dressing room. 'It was probably a bit of an over-reaction,' Phil Neal said. 'It was Joe's first big game in charge and he took the defeat more personally.'

The manager did not really need to say anything about his team. They knew the standards that were required and they knew when they were failing to match them. 'Every year started the same,' Dalglish said. 'We went out to win. That's all that mattered. We were under pressure only because we wanted to win.'

To the outside world, it seemed that competitive games had not even begun and the wheels were coming off. The naysayers were out in force, even in the *Liverpool Echo*'s letters page. They were led by a man who signed himself as Len Griffiths from Bebbington. 'I think the system is running out of steam and the change of boss will not affect us,' he wrote. Griffiths bombarded the paper with his negative thoughts on Liverpool throughout the late 1970s and 1980s. Even at the most glorious moments in the club's history a Griffiths missive would arrive at the paper's Old Hall Street office predicting chaos and failure and would find itself in a prominent position on the letters page of the newspaper's Saturday-evening sports edition, the Pink. Players who were winning footballer-of-the-year awards were castigated for their lack of vision and clumsiness of touch. Every managerial decision was doubted. Griffiths became a legendary figure among Liverpool fans, some of whom claimed he was an Evertonian, a practical joker or a madman. It was thought that there were a number of people who would assume the Griffiths alias for unfathomable reasons. Most people suspected he was what would today be styled a wind-up merchant, taking his pleasure from fooling the *Echo* and enraging Kopites. The pseudonym – if it is indeed a false name – is still often found in the correspondence section of Liverpool's local paper, no doubt now delivered by email rather than the Royal Mail.

In the wake of the Charity Shield defeat the Pink's letters page was filled by people expressing Griffiths-like opinions. It was no longer just a lone moan in the wilderness. It was clear: no one was going to give Fagan and his team an inch. Not even some of their own fans.

Inside Anfield, the thought process was very different, but there was a similar anger over what had happened at Wembley. 'Losing was abnormal,' Nicol said. 'No one expected it. No one liked it. It had better not happen too often.'

The main scapegoat was Phil Thompson. His appearance at Wembley, the scene of so many glorious days for the boyhood Kopite, was to be his last for the first team. For a man who had been captain and an integral part of the second Shankly revolution, it was a bitter blow.

Ten years earlier, Red Star Belgrade had taught Liverpool a footballing lesson in the European Cup, winning both legs of a second-round tie 2–1. The 4–2 aggregate score did not flatter the Yugoslav side.

Shankly reflected on the defeat and decided Liverpool could not win Europe's biggest prize with hulking, traditional English centre backs. Lumping the ball forward did not work against increasingly tactically astute Continental sides. Blunt force was no longer an option.

Thompson was promoted from the reserves at Larry Lloyd's expense. He was very spindly and less overtly physical than the average central defender but he was comfortable with the ball at his feet. He could bring the ball out from the back line into midfield and pass it forward as securely as most midfielders. Thompson's career had been kick-started with a Liverpool indignity in Europe. Now, with three centre backs ahead of him in the pecking order – all seemingly based on his prototype – a season of ignominy beckoned. The very bitter end was still some way off. Thompson's personal European humiliation was still to come.

Football is a brutal business. When a player is in the team, valued and part of a winning group, life is good. If injury strikes or he loses his place to a better performer, it is a different matter.

Up-and-coming reserves, those with a potential to improve and grow, are encouraged and made to feel part of the adventure. However, for men like Thompson, whose best days are behind them, the reserve team is a halfway house to departure or retirement. There is no pity from team-mates, either.

Few businesses turn a valued colleague into an outsider so quickly as football. Injured team members are marginalized. Being shunned puts psychological pressure on players to rush themselves back into first-team contention as quickly as possible. It means players hide injuries or try to return too soon. Liverpool were notorious for their harsh treatment of injured players. They were derided by the staff and their manhood was questioned repeatedly.

It was almost worse for players on the fringe of the team. Substitutes had a tough time. 'It's difficult because you do all the graft with the first team, listen to the team talk and get that build-up of nervous energy,' Johnston said. 'Then, just before kick-off, you're told you're not playing. Or you're on the bench.'

In 1984 only one substitute was permitted, making the job a lonely one as well as a thankless role. If the twelfth man did not get on the pitch, there was another drawback. Anyone who did not take part in the game was expected in at training the next morning. Those who had played got a lie-in but anyone who had not participated in the match had to report for training by 9.30 a.m. on Sunday. It left the No. 12 with a big Saturday-night decision: join in the traditional post-match drinking session and slog around Melwood the next morning with a hangover or miss out on team bonding and reinforce your status as an outsider. Either choice was painful.

The frustration was greater when a benchwarmer felt he could improve the side. 'It's worse if you don't feel the player who replaced you is any better,' Johnston said. 'And it's not just when you're at Melwood or Anfield. It's rammed home everywhere you go. You go out and all the fans are asking why you're not in the side. That's why a beer or twenty-five help. That's why you get into the drinking cycle.

'You do all the preparation the same as the first team and it winds you up. You go through all this preparation for six, seven, eight weeks in a row and you're not contributing on the pitch. You say no one's bigger than the club and try to be part of the team spirit but if someone says you're not good enough you ask yourself questions. You get tortured by doubts.'

Although the rewards could be great, it was a tough existence – however easy it looked from the outside.

Fagan was not as heartless as Shankly in his attitude to sidelined players. With Whelan, in particular, he took an almost paternal interest. 'Joe was always asking how I was doing and what was wrong,' the Irishman said. 'He was very keen to make sure I wasn't rushed back too quickly and that I was treated right. It was reassuring to know I remained part of his plans.'

Fagan's concern was not completely altruistic. There were few solutions to the weaknesses on the left side of midfield. The Lawrenson experiment at Wembley had failed. The team needed Whelan back.

The problem would not have been so acute had Fagan possessed a left back he could trust. Alan Kennedy, by his own admission, was the least stylish player in the team and prone to make mistakes. An air of chaos frequently surrounded Barney Rubble.

It started on the day he signed for the club. The ex-Newcastle United defender drove to Liverpool in a new car in dreadful weather. It was a perilous journey because the windscreen wipers did not work. Then the vehicle broke down in Leeds. 'I thought because it had a gold stripe along the side it was a good, reliable car,' Kennedy said ruefully. It was a haphazard start to a some-times anarchic career.

There was plenty to recommend the left back, though. His unusually slow heartbeat pointed to his remarkable fitness. He could run all day.

Paisley signed him in 1978, with the bullish declaration: 'If he doesn't play for England, I'll throw myself in the Mersey.' But the canny Northumbrian had been around long enough to hedge his bets by adding '. . . When the tide is out.' Paisley's prediction was eventually proved correct, though during the six years it took to fulfil it became part of dressing-room lore and a source of humour. 'We were always saying Bob wasn't a man of his word because he hadn't jumped in the Mersey,' Dalglish said.

The manager's qualifications appeared prudent right from the start. In the first half of the defender's debut against Queens Park Rangers in 1978, he was awful. He trooped off at half-time expecting words of encouragement from Paisley. Instead, the exasperated manager exclaimed: 'I think they shot the wrong Kennedy!'

It was a wake-up call. 'It was said in jest but the message was that I had to improve or I was out,' Kennedy said. 'You didn't last long if you weren't up to scratch.'

Fagan often felt the same sense of frustration with the player. On one occasion, rather than single Kennedy out, Fagan addressed the team as a collective. 'Joe got us all together and was talking about what we weren't doing right. The whole speech was intended for Alan,' Souness said. 'Of all the lads in the group, Alan was the one not paying attention and I remember Joe blowing his top. "Hold on a minute, son, this is all for your benefit. Work it out!" Everyone was taken aback.'

Kennedy was liked and his qualities were appreciated by his team-mates. 'He was a great laugh,' Dalglish said. 'Always great for team spirit. And he was underrated as a player. He was a big danger going forward.'

The left back scored big goals. He had already struck the winner in a European Cup final and had hit the net at Wembley in League Cup finals against West Ham United and Tottenham Hotspur. He may have been a weak link in Anfield terms but, with the right player in front of him, he was a huge asset to the team.

7

A Season of Change

Wolverhampton Wanderers (a); Norwich City (a); Nottingham Forest (h); Southampton (h)

Anfield was not the only footballing institution seeing change. The game was entering a new age. The First Division had a sponsor for the first time. Liverpool would now be competing in the Canon League after the camera manufacturer paid £1 million per year to have its name attached to the league's four divisions for three years. The Milk Marketing Board was paying to have its name attached to the League Cup, which now became the Milk Cup. The world of business was waking up to football's value in marketing terms. Liverpool had been at the forefront of this trend when they became the first club to carry a sponsor's name on their shirts by signing a deal with Hitachi in 1979. Now all the top-flight clubs' shirts carried advertising.

The businessmen who negotiated the deals were delighted by the breakthrough in television coverage. For the first time league games would be shown live, with ten matches scheduled to be screened on Fridays and Sundays. Liverpool, as reigning champions, could expect to find themselves involved in many televised games. Crown Paints, whose logo presently adorned Liverpool shirts, would get a wider projection than they had anticipated when they became involved with Anfield the previous year.

The decision to screen live games divided opinion. Many inside football believed that putting the sport on the small screen would affect attendances, which were in decline anyway. Fewer than 495,000 paying customers watched the first day of the 1983–84 season, the lowest number since records began.

It was one of many contradictions within the game. Sponsors and

TV were developing a bigger appetite for football at the same time that paying customers were staying away from the stadiums. Hooliganism kept many people at home. It had become a media obsession and scare stories involving violent behaviour were a tabloid fixture. The extreme right-wing groups found the disaffected young men who followed their teams around to be easy prey. The National Front and British Movement tried to recruit outside turnstiles across the country.

Liverpool, as usual, took a different path. The city had a strong culture of left-wing activism and Bill Shankly found this ethos dovetailed with his own views. The Scot encouraged the supporters to believe that their fervour had a direct influence on matches. He created a sense that football was a group activity that involved thousands of people and not just the eleven men on the pitch. He expressed it in political terms. 'The socialism I believe in is everybody working for the same goal and everybody having a share of the rewards,' he said. 'That is how I see football and that is how I see life.'

It was a potent message. The use of political imagery was one of Shankly's traits. After the defeat by Arsenal in the 1971 FA Cup final, the team came home to a civic reception and the Scot addressed the thousands of supporters who had gathered to welcome the team. 'Chairman Mao,' Shankly declaimed, 'has never seen a greater show of red strength.'

The supporters lapped it up. As the economic decline worsened in the 1970s, the iconography of the Liverpool shirt became increasingly a symbol of defiance for many on the terraces. The blood-red shirt and the Liver bird represented more than just a football team. They represented a city fighting back against injustice. Where the Crown Paints logo fitted into this view of the club was a question that was rarely asked.

When the Thatcher government set itself on a collision course with the city council the youngsters who flocked to Liverpool's matches became increasingly politicized. The travelling support was particularly vehement in expressing left-wing views.

This ethos was not reflected in the team. Paul Jewell, who was a reserve-team player at the time, has said that he was the only Labour voter at Melwood. This is not quite true – Michael Robinson had left-wing sympathies – but most of the squad were precisely the sort of people targeted by the Tories. They were earning good money by the standards of the day and were easily seduced by the promise of lower taxes. Yet there was a recognition that they were playing for more than just results, even if it was not consciously political. 'They were tough times,' Dalglish said. 'When we won, it made people happy. We wanted them to be happy. It lifted the mood during a difficult period.'

For Liverpool, the season opened in traditional fashion, at 3 p.m. on a Saturday, against Wolverhampton Wanderers at Molineux. Wolves had been promoted from Division Two and would be fired up by the visit of the champions on their return to the top flight. During the week between the Charity Shield and the first league game, Fagan worked on his side, trying to improve Craig Johnston's positional sense and build a balance in a midfield that still worried him.

On a day of blazing sunshine, Fagan took his place in the directors' box and embarked on a quest to emulate something so far achieved only by Huddersfield Town and Arsenal: winning the title three years in succession. The scale of the task was apparent within the first two minutes. Mel Eves broke free and shot and the ball rebounded to Andy Gray. Kennedy was close to him but could only bundle the Wolves striker over. '[Gray] was at a difficult angle and there was no need to trip him,' Vince Wright wrote in *The Times*. Barney Rubble had struck again. Palmer scored from the penalty spot and Liverpool were 1–0 down.

Half-time came as a relief. Wolves could have scored more. Rush equalized immediately after the break and hit the bar twice but it was an unconvincing performance against a promoted team missing four first-team players. Liverpool were forced 'to retreat in possession', *The Times* said. 'Robinson, in his first league match for Liverpool, was often on a different wavelength from Rush.'

A lukewarm start. Now it was time to show some character.

Bruce Grobbelaar was a character. He was a showman in a way

few goalkeepers have ever been. His long journey to Anfield took in three continents and a host of seemingly blind alleys. Along the way, he reinvented himself.

He was born in South Africa but grew up in Rhodesia, where he served a two-year period of national service in the army during the Zimbabwe war of liberation. By the time he reached Merseyside this role would mutate from propping up the regime of Ian Smith to that of 'freedom fighter'. There was plenty about Grobbelaar that didn't add up.

After leaving the army, he travelled to England, where Vancouver Whitecaps of the North American Soccer League were holding trials. His ability, agility and confidence earned him a contract in Canada. He spent his first season as a reserve and was loaned to Crewe Alexandra in the off season.

It was here Bob Paisley noticed him.

'I will never forget going to see Bruce Grobbelaar play for the first time,' Bob Paisley said later. 'I had an idea that he would become the next Liverpool goalkeeper even before the match had kicked off. He was playing in the Fourth Division for Crewe Alexandra at Doncaster in April 1980. Before the game, he had three of his team-mates lined up on the edge of the penalty area firing in shots at him. Bruce was dancing about like a cartoon character stopping every attempt. I turned to Tom Saunders, who was sitting next to me, and said, "We can go, I've seen enough."'

The swagger that attracted Paisley was a huge component of the goalkeeper's style. It wasn't exactly the Liverpool way but there was enough raw talent there to work with. Paisley imagined he could mould the new man and iron out some of his flaws. This would take time. The manager would not get it.

The goalkeeping role at Anfield had been a model of stability. Tommy Lawrence – 'the Flying Pig' – had kept goal for Liverpool from 1962 until he was eased out for Ray Clemence in 1970. Clemence took the shirt and held it until he left unexpectedly in the summer of 1981.

Both were solid performers. Clemence played regularly for

England, although the presence of Peter Shilton meant he won fewer caps than his talent warranted.

Neither goalkeeper courted the crowd like Grobbelaar. The Zimbabwean warmed up by walking on his hands or swinging from the bar. He bantered with the crowd, whether it was the friendly faces on the Kop or the snarling inhabitants of the Stretford End. There were other marked differences from his predecessors, though, and they were less attractive.

At Anfield it was generally estimated that Clemence saved them between ten and twelve points in a season. No one wanted to do the sums on his replacement. Grobbelaar was prone to lapses in concentration. He would make saves that would draw comparisons with the very best goalkeepers and then, minutes later, let an innocuous shot slip between his hands into the net.

Clemence directed his defence and was a vocal organizer. It was a knack his successor would take a while to learn. His inability to communicate made the back four nervous.

Grobbelaar trusted his own ability too much. Most goalkeepers would treat a cross dropped on to the penalty spot as a centre back's problem and stay on their line. Not Grobbelaar. He would chase the ball, sometimes through a forest of players, in an attempt to claim a catch. When it worked, it was a breathtaking sight. When it went wrong, and the ball went over his hands or squirmed away from his grasping fingers, the goal was left unguarded and forwards were presented with unexpectedly easy opportunities to score. Fagan warned his defenders to flock towards the goalkeeper when he came for the ball. 'He's bound to drop a few,' he'd say.

If that happened, suddenly the clowning wasn't so funny.

After the watershed game against Manchester City three years previously, Paisley had read his goalkeeper the riot act. 'If you don't stop the antics you'll be playing for Crewe again,' the veteran manager said.

'He walked out of the dressing room,' Grobbelaar said. 'It dawned on me I couldn't do all these things I used to do; sit on the crossbar and walk around the pitch on my hands and mess about. He made me realize my mistakes and made sure I put them right.'

And, for the most part, Grobbelaar did. But if you could take the boy out of Africa, you couldn't take the showman out of 'Brucie'.

They took the mickey out of him in the dressing room, and the goalkeeper was happy about it, especially if it took some of the pressure off younger, less experienced players. 'Bruce couldn't help himself with the ricks,' Johnston said. 'He would make himself look stupid for the benefit of others. He sacrificed his own integrity for team spirit.'

The sticks and stones of the dressing room washed over the man who had seen ugly things in the bush of southern Africa. 'If people were laughing at me, it was OK,' the goalkeeper said. 'We were having fun and no one was getting hurt. I enjoyed it all. I didn't mind when they took the piss. I gave it back.'

Around the league, Grobbelaar was perceived as one of Liverpool's weak links. Alan Brazil, who played for Ipswich Town, summed him up: 'Great talent and agility,' he said. 'But Bruce always gave you a chance. Put in a deep cross, get off a shot, and there was always a feeling he might get it wrong.'

Norwich City certainly had that feeling when they hosted Liverpool at Carrow Road for the second game of the season. As early as the sixth minute, Grobbelaar mishandled a Norwich corner and only the visiting side's profligacy meant the bad start to the season did not get worse. In a flat performance, Liverpool had the worst of the game. Although Souness rescued the match with a fine chipped goal just before the half-hour, it was a very scratchy victory.

'Joe Fagan can scarcely be happy with what he saw,' *The Times* wrote. 'Only Lee carried the true Liverpool air of authority.'

There were positives to be taken. Two awkward away games had produced four points. And the team, during the long trip home, were buoyed by news of their rivals. Manchester United, whom everyone imagined would present the biggest challenge, had suffered a shock result. After winning their first match against Queens Park Rangers at home the previous Saturday, they were beaten 2–1 by Nottingham Forest at Old Trafford. Cracking open the beer on the coach, Fagan and his team were relaxed and happy. The start had lacked fluency and conviction but things were looking up.

Now Anfield awaited Fagan's homecoming. The new manager's first match in charge in front of the Kop was against Forest on the first Saturday of September. The length of the shadows that hung over Fagan – and the scale of his task – were emphasized when Bob Paisley was presented with his manager-of-the-year award for the previous season on the pitch before kick-off. Fagan was delighted for his old friend but the symbolism was obvious. Could the new man come near to emulating the most successful manager in English history?

Yet again, Liverpool sputtered. Neal missed a penalty and it took until the eighty-fourth minute for Rush to break the deadlock and give Liverpool a 1–0 victory. Afterwards, Fagan talked of good sides grinding down the opposition and scoring late goals. It was a Liverpool characteristic. They did not enjoy it when it worked in reverse.

Three days after the Forest match, Anfield hosted its first night game of the new campaign. Southampton were the opposition and things seemed to be going to plan as Rush showed his predatory instincts by following up on a Souness shot on the hour mark. As the minutes ticked away, it looked like another 1–0 victory was on the cards. Instead, with six minutes left, Liverpool went to sleep at the back. Mick Mills took a free kick from outside the box and the static defenders left the ball for one of their colleagues to deal with. Grobbelaar, unsighted, was not at fault when the ball went in.

Fagan's side were still unbeaten but the concerns would not go away. Anfield was not quite the fortress it had been and a pattern was emerging. 'We didn't play that well at home that season,' Neal said.

It was a subdued crowd that left Anfield. Those who mooched back into town to the city's nightspots missed the jauntiness that came with Liverpool victories. This was not the heady cocktail of goals and glory they were used to.

There were mutterings about Robinson's suitability for the Liverpool team. Bustling and eager, he had the subtlety of a cosh and was not an effective foil for the elegant and intelligent Rush. The new striker was also finding it difficult to get on Dalglish's wavelength. In four league matches, Liverpool had scored just four goals. It was not the sort of return that wins titles. The doubters went right to the top. 'Not quick enough in thought and action,' Fagan wrote in his diary when assessing Robinson's impact.

Craig Johnston still irritated the manager. He relied on his engine rather than intellect. During pre-season, Fagan had made the damning judgment: 'He sounds as if he plays for Roy of the Rovers. He must grow up.' Player and manager were already butting heads. One unlikely battlefield was the pre-match meal. Johnston found it heavy and far from ideal for an athlete preparing to take part in a match.

'The starter was prawn cocktail,' Johnston said. 'You had it whether you liked it or not.' The main course was even more unappetizing. 'There were two options,' he said. 'Steak or fish. I'd read a book by Dr Robert Haas called *Eat to Win*. He'd helped Ivan Lendl and Martina Navratilova to improve their performances. I read it. It was a formula to maximize energy. It basically said you burn fat in the flame of carbohydrates.'

In the embryonic days of sports science, such notions generated hilarity in the Bootroom. 'I started to bring my own food,' Johnston said. 'Brown rice, soy bacon and a bit of egg for protein. Fagan said: "What's wrong, don't you like our food?" and called Ronnie over to have a laugh at it.'

As far as Fagan and Moran could see, the methods they had used for decades worked. They were not keen on departing from their tried and tested policies. An outsider like Johnston could spot the flaws in an otherwise successful blueprint, though. 'They had me in the office,' the young Australian said. 'I said to them: "If you had a jet fighter you wouldn't put diesel in it, would you? It needs jet fuel."'

Most of Johnston's team-mates took a similarly jaundiced view of his packed lunches. 'All the lads were saying: "What the fuck are you doing?"' he said. 'Then Sammy Lee said: "Can I have a taste?" He liked it and asked me to bring some for him.'

When outsiders noticed the impact of the diet in Johnston's performances, the mood swiftly changed. 'I was flying in pre-season and then the BBC said I'd covered every blade of grass in one game and it was because of a secret diet,' he said. 'It changed everyone in the dressing room's perception.'

Now, Johnston could eat his food openly, without being the focus of sarcasm. How did it feel? 'It was like coming out of the closet,' he said.

Johnston's fitness and appetite for hard work were never in question. Fagan was still unsure about his best position and tactical nous. He may have been out of the closet, but he was still no closer to being in the team on a permanent basis. The frustration would linger.

8.

The Master Bites Back

September 1983

Arsenal (a)

No one had seen anything like Kenny Dalglish. At a club that deified its heroes, Dalglish was different.

He arrived at Anfield in the summer of 1977 as replacement for the latest Kop idol, Kevin Keegan. The departure of the little Englishman was the only blight on a glorious summer. On 25 May, in Rome, the European Cup had been won for the first time with Keegan playing the pivotal role in the 3–1 victory over Borussia Mönchengladbach. He had been the team's flag-bearer and superstar. It was the highlight of his Anfield career and his swansong. The club's wage structure left the England forward feeling underpaid. By 1976, he was resentful and looking for a better salary.

It was widely known throughout the 1976–77 season that it would be Keegan's last on Merseyside. During the summer, he signed for SV Hamburg in Germany for a transfer fee of £500,000. It would not be the last time an Anfield hero would depart for better wages after producing a man-of-the-match performance in Europe's biggest game.

Many players are loved by the Kop. Few are worshipped. Keegan was in the latter category, following in the tradition of Billy Liddell in the 1950s and Ian St John in the 1960s. Almost everyone believed Keegan to be irreplaceable.

Bob Paisley didn't. He knew just the man for the job.

Kenneth Mathieson Dalglish was born in Glasgow's East End but grew up as a Rangers fan close to the Ibrox club's training ground. In the summer of 1967 – weeks after Celtic had beaten Internazionale 2–1 in Lisbon to bring the European Cup back to

Scotland – Jock Stein came calling and Dalglish crossed the religious divide to ply his trade at Parkhead. A year earlier, the young Scot had trained at Anfield but the fifteen-year-old was too immature and homesick to move south. That would have to wait.

For Celtic, Dalglish was sensational. His goalscoring exploits caught the attention of English scouts but the Glasgow club could not be bullied financially and the player was happy. It was not until 1977 that the twenty-six-year-old was ready to try his skills south of the border.

Manchester United were interested and, having beaten Liverpool in the 1977 FA Cup final, could make a persuasive argument that Old Trafford was the place to be. Paisley, however, was not to be denied. With the Keegan money in his pocket, the Liverpool manager went to Scotland with Peter Robinson to negotiate the transfer. The bid was £400,000. Celtic played hardball and asked for ten per cent more. After some theatrical wavering, Liverpool agreed to stump up £440,000. The deal done, Paisley whispered to Robinson: 'We'd better get out of town before they realize what we've done!'

Indeed, it was the greatest bit of business Anfield had seen. Within five minutes of his league debut away to Middlesbrough, Dalglish banished thoughts of Keegan with a beautiful, curling, chipped goal. In front of the Kop four days later, the new No. 7 repeated the trick against Newcastle United with a similar strike. But goals were only a small part of what made Dalglish great.

Many players have superb control, powerful shots and the ability to beat an opponent. Dalglish had something more. He had an almost supernatural awareness of the rhythms of the game. He could find space where none appeared to exist and seemed to know instinctively where his team-mates would be.

Short and thick-bodied, the Scot might have looked like a pushover for imposing, physical defenders, but underestimating Dalglish was a mistake. His quickness of mind was complemented by an intuitive speed and change of pace. He could ride the most savage challenges and wriggle away as if barely any contact had been made.

He is not the only player who has towered above everyone else on the pitch in terms of ability, but he was one of the few whose mere presence could visibly lift his team-mates' performances. He was unselfish on the pitch and made colleagues look good.

Paisley summed Dalglish up: 'Of all the players I have played alongside, managed and coached in more than forty years at Anfield, he is the most talented.'

Keegan, as good as he was, became a footnote to history. Dalglish was now the supreme presence in a team that was feared across Europe.

Dalglish's sense of understanding with Souness was particularly devastating for opponents. A team built around either player would have been formidable. A side that featured both was often unplayable. They enhanced each other in a way only supreme talents can. Here were arguably the two finest players in the club's history.

'Between the decline of Johan Cruyff and the emergence of Diego Maradona, Kenny Dalglish was the best player in the world,' Souness said with characteristic certainty. He was right. And even after Maradona made his mark, Dalglish was not too far behind.

They dominated the squad, too. Souness's steely, confrontational leadership style was more obvious but Dalglish was no junior partner in the dressing room. With a dry, sometimes crushing wit, he demanded the highest standards. He was generous in creating opportunities for his team-mates to shine and quick to praise hard work and excellence. Any lack of effort or concentration would earn the perpetrator a tongue-lashing. Few could match Dalglish's talent, and that was fine. But those who let their own quality slip would soon regret their mistake.

'The Scots had a rough, working-class ethos,' Johnston said. 'Particularly Kenny. He was a winner and a leader.'

Fagan was lucky in the sense that he inherited two players who 'managed' the team on the pitch. Where he may have felt less fortunate was inheriting Dalglish at the age of thirty-two. During the stuttering end to the previous season and the spotty start to the new campaign, there was a feeling that the forward was no longer at his dominant best. 'The reactions of Dalglish were a trifle slower than usual,' *The Times* opined after the opening match against Wolves. By his own elevated standards, it had been an ordinary start to the season for the Scot. Was it just a dip in form? Was he slowing down? Had fifteen years of robust tackling taken a toll? Was Dalglish on the decline?

These questions were thrown into harsh relief when Liverpool went to Highbury for their fifth league game. Arsenal, the hosts, had beaten Liverpool to the signature of another Celtic hero, Charlie Nicholas, during the summer. He was more than a decade younger than Dalglish and had been portrayed as the older man's heir apparent in greatness. When Nicholas signed for Arsenal, Terry Neill, the manager, pointedly described him as 'the most exciting talent to emerge in Britain since George Best'.

By this point Dalglish had outstripped Best in all departments. The romantics might laud the splendidly talented Ulsterman as the greatest player ever, but that leap of faith meant applying a wilful blindness to his selfishness and relative lack of medals.

All the clichés were out before the Arsenal match. The 'master versus pupil' and 'king against pretender' headlines focused the interest of the football nation on the two players. There would be only one winner.

Nicholas's positional play, movement and scoring ability made it easy to evoke comparisons to a young Dalglish. Early in the game, he produced the sort of breathtaking moment that had characterized the Liverpool man's career. The Arsenal forward chested down a chipped pass from Graham Rix and rattled a right-foot shot against the Liverpool bar. The false dawn was a motif for Nicholas's career. It was time for Dalglish to reassert himself.

Dropping deep behind Ian Rush and Michael Robinson, the Scot was central to everything his side created. Shortly after Nicholas hit the bar, Dalglish helped set up the opening goal for Craig Johnston. With twenty-three minutes to go, he then underlined his dominance with the sort of goal only the great players score.

Dalglish was lurking on the edge of the Arsenal box and attempted a one-two with Sammy Lee, who knocked the return ball down the inside-right channel. Robinson, still not displaying the awareness required by Liverpool, made a rather boneheaded run into the locale that Dalglish was heading for and the threat looked to be finished.

As Dalglish gave up the chase, the lumbering centre forward showed the sort of flash of alertness and skill that had caught Fagan's attention. He back-heeled the ball towards his No. 7.

Alan Sunderland had tracked back to cover Dalglish and the Arsenal man stood between the goal and the Liverpool striker. Instead of shooting, Dalglish let the ball run between his legs and back towards the centre of the penalty area. Languidly, without the slightest hint of bustle, the Scot shifted his weight and followed the ball. The dummy and change of direction left the Arsenal defence frozen. Five defenders watched in horror as Dalglish took one left-footed touch to tee up the ball and then curled it with the same foot into the far corner. It was a startling, sublime goal that sent a message across the league.

'As if to teach Nicholas a lesson for the future,' *The Times* said, 'Dalglish displayed all his mastery.'

The Scot laughs off the idea that he had a point to prove. 'We only thought about ourselves,' he said. 'We weren't thinking about Charlie or anyone else. We didn't worry about other players, other teams. I'd been feeling good. We knew things would click.'

The early-season jitters appeared to be over and just at the right time. European competition was about to begin again. The final was once again in Rome, which had an important and affectionate place in Anfield history. Liverpool's first European Cup had been won there in 1977. It was time to start dreaming of another glorious night in the Eternal City.

9.

Continental Credibility

September 1983

BK Odense (a), European Cup R1; Aston Villa (h)

Europe changed Liverpool as a club. It turned a provincial team into a global institution and a source of civic pride. The Continental success was timely because, as a city, Liverpool was undergoing a difficult time.

In the boom-time 1960s, with the Beatles conquering the world, other clubs overshadowed Anfield's Reds in competition against foreign sides. Celtic and Manchester United won the European Cup; Tottenham and West Ham brought home the Cup-Winners' Cup; and Leeds United and Newcastle captured the Fairs Cup, the predecessor of the Uefa Cup.

Shankly's team went close but missed out on glory. In 1965, they felt they were cheated out of a place in the European Cup final by Internazionale after a fractious and controversial semi. A year later they lost to Borussia Dortmund in the Cup-Winners' Cup final.

They finally imposed themselves in the 1970s and, as the city declined economically throughout that decade and became increasingly philosophically out of tune with mainstream British life, Liverpool began to dominate Europe.

Shankly's last great side won the Uefa Cup in 1973, beginning a rivalry with Borussia Mönchengladbach that would last for a decade. Paisley brought the same trophy to Anfield in 1976 after a thrilling 4–3 aggregate two-legged final against Bruges. This was just the warm-up.

In 1977, in Rome, Liverpool emulated Celtic and Manchester United by winning the European Cup, defeating their old adversaries from Mönchengladbach 3–1. A year later at Wembley they retained their trophy, beating a cagier Bruges 1–0. In 1981, the club joined European football's aristocracy when they won the premier Continental trophy for the third time, dispatching Real Madrid 1–0 in Paris.

At a time when Merseyside had little to boast about, the Liverpool team were strutting across Europe and bringing home trophies. Unemployment was spiralling out of control, the British government were discussing a 'managed decline' of the city at cabinet level, tear gas was fired on the mainland for the first time as Liverpool 8 burned in the Toxteth riots and the Scouse accent was associated with theft and violence.

Even the art coming out of the city was edgy and unnerving. In the 1960s, Merseyside had exported cheeky mop-tops, jangly, happy pop music and comedians who showcased the sunnier aspects of the city. By the depressed 1980s it was much darker. Now the world was presented with Alan Bleasdale's *Boys from the Blackstuff*, a gritty exploration of the effects of poverty. The new comedy from the likes of Alexei Sayle was suffused with rage. And although the music scene was vibrant and produced brilliant bands like Echo and the Bunnymen, Wah! and The Teardrop Explodes, only Frankie Goes to Hollywood had a massive national impact. To outsiders, everything about the place was in the doldrums.

Yet while all this was going on, the side that bore a despised city's name was the best and most powerful team in Europe. Liverpool's success provided a fillip for a beleaguered community. The team's exploits also indirectly created a new style of football follower.

Liverpool and Everton fans had long been at the cutting edge of the developing supporters' culture. The Kop choir became famous in the 1960s and elevated fanatical backing to an art form with an unprecedented range of chants and wit. Scousers' commitment to their football teams had been in evidence long before the media discovered Anfield's swaying, singing crowd, through.

In the late 1950s, when the post-war boom provided more disposable income for the working classes, Liverpool and Everton fans were among the first to travel to away games in large numbers.

Their exuberance and excitability led to them being dubbed the 'Mersey Manics'. Two decades on, they exported the mania to Europe.

In 1977, upwards of 25,000 Liverpool supporters flocked to Rome. They looked largely like any other group of fans: denim-clad, long-haired throwbacks to the mid-seventies. They showed few signs of the shifting currents of youth culture that had their most obvious manifestations in punk.

Almost unnoticed, on the streets around Scotland Road, there was another teenage movement growing. It had started in the mid-1970s and initially only demonstrated itself in the widespread appearance of Adidas Samba training shoes and shorter haircuts than were usual for the time. In the summer of 1976, all the teen-aged boys in the area seemed to be wearing Adidas tops, basic T-shirts with a trefoil on the breast and three stripes down the arm.

A consignment had been stolen from a lorry whose driver was spending the night in Arden House Salvation Army hostel on Scotland Road. The shirts sold rapidly in the factories around the docks. It signalled the beginning of a fascination with sportswear that would eventually come to be known as 'casual' style.

The trip to Rome whetted the appetite of young men for travel. Those who took the long overland journey enjoyed the experience. With few jobs around, there was nothing to keep them at home. Some of the groups of mates who went financed the excursion by shoplifting. They came back dressed in clothes and training shoes that had not yet reached Britain and sold any surplus to willing customers.

By late 1977, the T-shirt of choice was the classic Fred Perry polo. The look changed regularly but straight Lois or Lee jeans, Kickers boots and mushroom wedge haircuts – short at the sides and back and puffed-up and bouncy on top – were being seen increasingly on the trains to away matches and in the pubs where football fans drank as the 1970s came to an end. There was a post-Bowie foppishness about the fashions and punkish fluffy mohair jumpers abounded.

In Liverpool, these wild young men were referred to as 'Scallies', short for scallywag. The Scotland Road look became known simply as Scal. In the aftermath of each European away game a wave of new fashions swept across the city. Suddenly, people were wearing Lacoste shirts and flamboyantly coloured Trimm-Trab training shoes. The more colourful and rarer the sportswear, the more people craved ownership. Businessmen like Robert Wade-Smith spotted the developing market. His eponymous shop helped the style go mainstream. Now you didn't need to be a robber – or know one – to carry off the look.

Even those who blanched at shoplifting found a way to cut the costs of their European trips. The favourite method of transport for the growing numbers of young men who followed Liverpool to the Continent was the train. Most of those who travelled were under the age of twenty-five and booked their tickets through a company called Transalpino, based near the university. An enterprising forger found that it was possible to buy the cheapest fare and, by erasing some of the print on the voucher, trick any inspector into believing it was a much more expensive ticket that allowed a significantly wider range of travel. The 'Transalpino rubout' became part of fan legend and gave a generation of youngsters a chance to follow Liverpool across Europe even though they were on the dole.

The trip to the Italian capital in 1977 had helped kick-start this new youth movement. Its acolytes were looking forward very much to a return to the scene of the crime.

The road to Rome started in Odense in Denmark. It is the birthplace of Hans Christian Andersen but Liverpool were determined that there would be no fairy tales for the local side.

Fagan was light-hearted before the match, claiming to have sent an unlikely spy to watch Odense in their previous game. It was, he said, 'my best scout, a promising lad called Bob Paisley'.

The Danish part-timers were the usual collection of mechanics, bank workers and lawyers. They did not make their living from playing football and now they were facing a team that had reached the apex of the sport. Odense were top of their league but lacked the conviction that they could beat a team that contained Dalglish and Souness. Indeed, in the match programme, Liverpool's talismanic No. 7 was referred to as 'Mr Dalglish'.

It felt like a friendly. The tiny ground was packed full and the overhanging trees dripped with adolescent boys, clinging on precariously for a sight of the men in red. They were rewarded quickly when Dalglish scored in the fourteenth minute, pouncing on a rebound save from Robinson's shot. Once again, the Scot was at his unplayable best but Liverpool were slipshod at the back, with Hansen and Lawrenson making first-half errors.

There was a casual air about the team's approach that was summed up at half-time. During the break, two local blonde girls entertained the crowd by dancing in the centre circle. As the Liverpool team returned, a number of them ogled the blondes and were more intent on flirting than lining up. It was not the most committed return to European competition. 'They were content to do no more than keep control,' Sepp Piontek, the Denmark manager, said. Dalglish aside, it felt like a bare-minimum effort.

If Europe seemed like a holiday, then the league was a chore. Aston Villa were the next team to visit Anfield and they did not make things easy. Steve McMahon, who had spurned Liverpool's advances when he left Everton for the Midlands, kept close to Dalglish and produced an effective and combative performance.

Villa exploited Ronnie Whelan's absence, getting behind Alan Kennedy when he ranged upfield. With less than twenty minutes left in the game, the visiting side were starting to believe they could hold out but Dalglish discovered a yard of space away from his marker. Rush found him with a square ball and the Scot gave Liverpool the lead. Six minutes later, Rush sealed the game after Robinson headed down to the Welshman in the area.

Villa pulled one back but Liverpool's victory was complete in the closing seconds when Souness gave McMahon a late reminder about who was boss at Anfield by giving his opponent a hefty and unnec-essary whack after a tackle. Villa's young Scouser retaliated and was sent off. It was a triumph for experience and cynicism and Souness had once again marked his territory. No one played the tough guy at Anfield without being called to account. No one roughed up Kenny Dalglish without having to reckon with Souness. 'Charlie was cunning and devious,' Kennedy said. In the world of football's alpha males, Champagne Charlie was a snarling top dog. Young pre-tenders could expect to be bitten.

It was not a position he was going to relinquish, either for him-self or for his team. And next up were the main challengers. Even in late September, a visit to Old Trafford to play Manchester United had the feel of a watershed moment about it. Liverpool had lost twice already to United under Fagan's tenure. No one was keen to make it a hat-trick.

10.

Fire and Fury

September 1983

Manchester United (a)

Everyone had been expecting a titanic battle for the league between Liverpool and Manchester United but the first month of the season had confounded expectations. Despite their inconsistent start to the campaign, Liverpool were in third place in the table as they arrived at Old Trafford. It was no surprise that Fagan's team were within one point of the top two. What no one expected was who those two leaders would be, and that United would be struggling to keep up.

West Ham United headed the table, with Southampton in second place. United were fifth, having lost twice at home already. Although they were sitting just two points behind Liverpool, United were hardly showing title-winning form.

Ron Atkinson, United's manager, was a big-talking Scouser. He had spent heavily in the transfer market and the midfield was powered by Bryan Robson, the England captain who was considered one of the best players in Europe. Despite winning the FA Cup earlier in the year, there was massive pressure on Atkinson. It had been sixteen years since United had won the Championship. The desperation to wrest the title away from Anfield radiated from the Stretford End.

The pressure was on Liverpool, too. It always was at Old Trafford. Invariably, this match attracted the biggest league crowd of the season. On 24 September 1983, 56,212 people packed into the stadium. Outside, the antagonism between the two cities spilt over into violence across Manchester. The Stretford End, United's answer to the Kop, roared abuse at the 3,000 visiting supporters at the opposite end. In the scoreboard end, the Liverpool fans roared themselves hoarse trying to make themselves heard in the maelstrom of noise. The two most vehement sets of followers in English football howled their distaste for each other.

The spite on the terraces was mirrored on the pitch. United's mixture of envy and ambition had them fired up. Liverpool were determined never to let the mouthy pretenders from down the East Lancs Road usurp their rule.

There are few other occasions on which the game is reduced to such a gladiatorial essence. When the teams emerged from the tunnel, the atmosphere became frenzied. Liverpool were in all yellow and United in their traditional red, black and white. Football was never more raw and vivid. 'Aye, there was always a bit of an edge between us,' Dalglish said in wry understatement.

Almost from the start, Liverpool were second best. Still without Ronnie Whelan, the midfield struggled to contain the surging, driving runs of Robson. Norman Whiteside's physical approach seemed to unnerve Hansen and Lawrenson and United had more zip in their legs.

The only goal came in the fifty-second minute. Michael Robinson, looking even more leaden-footed than ever, headed weakly towards goal in the United area. Mike Duxbury picked up the ball and broke down Liverpool's left behind Alan Kennedy. The Liverpool defender's magnificent engine allowed him to catch the United full back just inside the away team's half but it was too late. Hansen had been sucked out to cover Kennedy and when Duxbury shifted the ball infield to the onrushing Arthur Graham, Liverpool were ragged. Hansen was in the position every centre half dreads: on his heels, isolated against a winger. His weak challenge on Graham barely slowed the United man down. Graham reached the byline and pulled the ball back to Frank Stapleton to side-foot home while men in yellow shirts streamed back to no obvious purpose.

Grobbelaar went to his knees and rose in rage but struggled to locate a victim for his anger. The culprits could have formed a queue. The goalkeeper took the ball from the net and booted it with a fury towards the halfway line. There were few recriminations, either, as

Liverpool trooped back into position with their shoulders slumped. Even Souness, usually so vocal, had little to say. With more than half an hour to go, they looked a defeated team. United were ebullient.

'In the context of the marathon race for the championship,' *The Times* said, 'such a fleeting moment may be of little significance. But United, who should have increased the margin of their richly deserved victory, have beaten Liverpool twice already this season and will go to Anfield on 2 January knowing their recent record there is impressive as well.'

There was a feeling that the tide had turned. United leapfrogged Liverpool into second place in the table. West Ham won again to stretch the gap between the leaders and Liverpool to four points. It was not a massive lead but the manner of the defeat and the strength of his squad worried Fagan. The Liverpool manager put on a brave face for public consumption but was deeply unhappy. All his early-season concerns were being confirmed. That the goal came down the Liverpool left served to underline his worries in that area. Kennedy remained a frustrating enigma. He needed more protection from the midfield than Johnston, Lee and Souness could provide.

Right back had suddenly become a problem, too. The only remarkable thing about the game from Liverpool's point of view was an injury to Phil Neal.

Neal had been at Liverpool for nine years. He was signed from Northampton Town for £66,000 in October 1974. At the age of twenty-three, he was not sure what his best position was and not quite certain where life was taking him. During his 187 appearances for Northampton he had played across the defence, in midfield and even had spells up front. His reputation was as a 'utility man', a useful reserve who could slot into a number of positions but without being first choice for any. The day Liverpool came to take a final look at the player before deciding whether to buy, Neal took his show of versatility to the extreme.

'Paisley often used to pay to go through the terraces and talk to people about the players, asking, "What's that Phil Neal like?"' the full back said. The Liverpool manager did just this when Northampton played Rotherham United at Millmoor.

'When Paisley saw me for the last time at Northampton he brought a Liverpool director with him. For the first twenty minutes I played at right back,' Neal said. That was until the goalkeeper was injured. 'For the rest of the game I played in goal. Bob said: "We came all that way to see you for the last time. I wanted to show my director what a good right back you were. The keeper got carried off and you put the green jersey on."'

It didn't matter. The decision to purchase was already taken. Geoff Twentyman, Liverpool's chief scout, had seen Neal play three times in the previous month and another of the recruiting team had run the rule over the player.

Two days later, on a Monday morning, Neal was summoned to the Northampton manager's office. Neal remembers: 'When I got there, the first thing he said was: "How do you fancy going to Liverpool?"'

Within hours, Neal was at Melwood. Leaving the third tier of English football for life with one of Europe's best clubs should have been the deal of a lifetime. It wasn't quite like that.

'I got ten pounds a week more than I got at Northampton,' he said. But, even if it did not make him rich, it was a move Neal had to make.

'On the day I signed, my wife was in hospital having our son and I couldn't even consult her,' he said. 'I had no option but to sign. I was twenty-three years of age and wondered what I was going to do for the rest of my life. I was playing Third Division football and going nowhere. I thought time had already passed me by.'

A little more than a month later, Neal was given his debut, thrown into a Merseyside derby at Goodison Park. But it was hardly the big time. 'I picked up my boots from Anfield in the morning and walked across Stanley Park early afternoon and got changed when I got there,' he said. As humdrum as it felt, it was the start of something special.

After the o–o draw with Everton, Neal was left out of the team for three games. Then he was given a chance at the left-back position in place of Alec Lindsay just before Christmas in the 2–0 win over Luton Town. Nine years on, Neal had played 417 consecutive games, not missing a match. In that spell, he had won three European Cups, six league titles, three League Cups, a Uefa Cup and a facetious nickname, 'Zico', after the brilliant Brazilian. He was also the team's penalty-taker. Not bad for a utility man.

The long run of consecutive appearances said much about Neal's attitude to the game. He was robust but no less susceptible to injury than any other player. Indeed, he had played through knocks that would have sidelined a lesser man.

'There were two occasions when I could have missed a game,' he said. 'One was when I got a fractured cheekbone.' This was in 1976.

'Roger Davis, the centre forward at Derby, gave me an elbow. I had my cheekbone lifted in line with the rest of my face to put my face back in shape. Bob Paisley came to me on Wednesday and said, "How are you feeling?" I said, "I'm OK. I'm over the operation and everything else." I chose to play against the specialist's wishes, who said that I shouldn't play for a month. I got away with it.'

There was no mask for Neal. And no escaping from more normal football injuries.

'I got over a broken toe, but I had to play for six weeks with size eight and a half on one foot and size seven on the other,' he said. 'Ronnie Moran made me a plaster cast on the little toe I had broken. It was uncomfortable with my normal-size shoes. I had to find some way to be still able to kick a ball, tackle and maybe have a little injection to keep the pain away for ninety minutes. There were little incidents when I could have missed a game but I was doubly determined not to. It was so exciting. I didn't miss a day's training in all those years I was there. I wouldn't ring in for a cold. Every day I had a smile on my face.'

There was another driving reason. At every club there are players in the reserves desperate to seize on a regular player's misfortune to stake a place in the first team. Neal was not going to let anyone else audition for his position if he could help it. 'You had to be careful,'

Steve Nicol said. 'If you got injured and were out, you might struggle to get back in. If you had a place, you didn't want to lose it.'

Yet now everyone knew an injured Neal would be drafted back into the side as soon as he was fit. There was too little quality in Fagan's squad. There were many times over the years when the full back's absence would have been hardly noticed. Now he would be sorely missed.

Weight of Expectation

September–October 1983

BK Odense (h), European Cup R1; Sunderland (h); Brentford (a),
League Cup R2; West Ham United (a)

At least Fagan had a relatively straightforward game to look forward to. Odense were due at Anfield and the 1–0 lead from the away leg in Denmark provided a cushion, the opportunity to experiment a little and build confidence by scoring a few goals.

Michael Robinson had shown only flashes of ability. There was always a battering-ram element to the forward's game but even his rather bulky physique did not explain his sluggish movement on the pitch. Fagan had been in the game a long time and was determined to find an answer to Robinson's problems. The striker had not scored in a competitive game since his arrival from Brighton.

Robinson had dreamt of playing for Liverpool but was finding the reality more difficult. When he played for the opposition at Anfield he had enjoyed the experience and had done well. There was no expectation to win. 'I felt like I always scored against Liverpool whoever I was playing for,' the striker told Simon Hughes in *Red Machine*. 'When I walked outside the left-hand dressing room and down the stairs and past the imposing "This Is Anfield" sign before hearing "You'll Never Walk Alone", you'd wait for the Liverpool team to run out. They seemed like giants.'

The expectations of wearing a Liver bird had the opposite effect on the man from Blackpool. 'I remember looking at the red shirt and the jersey weighed so heavy. I remember in some games half wishing that I was that lamb again being led to the slaughter, because there was no responsibility in that. Instead, I had to be at the level of Liverpool Football Club. And I wasn't too sure I could be. Anfield was far more imposing to me as a Liverpool player than as a visiting player. That played on my mind and I thought about it too much.'

Fagan went through every trick in his psychological book to try to change the striker's thought process, even to the extent of telling him before the Odense match that he was first on the team sheet on the insistence of Mrs Fagan, who was worried he might be dropped. Of course, said Fagan, there was never a chance that he'd even consider dropping his new striker, and that Lil would even ask the question meant she knew nothing about the game, but might he please reassure her that Michael was happy to play?

'The whole story may have been a load of bollocks but it made me feel like the greatest man on earth,' said Robinson.

The Liverpool manager also focused on the big man's feet. Robinson had suffered problems with fallen arches in the early days of his career at Preston. The answer had been to wear boots that contained metal supports. Fagan decided that the forward was heavy-footed enough already and insisted Robinson play against the Danes in normal footwear. A wary and reluctant Robinson 'agreed to give it a go'.

Plenty of others were even less willing. A mere 14,985 fans were scattered across the stadium. Gloom hung heavy over Anfield before the game that night. The players' shouts echoed under the roof of the Kop. It felt like a club in decline, rather than a team of champions marching to glory.

Odense might have even fancied themselves to be in with a chance: since the first leg of the tie, Denmark had come to Wembley and beaten England 1–0. The small crowd seemed to reflect a general pessimism about football that ranged far beyond Merseyside.

Robinson did not despair. Being literally lighter of foot – and, temporarily, of worry – helped remove the leaden quality from his game. After fourteen minutes he scored with a low, powerful shot. Boxers might load their gloves to add extra power but the added mass in his boots had made Robinson's striking of the ball awkward and scuffed. Now he hit it clean and with force. The goal came as a relief for everyone. The opposition were poor but it did not worry Robinson. He scored another, the fifth in a 5–0 rout.

Dalglish, too, had a good night. He became the most prolific British scorer in the European Cup when he emulated his fellow striker with a brace of goals. The Scot's fifteen goals in the competition passed Denis Law's record of fourteen. A Danish own goal padded the score to complete a very satisfying night all round.

This felt like the season that Steve Nicol should impose himself on the team. So far it had not happened. Fagan had tried him on the left of midfield in pre-season to fill the vacuum left by Ronnie Whelan but had not been convinced.

It was reflected in team selection. Up until the Manchester United game, Nicol had been picked as an unused substitute three times. With twelve minutes to go at Old Trafford, he came on for Neal. It was too late to have any impact on that game but the young Scot was the natural replacement for the veteran full back. Given Neal's record, he was expected back quickly and Nicol could return to the reserves to continue his education.

There was some question as to whether he would ever develop into the player Liverpool needed. Nicol had now been at the club for two years after a £300,000 move from Ayr United. He had been bought as a potential replacement for Neal but dislodging the man who never missed a game had so far proved impossible. After a short spell at left back, Neal had switched to the right side of defence and shed his utility-man reputation. The opposite happened with Nicol.

He was an uncomplicated nineteen-year-old, who accepted what the world threw at him. The day he learned about Liverpool's interest was typical.

'I was at training one day and the assistant manager told me to stay behind,' he said. 'Willie McLean, the manager, came in and said, "We've had an offer for you. From Liverpool."'

The teenager weighed up the bombshell and then reacted in his usual style. 'I said, "OK,"' Nicol said. McLean could not believe it. 'Just fucking OK?'

The ability to take life as it arrived without any fuss was characteristic of Nicol. 'I was pretty level about everything,' he said.

The young Scot was driven down to Anfield to sign. It all seemed natural. 'I went in, they said, "This is how much we want to pay you." I agreed. Then they asked me to step outside and wait in the corridor while they sorted out the fee.

'I sat there for an hour, with a fella asking me did I want a cup of tea every five minutes. It wasn't glamorous. Willie came out and said, "You're a Liverpool player now. I have to drive back to Scotland. Good luck." With that, someone came out and took me round the corner to my digs, a terraced house on the corner by the ground. As he left me, the fella said, "Oh, and don't be late for training."'

It was a low-key welcome but typical. 'Next day at training,' he said, 'I had Hansen and Rush on one side, Dalglish on the other.' Nicol was not overawed. 'I was used to that. At Ayr, I'd only played two half-seasons. The dressing room was full of older pros and they helped me. They taught me. It was the same at Liverpool. By the time I got back to my digs that night, I felt I'd been there a long time. I felt I was where I should be.'

His first impact at Anfield was to undermine the sense of Scottish ascendancy in the dressing room where Dalglish, Souness and Hansen formed the dominant triumvirate. The youngster from Ayr was photographed like a music-hall Scotsman, a Tam O'Shanter perched upon his head and clad in tartan. It horrified the more sophisticated Caledonians.

'We couldn't believe it,' Dalglish said. 'We'd convinced everyone that the Scots were the master race.' It was hard for the rest of the squad to argue back against these three powerful leaders. 'Then Stevie showed up. Everything we had built up, he destroyed in ten minutes because of the photograph that was taken of him when he signed. There he was with a Tammy on and a stupid grin. We nicknamed him "Chico" after one of the Marx Brothers.'

The impression quickly formed that thinking was not the young man's finest quality.

He became the victim of dressing-room jokers. 'He is so honest and nice that he is easily wound up, and that can be fatal at Anfield,' Souness said. 'Stevie let himself in for a ribbing right from the start when he turned up for an away match at the team hotel with a teddy bear on top of his bag which read something like, "I am sad Sam, will you cuddle me and love me and make me happy?"'

The young man would occupy a strange position in the Anfield pecking order. 'He was the butt of the jokes but because he was Scottish he was still an insider, at the top of the hierarchy,' Johnston said.

Nicol's innocence made him an easy victim for the rest of the team. Shortly after Nicol arrived at the club, Paisley went around the dressing room handing out brown envelopes. The only person not to be given one was the newcomer. He was concerned and naturally felt left out.

Dalglish takes up the story: 'He was looking at us and someone said, "Didn't you get one?" He asked what it was and we told him it was cash, from the kit-maker. We said to him, "Were you on the team photograph?" We knew he was. So we said, "They give you cash for being on it. You should get your share. Go and see Bob and tell him you want one." So he did. Bob said, "You can have the fucking lot, it's tax bills!" We were rolling around the dressing room.'

The mickey-taking could be vicious. On one occasion some senior players convinced Nicol that Dalglish was suffering from a terminal disease and that the striker wanted the news kept quiet. The charade was kept up until a distraught Nicol went to Dalglish's room to offer sympathy only to find out he had been on the receiving end of a malicious practical joke.

For all the ribbing, Nicol felt at home. He was learning quickly and being helped by everyone around him. 'I kept my head down and worked hard,' he said. 'I didn't over-think things.' The contrast with Robinson is startling.

Nicol's approach worked for a while, but playing in the reserve team can only be satisfying in the short term. Unfortunately, he was seen as a right back, and that position was taken by Neal, the immovable force.

Nicol had the qualities to be a star but the eating habits of a gannet. 'His fitness was astonishing,' Hansen said. 'Dietitians would be horrified at the amount he ate. He could eat for Britain. It was not unusual for him to go through six or eight packs of crisps in one go.'

Fitness and self-restraint were hardly overemphasized at Anfield but sometimes Nicol pushed it a little far. 'I've never seen a fella smoke and drink so much and still be so fit,' Gary Gillespie said. 'He was a freak of nature. He loved a cig, much to the annoyance of Kenny, and would spark a sneaky one up on the bus on the way back from matches.'

It was possible to take the mickey out of Nicol's easy-going nature and his lifestyle but everyone recognized his raw talent and athleticism.

'He never carried any excess weight, hardly missed a tackle and gave the impression of being able to bomb up and down that right touchline for ever,' Hansen said. 'Suffice it to say that after our first match together on the right, I thought, "Where have you been all my life?"'

Before he reached that point, even the happy-go-lucky youngster began to have dark thoughts. 'Lots of silly things go through your head when you're not in the first team,' he said. 'These players were European champions, had won loads of titles. You think, "Am I going to be part of the demise?"'

Every day he was pushing closer to the starting XI. 'You look back and you were learning without thinking. Nobody over-talked, nobody over-coached. But when they spoke, you listened. They – Joe, Ronnie, Roy – had something to say. They, and all the players, had a winning attitude and you just fell in with it. It's not until you leave that you see how special it is.'

Moran and Evans pulled Nicol aside at training one day. For once the bad cop and good cop were bringing the same message. Its perfect timing changed the direction of the young man's career.

'I felt I could play in the first team when Fagan took over,' he said. 'I'd had eighteen months in the reserves. Ronnie said, "Do you want to play in the team?" Of course I said yes. "Have you told Joe?" he said. "Have you been to see him and asked why you're not in the side?"'

The thought had not occurred to Nicol. Now he took a deep breath and knocked on the manager's door. 'Joe couldn't give me a reason why I was not playing. He thought of me as a right back. That's how I came to play in midfield. To find another place to give me a game.'

But for now there was a chance at right back. And he impressed. Against Odense, all Nicol's ability seemed to coalesce at the right time. He ranged up and down the right flank with a vigour that had been lacking in the team so far in the season and was confident enough to shoot at goal from distance with his weaker left foot. The weakness of the opposition meant it could hardly be considered a landmark performance, but it made a few people sit up and think.

Goals were still not coming. Aside from the stroll against Odense, it had been a slow start to the season. Despite Fagan's tinkering with the system in an attempt to develop a partnership between Robinson and Rush, the pairing hadn't clicked.

The manager could not complain about the production of Rush and Dalglish. The former had netted four in the league and the Scot had added two. The lack of support from the rest of the side was a worry, though. The team's scoring rate was half the previous season's.

Every game was a struggle because the defence could not afford to concede. As good as the back four were, they could not take on all the strain. They had conceded only four goals and never more than one in a game. That sort of rearguard action should have earned the defenders more win bonuses. As it was, two draws and a defeat from seven games seemed like meagre pickings.

Liverpool's lack of punch had been noticed. Sunderland, who were limping along in seventeenth place in the table, came to Anfield and shut up shop. It made for a dispiriting afternoon for the Kop. It got worse when Gary Rowell scored a penalty on the half-hour after Craig Johnston punched away a header from Gordon Chisholm. It was Liverpool's second successive league loss.

The cost of defeat was not just points. Win bonuses made a big difference to a player's weekly wages. In 1984, the average annual salary in the First Division was £24,934. To put this in perspective, the UK average income was £9,984.

Liverpool were far from the best payers in the league, but sustained success brought add-on rewards. Bonuses were important. The anger in the dressing room at an individual error that cost points was mainly about pride. 'You weren't thinking about money, you were thinking about winning,' Dalglish said. However, the knock-on effect could be seen in the bank account.

Although the defenders were clearly doing their job, the rest were another matter. There was too much reliance on the front two. The Rush–Dalglish combination had racked up the goals during the previous two seasons but, as good as they were, they now needed better service and better support.

Dalglish had been an instant hit when he'd arrived from Scotland and the whole of Europe was aware of his talent, but it took Rush much longer to emerge as a superstar.

The eighteen-year-old Welshman had arrived from Chester City in 1980 for £300,000, then a record price for a teenager. Manchester City were sniffing around the boy from St Asaph and this perhaps forced Liverpool's hand too early. Geoff Twentyman, the club's legendary scout, later explained why he put his reputation on the line to sign Rush: 'I watched him six times and, finally, at an away game at Rotherham, I decided that despite his youth we had to strike quickly. A lot of other clubs were holding back, waiting for further proof. Liverpool took some criticism at first when people said it was too much for a teenager.'

The move almost *was* too much for the teenager in question. Rush did not believe he was good enough to play for the champions and tried to scupper the transfer with an outrageous wage demand. He asked for £100 per week. The gambit failed. Liverpool were offering £300 per week. Whether he liked it or not, the Welshman was moving to Merseyside.

Bob Paisley believed he had a fine prospect on his hands but there were plenty who shared Rush's scepticism. Quite a few senior players took one look and decided the young striker did not have the right stuff. The newcomer was tall, remarkably willowy and looked as though he would break under a tackle. He did not like being on the end of the savage dressing-room humour. And he did little to help himself fit in.

In training, he looked like a waste of money. He was sloppy, uninterested and laboured. The view from Melwood was echoed in the boardroom: 'That's a lot of money you've spent on a dud,' Twentyman was told by one director. Others thought it was a classic football transaction: with the end of the tax year looming, the club had spent its spare cash rather than have to pay tax. Better to buy a player and take a chance than surrender money to the exchequer.

Rush's laxness in training was a characteristic he would never lose. 'If they put a heart monitor on Rushie, you'd be trying battery after battery thinking it wasn't working,' Steve Nicol said. 'But Bob, Joe and the staff knew what he had to do. They didn't need a machine to tell them when a player needs to do something different. They saw he didn't need to be flat out in training.'

Paisley had the knack of being able to see talent that was not obvious to lesser football men. The manager, in his obtuse northeastern way, liked to say that the striker was 'not fast, but quick'. In a fair race, Rush might lose. The problem for defenders was he was off and gone before his marker knew the starting pistol had been fired.

Rush made his debut in December 1980 and played for the first team nine times before the season was over. He was banging in goals for the reserves – twelve in thirty appearances – but was unable to put the ball in the net at the higher level.

He also struggled to adapt to the unforgiving world of life at

Anfield. Rush was very shy and was cowed by the dominant personalities in the dressing room. All newcomers were given a rough ride
by the likes of Dalglish and Souness, especially if they carried a
record price tag. 'He was a dressing-room victim when he first
arrived,' Johnston said. 'New boys always got it.'

The young Welshman's homesickness was an obvious line of
attack. He was quickly christened 'ET' because he was always on
the phone, calling home.

'It took me a while to settle,' the striker said. 'It was a tough
dressing room to go into. I was very young and not happy at first.'

Respect needs to be earned. Nicol found his place alongside Liverpool's top dogs by dint of hard work and unfailing good humour.
Rush showed little of either quality. The only other way to develop
status was to perform in the First Division, where it mattered. To do
that, the striker needed to break out of the reserves.

By the summer of 1981, the boyhood Evertonian was ready to
call it a day at Liverpool. Again, he came up with a gambit which he
thought would force Paisley's hand.

Rush demanded a first-team place or a move. The manager
shrugged and agreed he could leave if he felt that way. Having
expected a little more resistance, the striker's pride was piqued. He
went back to the reserves with renewed determination and slammed
in another five goals in four games. When he got his chance in the
first XI, though, everything changed. 'At first, he couldn't score a
goal to save his life and what little self-confidence he had started to
seep away,' Paisley said. 'But once he started scoring he couldn't
stop. At first, they were all walloped in with his right foot. Then he
got the odd one with his left. Soon they were going in so frequently
with either foot that we couldn't remember which was his strong
one. Before we knew it he was heading in goals like they were going
out of fashion, too.'

Like Robinson, Rush opened his account against weak European
opposition, Oulun Palloseura, a Finnish team. After that, the goals
came thick and fast – more than thirty in each of his first two
seasons. The crowning glory was his haul of four in a 5–0 derby

victory over Everton at Goodison in November 1981. He was a once-in-a-generation goalscorer and his anticipation, pace and clinical finishing complemented Dalglish's genius perfectly.

The strained relationship off the pitch was not reflected on it. Rush's partnership with Dalglish bordered on telepathic. 'When he came he was only a kid. It took him a while to settle,' the Scot said. 'Then he played in the League Cup final replay at Villa Park. He didn't score but you could really see how good he was. When he started scoring, he took off.'

Once the pair clicked, they were unstoppable. 'He is one of the most instinctive finishers football has ever seen,' Dalglish said. 'My partnership with Rush proved so good because he could run and I could pass. I would just try to put the ball in front of him. Rushie said that he made runs knowing the ball would come to him. That was true, but only because his runs were so clever. His run was more important than my pass. Rushie was a good passer himself. He could have been a midfielder because his range of passing was great. Rush was easily the best partner I've ever had. We could have been made for each other.'

Rush had an acute positional sense. 'He was easy to set up,' Dalglish said. 'He took up good positions. He sat on the last defender's shoulder and went into the space behind him. No one could catch him.'

The striker was at his most dangerous against teams that played the offside trap. Sides that pushed their back four up to the halfway line were most vulnerable. 'Everton were the team who played with the highest defensive line at the time,' Dalglish said. 'And look at his record against them.'

Nicol, as usual, distilled Rush's genius down to its essence. 'He was phenomenal. With most players you hope they are going to score. With Rush, you *knew*. You just knew.'

In football, goals solve most problems. The more Rush scored, the less vehement the ribbing from his team-mates became. Rush was contributing and was no longer an outsider. Suddenly, he was at the heart of the squad's socializing and his thirst for drink was as strong as his appetite for goals. He didn't know how to stop in either arena.

Naomi Jacobs, who socialized with the team in Spain as a young woman, remembers an incident on the Costa del Sol. 'Ian once came to my friend's parents' place unexpectedly,' she said. 'He turned up in a taxi. He was so drunk he fell asleep on the couch and we couldn't wake him. My friend's parents thought he was going to die and were saying, "Get him out of here!" They had no idea who he was. They didn't believe us when we told them.'

That flat was about the only place in Europe where Rush went unrecognized. He was the object of desire at most of the Continent's richest football clubs. Like Dalglish, Souness and Hansen, he exuded class. If anyone was going to get Liverpool's season back on track, it would be the Welshman. And with an away match at West Ham, the surprise First Division leaders, next up in the league, Liverpool were hoping he was ready to go into overdrive.

Before that, there was another trip to London to negotiate, in less glamorous surroundings than Upton Park. In the second round of the League Cup, Liverpool had drawn Brentford of the Third Division. While Anfield fretted about the lack of goals, the west London club had more serious worries. Getting enough players on the pitch was the most significant concern. Just a week earlier, Brentford had been forced to abandon their match against Rotherham United because of illness and injury.

They were in no way prepared for the visit of the champions. Football's aristocrats were forced to slum it. Literally.

Griffin Park was in the throes of repair work after a fire in the stadium. Liverpool were forced to change in a Portakabin behind the stands. They had to jog to the pitch by running the length of the back of the East Terrace, to the delight of late-arriving supporters.

'Dressing rooms were pretty sparse anyway, even at the biggest grounds,' Johnston said. 'It was spartan. There was no luxury in those days.'

Even so, a Portakabin was a step down from the norm.

If changing was an uncomfortable experience, the match proved less of a trial. Rush punished the lesser opposition with two goals, Robinson helped himself to another and Souness contributed a strike from the midfield in a smooth 4–1 first-leg victory. Next was Upton Park, where at least Liverpool would get a shower. They wanted more, though. A defeat would leave them seven points behind the leaders. A win would cut West Ham's advantage to one. It was time for the champions to lay down a marker.

With West Ham flying high at the top of the table and Manchester United tucked in their slipstream two points behind there were those who thought there was a wind of change blowing through English football. The jury was out on this but one thing was certain: there was a gale blowing at Upton Park when Liverpool arrived on a dreadful autumn day. It was not an afternoon for silky skills and fancy dans. It was a time for ruggedness and physicality.

'Souness was a master in these situations,' Nicol said. 'In the dressing room he'd make it clear: no football. Get it, bang it long, don't try anything stupid. The squalls made it treacherous. You can't play football in those conditions.'

West Ham cherished their stylistic reputation. The east London side were having their best season in decades and the team was built around Trevor Brooking and Alan Devonshire, two skilful but lightweight ball-playing midfielders. When Liverpool looked at the opposition team sheet, there was a strong feeling that they would be given space to manoeuvre. Upton Park felt like a place the away team could play. The hostile reception from the famous 'Chicken Run', the section of terrace where the hardest characters in the East End gathered, was rarely replicated on the pitch. This was the club of Bobby Moore, Martin Peters and Geoff Hurst; of Ron Greenwood and the mythical 'footballing academy' that provided the raw materials which won England a World Cup. They loved to boast that Peters was a midfielder 'ten years ahead of his time'. Yet they rarely produced a man for the moment. That was Liverpool's speciality.

These were the sort of conditions that would suit a tank: and Michael Robinson seized his opportunity.

The big centre forward opened the scoring with a wind-assisted goal. On fifteen minutes a Grobbelaar clearance bounced down-field, eluding defenders, but Robinson barged into the area to nod the ball home. Phil Parkes, in the West Ham goal, levelled the Liverpool man but left no lasting damage. This was a striker built for contact.

Fagan was even more pleased by his new man's next two goals. The second came after Robinson turned in a poor clearance but the move that put the ball in the box contained a sublime passage of play that belied the conditions. Robinson, back to goal thirty yards out, tapped a pass from Kennedy to Dalglish, spun and set off for the penalty box while the Scot released Johnston to send in a cross.

The hat-trick goal was perhaps the best of all. Dalglish dinked the ball towards the edge of the area and Robinson, showing a Rush-like turn of pace and sharpness of instinct, struck the ball smartly as two defenders hurled themselves to stop the shot. 'People always underestimate Robbo,' Dalglish said. 'But he put everything into his game and was an important player for us.'

The Scot might have thought that but his first instinct was to take the mickey out of Michael. Offered the hat-trick ball to sign, Dalglish scrawled: 'I don't believe it!'

The 3–1 win sent out a warning. The First Division got the message. But did Europe hear?

12

Confronting the Beast

October–November 1983

Athletic Bilbao (h,a), European Cup R2; Queens Park Rangers (a);
Brentford (h), League Cup R2; Luton Town (h)

Javier Clemente was the opposite of Joe Fagan. The man in the Bilbao dugout was just thirty-three and the bright young thing of Spanish coaching. He had played as a striker for Athletic Bilbao in the late 1960s but had been forced to retire through injury.

Clemente did not take his attacking instincts into management. When he took over the Basque club in 1981 he set about creating a team that was difficult to beat. His side would play with two defensive midfield players and a solid back four. They won the Spanish title in 1983 but few friends in Madrid and Barcelona.

In the Nou Camp, especially, Clemente and his tactics were despised. Yet it was clear Bilbao were never going to win by entering into shoot-outs with Barcelona. The Catalan club had brought Diego Maradona to Europe in 1982. The young Argentinian had shown in that summer's World Cup in Spain that he was on the verge of being unplayable. In combination with Bernd Schuster, Barcelona's German playmaker, it seemed Maradona would dominate Spanish and European football.

It took something special to overcome Barcelona's skill players, but Clemente had a plan that involved a rugged approach, to put it kindly: Bilbao's savage tackling would overstep the mark.

On 24 September, as Liverpool returned to Merseyside with their tails between their legs after the defeat by Manchester United, Bilbao were kicking off a league fixture in the Nou Camp. Clemente had a special mission for one of his trusted veterans, Andoni

Goikoetxea. The defender was charged with making life uncomfortable for Barcelona's stars.

Goikoetxea's choice of weapon was the tackle from behind. He hit Maradona as he received the ball and gave similar rough treatment to Schuster. The defining moment of Goikoetxea's career occurred in the thirteenth minute of the second period. As Maradona took a pass inside his own half, the Bilbao No. 5 came sliding in from behind and, at full stretch, connected with the Barcelona player's ankle. Julio Alberto was close to his team-mate when Goikoetxea made impact. 'I heard the yell and his ankle went crack,' he said. 'We immediately knew how serious an injury it was. They had just broken the best player in the world.'

The transgressor was given a yellow card and Maradona taken to hospital. 'If I would have seen him coming I would have got out of the way, like I'd done so many times before,' the Barça superstar said. 'It sounded like a piece of wood snapping.'

Barcelona won 4–0 but that was barely noticed. Shock waves went through the football world. Maradona's ankle ligaments were in shreds. It would be four months before he played again. The defender was immediately dubbed 'the Butcher of Bilbao' and the Spanish FA came down hard, handing down an eighteen-game ban. Legend has it that Goikoetxea kept the boot that poleaxed Maradona in a glass case in pride of place at his home. When Bilbao were drawn against Liverpool in the next round of the European Cup, it looked a very tough draw. The only consolation was that 'the Butcher' would still be suspended.

Perhaps with one eye on Bilbao's European Cup campaign, the Spanish FA relented. Goikoetxea's ban was cut down to a mere eight games. There was rage in Barcelona and Argentina but the talismanic Basque defender was available for the tie at Anfield.

Just 33,063 watched a largely uneventful and scoreless game. 'The Butcher' allowed Rush and Robinson little space but was relatively mild in the tackle. Clemente's team gave nothing away; they niggled and nipped at Liverpool but were no worse than any other Continental opposition. Miguel De Andrés kept close to Dalglish, fouling him repeatedly, but it was well into the second half before the Basque was booked. 'The Kop, a cathedral choir in full voice every other Saturday, became a whisper of individual cries until they rose as one to condemn Goikoetxea on the hour,' wrote *The Times*. 'The Butcher' was inevitably shown the yellow card for a foul on Rush but it was another flat night at Anfield.

The mood in the dressing room was not quite so downbeat. 'They were a good team,' Kennedy said. 'As soon as we got off the pitch Joe said right away, "I'm happy with that." He knew we'd played a decent side and conceding no goals at home was vital.'

Rush concurred. 'Bilbao thought they were all but through and we expected Joe to have a right go at us when we got back to the dressing room,' he said. 'But he was surprisingly calm and came in after the match saying what a good result it was for us.'

'They couldn't just sit back at their place,' Dalglish said. 'It would open up. We were confident about that. We were always confident.'

Fagan may not have been a master tactician like Clemente but he had been around for a long time. He knew Bilbao would have to take a different approach in the San Mamés Stadium in the second leg. The Liverpool manager had won on alien territory before. He aimed to do it again.

Different away games present different problems. The San Mamés Stadium in Bilbao would be hostile and foreign. Before that, Liverpool had to face an even more alien situation.

The next league match was at Loftus Road. Two years earlier, Queens Park Rangers had laid an Astroturf pitch. This was to be Liverpool's first experience on plastic. It made for an awkward afternoon.

Almost nobody liked playing there. '[The ball] bounces and it runs, sometimes in the most diabolical way,' Brian Glanville wrote in the *Sunday Times*. 'It makes things devilishly difficult for visiting sides.' It was lucky for Liverpool that Steve Nicol had such a heavenly touch.

With Phil Neal back in the team after a two-game absence – which earned him the ironic nickname 'Crock' from the other defenders – the Scot was relegated to the bench. He would come on to score the goal that would transform the way Fagan thought about him.

'Craig Johnston had been sent off the week before at West Ham,' Nicol said. 'He got booked early on in the second half. The bench was cramped; you were all sitting together so I could hear everything that was said. Ronnie said to Joe: "This booking's too early, we don't want him getting sent off two weeks in a row." They put me on because they didn't want to risk it.'

The substitution gave Fagan a solution to his problems in the middle of the park. In the twenty-one minutes he played, Nicol was tireless and solid. The gaping hole left by Ronnie Whelan on the left did not look so huge now. To cap a fine performance, Nicol scored the only goal of the game with seven minutes left, showing remarkable balance and control to ram an awkwardly bouncing ball into the net from twenty yards out. Typically, Nicol remembers it differently. 'When I hit it I thought I'd not connected properly. Peter Hucker, the goalkeeper, dived under it. But it was huge. It was a massive result for the team and suddenly I was playing in the midfield.'

Loftus Road was bouncing. While the home crowds were dwindling, the away support was even more vehement than before. The gates were shut at the away end half an hour before kick-off and a large proportion of the travelling fans were not even in the vicinity of the stadium. The Football Special from Lime Street station had been delayed and eventually dumped hundreds of Scousers on a platform that was some distance from Shepherd's Bush. In London, especially, the centre of government and the chief beneficiary of Thatcherism, young Merseysiders liked to put on a show of strength. The deteriorating economic system meant that it was not just about football when they sang: 'They all laugh at us, they all mock us, they all say our days are numbered. But I was born to be Scouse. Victorious are we.' To the young fans who journeyed the length and breadth of England, every win felt like a two-fingered salute to the Establishment.

A decidedly tricky match was out of the way and suddenly the league table was shaping up the way the pundits had predicted. After ten games, Manchester United were on top with Liverpool two points behind. The battle was well and truly on.

If the intensity of competition was building by the week, the next game brought a chance for a breather. The League Cup's second round was a two-legged affair and Brentford came to Anfield trailing 4–1 from the game at Griffin Park. If the Third Division side expected an easy ride, they were mistaken. Even without Rush, rested with an eye on the trip to the Basque Country, Liverpool scored another four. David Hodgson, making his first start of the season, got on the scoresheet at last, adding a second goal to Souness's first-half penalty. Dalglish and Robinson got the other two, before a crowd of 9,902, the lowest there has ever been for a competitive game at Anfield in the modern era.

They saw a team that was beginning to purr. Suddenly, the goalscoring worries of early autumn were long forgotten. Next, Luton Town came up the M6 full of confidence and returned crushed after being used as a punchbag. Less than two minutes had gone when Rush – who had struggled with a virus until lunchtime – opened the scoring. Three minutes later the striker was netting again. Before the break he headed in a Nicol cross from the left to rack up a hattrick. Dalglish added another and, at 4–0, the game was over.

At least that was the hope in the Luton dressing room. In the home area, the mood was different. 'During the interval, Joe told us not to ease off,' Rush said. '"The job isn't done," he said. "Keep going. The crowd are loving it."'

Fagan's old prizefighting instincts were in full flow. Knock them down, keep them down, keep hitting until the final bell rings.

Rush did just that, running up his tally for the season with another two goals, a brilliant volley ten minutes after the break and another tap-in near the end. The Welshman's five goals in the 6–0 win were the work of a goalscorer at his peak. It was only the third time a Liverpool player had scored five in a match and the first time it had happened for twenty-nine years.

This game changed Rush's pre-match routine. The striker had signed a new boot deal and was playing for the first time in his sponsor's footwear. Before the match, the twenty-one-year-old had tried the boots on and felt the leather was too stiff. To soften them up, he filled a sink and soaked them, twisting them in all directions in an attempt to make them more supple.

After scoring five, Rush felt attached to the wet look. 'I'm not superstitious but I convinced myself I liked playing in wet boots,' he said. 'They seemed to fit better and hug my feet. I did it for the rest of my career.'

It was a brilliant feat of goalscoring and it gave Bilbao a hint of the challenge they would face, but the praise for Rush meant some of the other positive signs were overlooked. Nicol rampaged down the left. The youngster also gave Kennedy a level of protection he had been missing since Whelan's injury. Sammy Lee was back to his best, a buzzing irritant when the opposition had the ball and a precise passer when Liverpool were in possession. Dalglish, too, was flying, lining up Rush at will and providing intelligence and incisiveness up front. The team was brimming with enthusiasm and killer instinct. The time had come to export it to Europe.

The San Mamés Stadium, known as 'La Catedral', is tight, noisy and intimidating. It is one of the epicentres of Basque identity. The ground was full early, myriad drums beating. It was a pulsating, passionate and daunting atmosphere. Liverpool fans – 'sponsored by Transalpino', the young Scallies joked – were in a small minority but they knew they were about to see something special.

Bilbao had lost only once at home in thirty-one European matches. It was the sort of scene that set Souness's competitive juices flowing.

'We looked at the pitch and you could see that everyone fancied it,' the captain said. 'Warm weather, a tremendous atmosphere . . .

you just wanted to go out there and play. We fancied ourselves there.'

The doubts about their ability to progress only sharpened the steely determination in the Liverpool camp. 'We were written off by a lot of people,' Kennedy said. 'It was a bit surprising when you considered our record on the Continent.'

There was something truly imperious about Souness that night. He marshalled the side and was flawlessly calm in the first frantic fifteen minutes when the Basque side threw themselves towards the Liverpool goal. Before long, the home fans' drumming petered out and their chants trailed off into grumbling dissonance. Scouse voices made themselves heard as the roar became a hubbub. The first two jobs of the night had been completed: silence the crowd and take the sting out of the early wave of attacks.

There were fine performances across the pitch but Souness was in a class of his own; unhurried, elegant, merciless when necessary but always exuding class. 'He really intimidated their midfielders,' Kennedy said. 'It was cat and mouse early on, but we were definitely the cat.'

The Times captured the mood of the night: 'Souness strode through the bustling midfield traffic, directing his yellow-shirted colleagues with a deceptive nonchalance.'

Bilbao and their 'Butcher' had realized the size of their task, but the visiting side still needed a goal. Clemente had schooled his team so that they would not concede easily. Yet containing Rush for ninety minutes would prove too much for even the master of defence.

After sixty-six minutes Kennedy broke down the wing, found himself blocked from centring with his natural left foot and turned back on to his right. The full back clipped in a flat cross and Rush ran on to it, heading downwards in classic style with such power that the rising ball passed the goalkeeper at shoulder height.

The striker ran to his provider, celebrating in a manner that made it clear Liverpool believed the tie was over. 'Ian Rush, the cheeky bastard, told me later he thought there was no chance of me crossing it with my right foot,' Kennedy said. 'I don't know what was more surprising, the fact that I crossed with my right peg or he scored with his head.'

Rush was giving out some stick but he had to take it, too. 'That was the night he got a new nickname,' Nicol said. 'He didn't get many with his head so we called him "Tosh" after Toshack. We were always taking the piss.'

Fagan was bursting with pride. 'Our fellows love this atmosphere,' the manager said. 'Big hearts and big chests stand out on a night like this.'

Clemente, his team and the fans were generous in defeat. The San Mamés crowd applauded the men in yellow off and the coach was admiring afterwards. 'Liverpool are so difficult to handle because they never let you rest, not even for a second,' Clemente said. Outside the ground, the Basques plied the visitors with drink. 'The fans were great afterwards,' Souness said. 'As we got on the coach they were giving us those little leather pouches of wine for us to have a drink. It was a good celebration.'

The drinking did not stop there. Or on the flight home, despite it being the early hours of Thursday morning and a derby match against Everton on the horizon. 'We were all still buzzing when we got off the plane and decided to head out for a few drinks to celebrate,' Kennedy said. 'It was about two in the morning but we knew a place on the Wirral, so we went there and had a bit of a sing-song. We had Everton on the Sunday but nobody worried about that. It was still three days away.'

Europe could now be forgotten until March. The focus could turn to the neighbours and a little local difficulty at Anfield. But the happy bunch boozing until dawn on the Wirral were ready for anything football could throw at them.

'Big hearts, big chests, big thirsts, big ambitions, we had them all,' Kennedy said, echoing his manager. It was beginning to feel like something special was happening at Anfield.

But not for everyone. The day before the game, Fagan had taken the squad off the training pitch and named the team. When he got to the midfield, someone was going to be disappointed. The players sat quietly, paying attention, as was the custom. 'He read my name out,' Nicol said, 'and Craig groaned and broke the silence.' Johnston was appalled to be left out. 'I was in and Craig wasn't. He was shaking his head.'

In the harsh environment of the dressing room, some thought the Australian's pain was a source of amusement. 'It was a standing joke how often I was knocked back,' Johnston said. 'If I wasn't in the team, I'd take it to heart and almost cry. Rushie loved it. He thought it was funny. It was all right for him. He was always in the team.'

He was now. The days when the Welshman was an outsider were long gone. Despite having suffered similar treatment, there was no empathy from the striker.

Amid all the excitement, Johnston's eagerness and disappointment was a growing problem for the manager. It would soon come to a head.

13

Local Difficulty

November–December 1983

Everton (h); Fulham (a,h,a), League Cup R3; Tottenham Hotspur (a);
Stoke City (h); Ipswich Town (a); Birmingham City (h)

There was always an unusually close relationship between Liverpool and Everton. Both clubs can trace their roots to the same team: St Domingo's Methodist Sunday School football club.

The Sunday School team proved so popular that non-parishioners wanted to become involved and so in 1879 the St Domingo side was renamed Everton, after its parish. Initially, their home ground was in Stanley Park but the Football League required them to play in an enclosed area and they moved to a pitch off Priory Road.

Everton were an immediate success, so much so that the crowds irritated the owner of the land at the new ground and the club were on the move again – this time to Anfield – and so Everton became the first tenants of the famous old stadium whose name evokes Shankly, the Liver bird and the blood-red shirts of Liverpool FC. Their first League Championship was won at Anfield. Then, in 1882, a boardroom spat split the club and led to Everton's departure.

John Houlding, a local MP and brewer, was heavily involved in the growth of Everton but, when he attempted to buy Anfield, it sparked divisions on the Everton board. Houlding bought the ground but lost a vote of club members and Everton decamped to Goodison Park, leaving the brewer with a football stadium but no team.

Houlding's answer was to create his own club and Liverpool FC was born after a meeting in the Sandon Hotel, just yards from Anfield. In 1892 the upstarts played their first game. For a long time

Everton would look down their noses at the newcomers across the park with an older brother's contempt for his sibling.

Liverpool were the city's poor relation in footballing terms for a long time. Everton, owned by the Moores football pools family, were known as the 'Merseyside Millionaires'. It was not until Shankly arrived in 1959 that Liverpool began to close the gap between the clubs.

By the late 1970s, things had changed. The Reds were ascendant not only in the city but were also dominating Europe. Across the park, Goodison was in decline and Evertonians in gloom. As the Anfield trophy room overflowed with cups and honours, the ground's former tenants struggled. It had been thirteen years since Everton had won the title. In the intervening period, only a League Cup final defeat by Aston Villa gave Evertonians even a sniff of silverware. Only those with long memories could recall the days when Blues swaggered around the city, looking down on their red friends and relations.

The ultimate indignity had occurred almost a year earlier. In a derby match at Goodison Park in November 1982, Rush had scored four goals in a 5–0 rout. That Rush was a boyhood Evertonian sharpened the pain. It was the lowest point, and even a year on Everton had not climbed too far from that nadir.

The latest meeting of the two sides, one of the televised live matches, kicked off at the unusual time of 2.35 p.m. on Sunday at Anfield. The visiting team never looked like making Kennedy and his team-mates regret their early-hours sing-song on Thursday. The atmosphere, so often frenzied on derby day, was flat and so were Everton. The home team kept up the standards they had shown in Europe. 'The performance was built around accurate passes and intelligent runs,' *The Times* cooed. 'The game suddenly seems as absurdly simple as it should always be.'

The 3–0 victory was not quite as crushing as the previous year's five-star performance but it was emphatic enough. Nicol, rampant on the left, crossed for Rush to open the scoring. Rush then hit the post, the rebound giving Robinson the most straightforward of tap-ins for his first league goal at Anfield. With five minutes left, a flowing move ended with Nicol heading home the third goal. Manchester United had gone top of the table the previous day but Liverpool leapfrogged them with devastating ease. As for Everton, they appeared to be in free-fall. The speculation suggested that a change of manager was imminent. The Kop gleefully reminded the incumbent at Goodison that time was running out, singing: 'Howard Kendall, Howard Kendall, there's a taxi at the gate!'

Fagan seemed to echo the sentiment in his diary. He was disappointed with the lack of passion and fight from Everton. 'It wasn't like a derby game,' he wrote. 'It was too easy for us so there wasn't much excitement. Nothing much to say, other than three more points.' Everton, just three places away from the relegation zone, were a long way adrift. It was hard to imagine when derbies would again be competitive. 'We didn't think they'd give us much trouble again that season,' Dalglish said.

The games were now coming thick and fast. Too fast. On the Tuesday after the derby the team travelled to London for a League Cup game against Fulham. In this round the competition reverted from a two-legged format to a single knockout match. At least in theory.

Liverpool had not been beaten in this tournament for four seasons. They had won three consecutive finals. This minor domestic competition had once been derided by Kopites as the 'Mickey Mouse Cup'. Now they were taking it seriously.

Fulham, from the Second Division, attacked their superiors with a vigour that Everton had lacked. The champions were on the back foot. When Lawrenson tripped Gordon Davies to give away a penalty that Kevin Lock scored, they looked to be in trouble. However, the home side were overexcited by taking the lead and Rush equalized within a minute. There was relief that a draw had been salvaged but the prospect of a replay did not impress Fagan, who could see signs of strain.

And it didn't take a man with the Liverpool manager's experience to see what the problem was. The issues were obvious. Four days after the Fulham draw, Liverpool were back in London to play Tottenham Hotspur at White Hart Lane. The visiting side led twice but surrendered the lead each time. 'They do bear the marks of a side which has been playing rather too much football,' Brian Glanville wrote in the *Sunday Times*. The headline said it all: 'Staggering to a Stalemate'. When, back at Anfield a week later, they barely scraped past Stoke City with a late Rush goal, Fagan's anger was building.

For the moment, he turned it on the away team, lashing out at Stoke's style of play: 'What a depressing game,' the Liverpool manager said. 'In all my twenty-five years here I have never been so disappointed by the visiting side's display. Stoke wanted to defend and they did. The enjoyment went out of it for our spectators and players just because of their tactics.'

It was unlike Fagan, a man schooled in pragmatic football, to be so outspoken. The pressure was beginning to show.

After the replay against Fulham, the rage was focused on his own side.

Yet again Liverpool sputtered against the London team. With Rush struggling to find room and chances, the home side had to rely on their other attacking talisman, Dalglish. The Scot scored early in the second half and it looked to be enough to see the holders through to the next round. Yet, to the shock of the Kop, the almost infallible No. 7 gave Fulham a lifeline.

With five minutes to go, Dalglish decided to try to thread a back pass to Grobbelaar with two Fulham forwards lurking in the vicinity. It was almost a repeat of the situation at Craven Cottage. Davies latched on to the ball, the goalkeeper brought the Fulham forward down, and Lock calmly put the penalty into the net.

Liverpool could have done without the thirty minutes of extra time that followed. Even worse, Fulham held on to force a second replay. Fagan was furious.

'I'm not happy with our displays at the moment,' the manager observed. 'We seem to be hanging on. We are just not performing.

Too many players below par. Our fellows were just not as sharp as they were.'

Dalglish, so often above criticism, was in the line of fire, too. 'Dalglish has lost his edge,' Fagan went on. 'Started the season brilliantly but now being caught in possession too much.'

Smokin' Joe's decades in football had given him the knowledge to find a solution. He decided the problem was based in the midfield. Nicol's energy and enthusiasm had made a difference in the middle of the park but using a front three of Rush, Robinson and Dalglish put too much strain on the trio behind them. Lee, Souness and Nicol were being swamped and were required to do too much running. Fagan could see this.

'Our three-man midfield is being over-run by other teams with four in the middle. The strain is telling.'

There was an answer readily at hand. Ronnie Whelan, missing since August after a hip operation, was ready again. Whelan's first game of the season came away at Ipswich Town. Despite his annoyance at Dalglish, Fagan left out Robinson and reverted to his tried and trusted attacking pairing. The Scot rewarded his manager when he scored his hundredth goal in a Liverpool shirt, a classic, curling chip from close to the byline into the far corner. The 1–1 draw against a fine Ipswich side was satisfying and Fagan was pleased. 'A cracker of a game and a cracker of a goal,' he said. 'We were the better side, no doubt about that, but at the end of the day the result was right.'

The results may have been right but getting them was a strain. The underlying problems were obvious. The goals were not coming. The team were making things hard for themselves and the perfect example was the second cup replay against Fulham.

After the draw at Anfield, the London club won the toss for home advantage and an unnecessary third match against lower-division opposition loomed. As usual, Fagan's side made hard work of things. Dalglish dropped out with a niggle and Robinson came back into the side. By now, David Hodgson was boiling with frustration. He was not the only one.

Hodgson had never stepped up to the challenge of playing for Liverpool. He was deeply unhappy with his playing time and had seen Robinson jump in front of him in the pecking order. It might have been easier to take had the newcomer been banging the ball into the net regularly, but he was not. After more than a year at Anfield and with a hefty fee of £450,000 hanging around his neck, Hodgson was resentful and angry. He repeatedly asked for a transfer.

Johnston was in a similar position. He was in the team for Fulham but felt as marginalized as Hodgson. Nicol's emergence had increased competition in the midfield and the Australian struggled to cope with the situation. 'When I wasn't in the team I took it personally,' he said. 'So when I wasn't playing it was almost like a knife through my heart to see the lads running round the pitch without me.' Johnston rowed with Fagan on frequent occasions and demanded a transfer, too. Yet with the matches piling up, the manager needed all the bodies he could get.

The final match of the Fulham trilogy went largely like the previous two. The Second Division team more than matched their betters and the tie was 0–0 after ninety minutes. It took until the 116th minute of the game for Liverpool to break the deadlock in a decisive manner.

As so often when Liverpool were in trouble, the captain stepped up. Souness's strike put his team in the fourth round, to everyone's relief. 'The game is cruel at times and it is cruel to Fulham at the moment,' Fagan said magnanimously. 'Thank God the round was over.'

Johnston played the entire 120 minutes but events left it clear to the Australian that he had done little to advance his cause to be a regular in the team. The game was turned by Fagan's introduction of Ronnie Whelan for Steve Nicol. The Irishman made the difference.

'All I did was put on a pair of fresh legs to break the deadlock,' Fagan said. 'It worked. There was no ulterior motive about it, nothing tactical as one or two of the press tried to make out. Just fresh legs.'

Whelan was still easing himself back to full fitness after his hip operation. When he reached peak condition, he would be one of the first names on the team sheet. Johnston's frustration remained unabated, even though he was named in the side for the next league match, at home to Birmingham City.

With Christmas on the horizon and cash at a premium, fewer than 25,000 trooped into Anfield for the visit of Birmingham. Despite the team being top of the league, there was uncertainty around the old ground. December was shaping up to be a crucial month but the fans were staying away, and those who did turn up struggled to generate any atmosphere. The vibrant youths who made the away support so fervid were strung out across the Kop and scattered around the ground. Their passion often failed to penetrate the void left by 20,000 empty spaces. Shankly had proclaimed that the home crowd gave Liverpool a goal start. Like Fagan's back-up strikers, they were not contributing their share.

Rush, as usual, obliged with a goal to give the home team a 1–0 win but it took until the eighty-sixth minute to break down the opposition. It was the striker's thirteenth league goal – half of the team's production in the league. They were relying too much on the Welshman. His goals, and the results of other teams, were papering over a number of cracks. While Liverpool edged past Birmingham, West Ham, Manchester United and Tottenham, the three teams below the league leaders lost. It meant Liverpool had opened up a four-point gap at the top of the table.

The Times suggested the title race was turning into 'a foregone conclusion by Christmas'. But nothing is ever certain in football.

14.

Month of Madness

December 1983

Coventry City (a); Notts County (h); Birmingham City (a,h), League Cup R4; West Bromwich Albion (a); Leicester City (h); Nottingham Forest (a)

Every team has a bogey ground, a place where they don't feel comfortable, where results seldom seem to go to plan. For Liverpool, Coventry City's Highfield Road was near the top of the list.

Of ten games in the East Midlands since Bob Paisley took over in 1974, Liverpool had won just two – and one of those was a League Cup match. In the First Division, they had lost twice, drawn six times and achieved victory once.

Still, Liverpool feared no one. For all their stuttering form, they were on a fifteen-game unbeaten run. There was rancour in the air at Anfield, though. Joe Fagan shuffled his team before the game. Although things appeared to be running smoothly, the Liverpool manager was unhappy with his midfield. Ronnie Whelan was picked instead of Craig Johnston, who was relegated to the bench.

The Australian was furious. He confronted Fagan and handed in a written transfer request. 'Craig has given me a letter asking for a transfer and doesn't feel I've been fair to him,' the Liverpool manager told the press, attempting to calm the situation. 'He has a case. He's played in most of this season's games, done well and I can understand how he feels. He's entitled to his opinion and is quite right to express it. Dropping him wasn't easy and I might find I've done the wrong thing.'

It was hard for Johnston to understand. Fagan frequently said he was opposed to changing a winning team. Except, of course, where the Australian was concerned.

'I thought it was unfair,' Johnston said. 'That's why I asked for a transfer. I took it very seriously. I thought, "If I'm trying this hard and it's not appreciated then I might be appreciated elsewhere." I went to see Joe and said I thought I was doing as good a job as anyone else in the role. He was nice, friendly, but kept saying he couldn't change a winning side. I got into the team and we won. Then he called me in and said he was going to drop me. Maybe he understood the game better and saw the bigger picture. I was in my early twenties. I went off the rails.'

On this December Saturday, the entire side were on the wrong track. The horror show at Highfield Road shocked the league.

Coventry were fifth in the table but hardly one of the division's powers. If the results of the previous decade were anything to judge by, the game would be a sterile 0–0 draw. It didn't take long for any preconceptions to be challenged.

Within forty-five seconds, the visiting side were a goal down. Grobbelaar fumbled a tepid drive by Terry Gibson and Nicky Platnauer headed the ball into the net from a prone position. If he took it lying down, so did Liverpool.

By half-time, they were three goals behind, with Gibson scoring twice. Grobbelaar was having a nightmare and Kennedy was suffering humiliation. Dave Bennett, the Coventry winger, was exposing all the full back's flaws. 'Kennedy can't have been turned so often since he last played blind man's bluff,' the *Sunday Times* commented unkindly. The newspaper's verdict was mild compared to Fagan's.

'He went absolutely berserk at half-time, at everybody,' Kennedy said. 'We couldn't get near Gibson.'

Things escalated fast. 'It was probably the most annoyed I ever saw Joe,' Kennedy said. 'Unfortunately for me, I was the one he picked on. There were others who hadn't pulled their weight but he targeted me.'

Strident exchanges of opinion were not unusual in the Liverpool dressing room but the rows rarely spun out of control. They did now. Kennedy attempted to answer back and this infuriated the manager, who hurled his half-time tea across the room.

'Some cups got thrown,' Kennedy said. The situation escalated immediately. 'I threw some cups, too. It was not the best idea.'

The dressing room was in meltdown. Jim Beglin had been taken down to the match to give him some experience of travelling with the first team. He found himself in the middle of a battle zone. 'I didn't know where to look,' the twenty-year-old reserve said. 'There were cups flying around all over the place and a lot of raised voices.'

As the argument spiralled out of control, others joined the fray. 'Souey and Ronnie Moran started barking in and Roy Evans had to come in from outside to calm it all down,' Kennedy said. 'It got out of hand quite badly.'

Fists flew with the teacups and Beglin was frozen with fear. 'Alan Kennedy, the player I was hoping to eventually displace in the team, came in for a lot of stick and I was thinking to myself, "Do I really want to get into this team?"'

Nicol, who was no longer naive in the way Beglin was, knew what Kennedy's mistake had been. 'Blasting was very rare,' he said. 'Don't have a go back. If Joe spoke, you listened. You didn't waste words arguing. Most of the time it was not so much screaming, it was just straight to the point. Telling people the truth. Joe, Ronnie, Roy, they knew their shit. Suck it up, be quiet and listen to them.'

'We were accusing each other of not doing the job,' Kennedy said. 'Things were said. Some harsh things but they probably needed to be said. We were trying to put things right.'

Barney Rubble recognizes that his biggest error that day was not on the pitch. 'Joe Fagan was not a man to be messed with,' he said ruefully. 'If he spoke. You listened.'

Among the sub-plots was a disagreement between Souness and Dalglish. The big beasts of the team were friends and room-mates and rarely crossed swords. 'It went out of control,' Johnston said. 'Kenny and Charlie were going for it. It started over something small, like "you didn't pass to me, you greedy bastard" and blew up. I'd never seen it before or since.' Johnston chuckled. 'It was excellent viewing.'

A frazzled and frantic Liverpool team took to the pitch on a damage-limitation mission. They barely achieved that, losing 4–0 eventually after Gibson struck again near the end. Fagan was shell-shocked.

'I need a pint of whisky,' he told the press. 'I feared something like this was going to happen because we haven't been playing too well recently. But that was a pathetic performance. It's so long since a Liverpool team have needed to be given a blasting I'd forgotten what to say. I'm confused at the moment. At times like these we haven't got a prayer.'

The coach ride home was subdued. 'You were scared to talk on the way back,' Nicol said. 'Losing was a no-no. If you got caught laughing, you'd get your lungs ripped out.'

Even Johnston kept quiet, though he felt vindicated. Perhaps Fagan had made a mistake dropping him.

Back in Liverpool, the players headed off to their usual haunts but not for sing-songs. That night they were drowning their sorrows. They didn't like it.

On a sober Sunday morning, the heat had gone out of Smokin' Joe. The manager and his staff gathered and wrote off the result as an aberration. The players reached their own verdict. 'We were becoming a little complacent,' Souness said. 'We needed to be brought to our senses and that result was just the trick.'

A rather raw Kennedy put the game behind him. 'The only thing you can do is learn from it,' the left back said. 'It was one of those days when nothing worked.'

Nicol agrees. 'Joe realized there'd be games when it didn't happen for you,' he said. 'Move on, win the next one. The mentality was incredible.'

Dalglish was even more phlegmatic. 'Nearly every year we got hammered once,' he said. 'Wolves beat us four–one a couple of years before, for example. It didn't matter. We moved on and put it behind us.'

The *Echo* summed it up succinctly: 'Destroyers Given a Taste of

Their Own Medicine', ran the headline. There was only one way to bounce back and that was to inflict pain on someone else.

The backlash began. The victims were Notts County, who were struggling near the bottom of the table. The 5–0 thrashing at Anfield saw Liverpool at their most brutal and, as usual, Souness led the way. The game was never a contest and by the time Nicol scored after twelve minutes County knew they were in for a pounding. More than the goals, the visiting side were left battered and bruised. Martin O'Neill, who had been part of the Nottingham Forest team that went toe-to-toe with Liverpool in the late 1970s and part of the Northern Ireland side that had beaten Souness's Scotland four days earlier, was left writhing in agony by the Liverpool captain. Souness started his assault on O'Neill early, fouling him within seconds of the match starting. When County's captain tried to take the initiative and show a bit of muscle in the fifth minute, Souness was ready for it and emerged from the confrontation with a smirk on his face. O'Neill, meanwhile, was left requiring stitches to close a cut on his knee and a stretcher to carry him off the field.

There was bloodlust in the air at Anfield. Fewer than 23,000 people were in the ground but they relished the vicious spectacle, cheering each pass as the men in red zipped the ball across the pitch and wallowing in the humiliation of the opposition.

It was precisely the message Fagan wanted to send out. 'We knew we were bloody awful last week but the lads were more upset about it than I was,' he said. 'They thought they'd let the club down.'

This was not the time for let-downs. The team now faced five games in twelve days. The first was a League Cup match against a rugged Birmingham City side at St Andrew's. In characteristic style for this season, Liverpool stuttered and drew 1–1 on a freezing night. Souness gave his team the lead in the first half but a late goal by Mick Harford forced a replay two days later. Another game in the crowded Christmas schedule was the last thing players and fans needed.

Fagan was relieved. Another bogey ground had been negotiated. 'I've always dreaded coming here as a player because we always got kicked out of sight,' the manager said. 'It's a place most clubs hate to come to. They give you nothing and generally you go home crying. At least we are not crying tonight.'

A mere 11,638 fans came to Anfield on the Thursday night before Christmas to witness a 3–0 win that took the home side into the semi-finals of the secondary cup competition. It was an eerie atmosphere: to cut the cost of paying underutilized gatemen, the club left the Kemlyn Road stand shut. The other three sides of the ground were sparsely occupied, too. But at least another replay was not required.

After the game, it was off into town for the Christmas party at a nightclub owned by Tommy Smith, a former team-mate. It was a lively, almost riotous affair. As usual, the dress code was fancy. Sammy Lee and Ian Rush went for the almost traditional Nazi uniforms, Phil Thompson captured the mainstream mood of the age by dressing as Boy George.

By then, though, the zeitgeist had moved on. The young scallywags who had braved the empty and frozen terraces of Anfield to support the side against Birmingham flocked into town to a different kind of party, one that attracted football's underclass rather than its ruling class. The players went in fancy dress to Tommy Smith's club; the parallel-universe hot-ticket bash was round the corner in the shape of Joe Wagg's Christmas party at the System club.

Joe Wagg was a character in the groundbreaking football and music crossover fanzine, *The End*. It was one of the first indicators that the matchgoing culture – derided as hooliganism by the mainstream media – was not merely nihilistic and violent. It contained interviews with internationally renowned bands like the Clash and local favourites like the High Five.

Wagg is a Scally Candide, an ingénu who travels to London on an 8p platform ticket, is surprised to find two jumpers on a coat hanger when he tries the garment on in a shop and is even more shocked to discover after leaving the premises that one of the sweaters has found its way into his holdall. It is a faux innocence to explain away 'bunking' the train and the theft of clothes. It is a ludicrous, hilarious visit to the city's counterculture.

Among the bands on the bill that night were the Farm. Peter Hooton, the lead singer, was one of the brains trust who created *The End*. He was one of the young men who travelled religiously to matches and remembers the Christmas of 1983 as being characteristic of the era. 'There wasn't a great deal of money around but people weren't going to let that get in the way of having a good time. There was always something going on every night in the city at the time: a new band, a political meeting, a writers' workshop. It was a very creative time and lots of the young lads at the match were involved in politics, even if it was only in a loose way.

'We thought the fancy-dress thing was funny. You'd see the players out and about but they seemed like a different generation to us, with their muzzies and perms. You'd see Souness in the Conti [Continental club] and he'd be dressed like he was going to Studio 54. But you'd bump into them everywhere. Everyone knew the ones who lived in West Derby would be in the Jolly Miller on a weekday afternoon and some of them would be in Streets, off Hardman Street, after the match on Saturday. Hardly anyone bothered them. But our Christmas party was a very different thing.

'How did we feel about them? They were a bunch of dopes. When they had a red shirt on, they were heroes, you'd get behind them. When they were off duty and on the ale they were your average bunch of knobs. Just like us. Only dressed more badly and with a few more quid.'

In Smithy Manor, the assorted bunch of Nazis, New Romantic pop stars, Klansmen and judges that comprised the costumed Liverpool squad partied long into the night. Some of their most vehement supporters were enjoying the same high jinks and downing pint after pint, dressed in a more subdued selection of sportswear. No one was thinking about tomorrow. They were drinking for today.

The festive season, after all, was a time of excess, even if it was followed by four games in a week.

'The culture in those days was to have a drink,' Alan Kennedy said. 'We still like a drink. I can't imagine the players of today going up to their colleagues and saying, "Shall we have a Coke? Shall we have a glass of water?" We all liked the beer and we all socialized together and that was a good thing about what Liverpool were all about.

'We went out after a game and used to have a couple of beers, but that was normal. Everybody did that. Generally speaking, it didn't do us any harm, and if it didn't do us any harm we continued to do it. Over Christmas it was the same.'

By Boxing Day the team were sober enough to beat West Bromwich Albion at The Hawthorns. The visiting side brought the festivities in the Midlands to an end with a splendidly assured performance and the scoreline of 2–1 did not reflect Liverpool's dominance. Aside from a two-minute spell when Albion equalized Nicol's first-half goal, Fagan's team were in charge. Souness sealed the victory with a shot of 'characteristic arrogance', observed *The Times*. The margin was narrow but Fagan laughed it off. 'They must have had it in their minds that they have another match tomorrow,' he said. Two games in two days was as much a part of the Christmas tradition as the festive booze-ups.

'You didn't complain or even think about it,' Souness said. 'Playing twice in forty-eight hours was the sort of thing that happened at Christmas and New Year. No one said they were tried or moaned.'

The punishing schedule – or the ale – seemed to have caught up with Fagan's men at Anfield, though. With sixteen minutes to go, Leicester City were 2–0 up, the Kop silent and shuffling rather than loud and bouncing. Then Liverpool woke up. Lee pulled one back, Rush equalized with seven minutes left and suddenly the visiting side were under siege and the crowd in full cry. And Leicester cracked with two minutes left and gave away a penalty. Souness stepped up to take it and the three points looked to be in the bag. Yet Champagne Charlie was a little too casual and Mark Wallington, the goalkeeper, saved the shot. It was an opportunity missed.

While Liverpool had clawed back a two-goal deficit, Manchester

United had thrown away a 3–1 lead at home to Notts County. Suddenly, a point recovered looked like two lost. United were due at Anfield in six days' time in what would be the start of the second half of the season. First, there was a difficult trip to the City Ground to face Nottingham Forest on New Year's Eve.

The sting had gone out of the rivalry with Brian Clough's Forest over the past couple of years. Between 1977 and 1981 it had been one of football's most anticipated contests. Forest were European champions in 1979 and 1980 but were on the decline. Clough, an opinionated and abrasive manager, tried to put pressure on his Liverpool counterpart by claiming that Fagan was responsible for the sacking of Richie Barker, the Stoke manager.

The previous month, Fagan had roundly criticized Stoke's defensive approach at Anfield. Clough blamed this for Barker's dismissal. The Liverpool manager was naturally combative but this time he let his team do the talking. Rush made it a happy New Year, scoring just before the half-hour to give the team a vital advantage and earn a 1–0 victory. The goals were still hard to come by, the performances stuttering, but Liverpool were on top of the table at the halfway point in the season, three points clear of United. It looked increasingly like a two-horse race. The combatants were about to meet on 2 January. What a way to open 1984.

15.

Damned Cheek

January 1984

Manchester United (h)

The antagonism between Liverpool and Manchester runs far deeper than football rivalries. Its basis is economic. In the nineteenth century Manchester was a cotton town and needed the port of Liverpool to export its goods worldwide. Resentful that the docks on the Mersey were trimming their profits, Manchester's city fathers built the ship canal to ensure that the trade was entirely their own. Five years before Liverpool FC came into existence, spades went into the ground to build the canal.

Both Manchester clubs, United and City, have a sailing ship on their badge, despite their city lying forty miles inland. The competitiveness then seeped into almost every area of life: music, literature, fashion and attitude.

Football was to become the main battleground. The combativeness grew into hatred in the 1970s and was reaching a crescendo in 1984. Liverpool had dominated proceedings for a decade but United's status and fan base were massive. The Old Trafford club were newsworthy – turmoil always earns more column inches – and had some of England's biggest stars in the squad. Liverpudlians resented the attention that United drew. Mancunians hated the sight of Liverpool's trophy cabinet. Now, under Ron Atkinson, United believed that they could usurp their rivals. They thought the new year would herald a new age.

The atmosphere at Anfield can be flat at times. The old ground's reputation is daunting but, like anywhere, it can have off days. In 1983 there were a lot of off days. Small crowds caused by a combination of economic hardship and success burnout created matchdays where players could be heard shouting to each other.

Shankly's 'bastion of invincibility' seemed an idle threat on the cold afternoons and nights of the autumn. Even the derby match, played on a Sunday, had been subdued.

It was different in January. It was different whenever Manchester United were in town. Anfield would never accept the presence of the enemy without whipping up a frenzy. Everton were rivals but Kopites had brothers, sisters, cousins and friends who supported the Blues. The momentary bile was quickly forgotten in the hurly-burly of everyday life. There were few such bonds to weaken the spite towards those from the other end of the East Lancs Road. The queues up Walton Breck Road started early on this cold, windy Monday.

Behind the Anfield Road end was Stanley Park, a leafy expanse of green. The other three sides of the ground were hemmed by terraced streets with warrens of back jiggers that were impossible to police. It was crowded, cramped and intimidating to outsiders, especially Mancunians. One of the main approaches to the Kop was down Back Rockfield Road which was more commonly known as 'Dog-Shit Alley'. On days like this the mood around the stadium was tense and threatening.

The United coach ran a gauntlet of abuse on its way up Anfield Road and was met by a couple of hundred hecklers as the players disembarked. Inside the ground, the corridors were as pinched as the terraced streets outside. The dressing rooms were basic – wooden benches, coat pegs above and a table in the middle.

Paint flaked from the walls. There was not a shred of glamour. It was spartan by design, though the home area was hardly more luxurious. These were not places to be comfortable; they were places to prepare for battle.

Five minutes before kick-off, the referee knocked on the dressing-room door. Souness led the Liverpool players out into a small corridor that could barely accommodate twenty-two players, let alone the assorted coaching staff, substitutes, stewards, cameramen, press and random others who gather outside dressing rooms. He moved slowly, strutting. This was his territory. He was marking it. He waited for United to emerge and looked the enemy in the eye before leading the way on to the pitch.

The teams went down a dozen steps, studs clattering on the concrete, with the Liverpool players reaching up to touch the 'This Is Anfield' sign for luck. Three more strides brought Souness and his men into the open and up another flight of stairs to be met by a blast of appreciative noise that rapidly turned to howling nastiness at the sight of United in their white shirts and black shorts. Souness led his team towards the Kop, where 12,000 people craned up on their tiptoes for a better view and leaned forward, pushing the spectators in front of them. A stumbling wave of humanity rippled from the back of the terrace down towards the pitch.

United ran to the Anfield Road end, where some 3,000 of their fans were fenced away from the home supporters. Small pockets of Mancunians were dotted around the ground, some even sneaking into the Kop. It was dangerous – the rancour between the two groups of supporters meant that punches were thrown freely – but worth the risk to see a game like this.

The Times captured the scene inside the stadium: 'The famous arena resembled a battleground of old and the conditions might have detracted from the spectacle but did nothing to limit the drama.'

Things appeared to be going in Liverpool's favour. Bryan Robson, who had already produced two excellent performances against Fagan's team this season, was ruled out with a bruised instep before the game. Without their talisman, the United midfield lacked thrust and firepower. Fagan had worried about Dalglish's fitness. The Scot had felt discomfort from a stomach injury. It was determined he was fit to play on the morning of the game. Liverpool were delighted, though they would come to rue the decision.

The game started badly for United. They had problems at the back when Gordon McQueen, the centre half, limped off after twenty minutes. By then United were in the eye of the storm. The home side swarmed all over them.

After half an hour Liverpool got the reward they deserved. A Dalglish corner hung in the wind, allowing Souness to adjust his body and lash the ball goalward. Arthur Albiston was on the line to block the shot but the irrepressible Johnston followed up to bundle the ball into the net. The Kop celebrated wildly and suddenly there was a real possibility of a six-point gap opening up at the top of the table. Half-time arrived with Liverpool satisfied and Ron Atkinson desperate to rally his United side during the interval.

Whatever the United manager said, the match changed in complexion early in the second period. Dalglish jumped for the ball with Kevin Moran, who was famous for his physical approach. 'The ball came in to Kenny and he tried to flick it on and Moran caught him,' Souness said. 'He caught him. It looked bad.'

Moran had played Gaelic football and tended to crash into opponents, often injuring himself as badly as his victims. The Liverpool No. 7 had dealt with defenders like this throughout his career but there was something different this day. The United defender had injured a wrist over the Christmas period and had his arm in a cast. The referee allowed him to play, despite the potential damage the hard sheath could cause to other players. As he clattered into Dalglish, Moran's wrist pounded into the Liverpool player's cheek. There was blood everywhere and the damage not just superficial.

The referee did not even blow for a foul. The official may not have seen it, but the Liverpool players had. 'I was first to him and he was up on one knee by then,' Souness said. 'He had his hand on his face. When he took it away his cheek was sort of concave. It was pushed in, depressed.'

The furious Liverpool captain charged at the United player. 'It was lucky it was near the bench,' Souness said. 'They stopped me going after Moran.'

Fagan was up quickly to restrain his captain. As the players milled around, it became clear Dalglish was in trouble.

'I didn't know anything about it,' Dalglish said. 'I went to flick on a header and bang! After that, I can't remember much.'

Half a pitch away, Alan Kennedy knew the injury was bad. 'I didn't realize what had happened,' he said. 'But everybody heard a crack.'

The bleeding was from a cut on the eye. The real damage was below. Moran's cast had inflicted a depressed fracture of the cheekbone on Liverpool's superstar. Ronnie Moran gave him perfunctory first aid but it was obvious that Dalglish could not continue. It was also apparent that he faced a long lay-off.

For the rest of Fagan's team, it was a shock to see such a resilient team-mate injured. Over the years the striker had seen more than his share of ferocious treatment and proved equal to it all.

'We all know he was a great player but he could look after himself,' Johnston said. 'He wasn't dirty, just very, very tough. He actually wanted to finish the game. He tried to stay on but his face was a real mess. He was as white as a ghost and was obviously told "no way".'

As the injured player was led off the pitch and taken to hospital, the United fans cheered derisively, happy to see their tormentor helped away. Dalglish shook his fist at them. It was unlike the Scot to act so emotionally but almost everyone inside Anfield believed this was a turning point in the season. 'I don't remember doing that,' Dalglish said wryly. 'I'd just had a blow to the head.'

'I didn't see what happened,' Nicol said. 'But I know what I thought: one time, one day, one game, Kenny would get Moran back. You did not take liberties with Kenny.'

Yet Dalglish did not see it quite the same way. 'It wasn't malicious,' he said. 'Kevin isn't a malicious guy.'

The loss of their best player in such circumstances had a huge effect on the team. Liverpool were subdued afterwards. With just two minutes remaining, Garth Crooks nodded the ball down to Norman Whiteside in the Liverpool area and the young Northern Irishman fired home despite the attentions of Lawrenson and Grobbelaar. 'By the time United equalized, I was in hospital,' Dalglish said, with a hint of regret in his voice.

Moran had also left the pitch, bleeding profusely from a gash that Atkinson claimed was 'as wide as the Grand Canyon'. Yet the retribution seemed paltry. Dalglish faced an operation and two months out of the game. It was generally believed that Moran's cast had turned the title race in United's favour. Fagan recognized the severity of the problem. 'It wasn't the loss of two points that was significant, it was the injury to Kenny,' he said. 'Who knows what will happen with him out?'

Dalglish had not faced such a prolonged spell on the sidelines since his arrival at Liverpool in 1977. He was the symbol of Liverpool's greatness. The Scot's mere presence brought a surge of belief in the dressing room and on the terraces. In one swing of Moran's wrist the new year had soured. The anger at Anfield was palpable.

Souness was the angriest. He turned his fury on Fagan, the man he had rallied the team around the previous summer. 'Yeah, I had words with Joe,' he said. 'I thought we'd gone soft. We let them into a game we should have won. They were going to win the league unless we shaped up quickly.'

Johnston, who had scored the goal against United, had some sympathy for his captain's point of view but thought United lacked mental strength. 'I always did well against them,' he said. 'But they had better players than us across the squad, position for position. We had something special, though. They lost games they should have won. We won games we should have lost. We had that magic teamwork.'

Part of that magic was recovering in hospital. The two lost points were bad enough but the mood got worse when the players trooped to the ward to see their injured team-mate after his operation.

'When they walked in the door all their faces fell,' Dalglish said. 'Lawro had to be taken outside for a cup of tea he was so shocked.' The Scot was not concerned about vanity, only victory. 'It didn't bother me my face was a mess.'

It bothered the others. Even Fagan, the bare-knuckle fighter with the 'sausage' nose, could hardly force himself to look at the injury.

'When Joe came in with the players he obviously got a fright as well,' Dalglish said. 'He left the papers, said he couldn't stay and left. He couldn't look at me.'

At Liverpool, injuries were frowned upon. Shankly would not speak to players who were out of the team, feeling that his disapproval would encourage them to rush back to fitness more quickly. Almost every member of the squad had niggles throughout the season and could have cried off on many occasions but management and peer pressure meant they took to the pitch when they probably should have rested. It was a macho culture and injured men felt like outsiders.

This was different. The damage to Dalglish's face upset both his manager and his team-mates. It was sympathy combined with horror that caused everyone to keep their hospital visits brief. Still, the star man felt alone and isolated. He was a huge loss to the team, too. As *The Times* noted, without him Liverpool 'were reduced to a more mortal level'.

Yet not everyone shared Souness's doubts or the newspaper's sense of mortality. 'I don't remember being down,' the ever-level Nicol said. 'We knew we were going to win. There was never a sense of being up or down. Even when Kenny was out, we had a conviction about us that we would come out on top.'

16.

Filling the Vacuum

January 1984

Newcastle United (h), FA Cup R3; Wolverhampton Wanderers (h);
Sheffield Wednesday (a,h), League Cup QF; Aston Villa (a)

There are few players who are impossible to replace. Once, the Kop believed Kevin Keegan was a player who would leave a permanent vacuum behind him.

Shankly had signed the twenty-year-old attacking midfielder for £35,000 from Scunthorpe United in 1971 on the eve of the FA Cup final. He became the star of the Scot's second great team, the league's most famous footballer and an England hero.

Although Keegan went on to win the Bundesliga title with Hamburg in 1979 and the Ballon d'Or twice, his years in Germany never quite reached the heights Liverpool were achieving. He returned to England in 1980, after playing in his second European Cup final, a 1–0 defeat by Nottingham Forest. His first stop was Southampton but then he had dropped a division to play for Newcastle United in the second tier of the league. There, he had become a Geordie hero. Now, on a freezing Friday night, he was back at Anfield after Newcastle had been drawn against his former club in the third round of the FA Cup.

There was always a smugness about the Kop when Keegan returned to Anfield. They had been spurned by the object of their affections only to find someone better almost immediately. And he had not quite moved on to better things.

On his first return to Merseyside, with Hamburg in the European Super Cup in 1977, six months after leaving Liverpool, Keegan was on the receiving end of a 6–0 rout. He had swiftly become living proof that even the finest of players can be replaced.

There was a national audience watching the former England cap-tain return to the stage where he had made his reputation. This was the first FA Cup tie other than the final to be televised live. On a wet Friday night Newcastle fans took up their full allocation and the ground bounced to the sound of 'The Blaydon Races'. At least until Michael Robinson opened the scoring after eight minutes.

Even without their injured superstar, Liverpool were too good for Newcastle. Gratifyingly for Fagan, the man who would have to fill Dalglish's boots opened the scoring. However, there was always a suspicion that Robinson had found his level playing against Sec-ond Division sides.

That could never be said of Rush, who was a massive threat with or without his strike partner. He added another two goals. John-ston, his transfer request reiterated on an almost daily basis, buzzed around to create a passable impression of a young Keegan and scored the fourth goal.

Newcastle, featuring Peter Beardsley and Chris Waddle, two young men who would earn international reputations, the former inherit-ing Dalglish's No. 7 shirt at Anfield, were swept away. The player to emerge with most credit was Terry McDermott. The man from Kirkby showed the energy and intelligence that had characterized his spell in a Liverpool shirt. McDermott was hailed affectionately by the Kop, a contrast to the slightly sneery treatment of Keegan. What the crowd did not appreciate was the legacy McDermott had left in the dressing room. 'The attitudes had been passed on from the 1970s,' Johnston said. 'Terry Mac had educated Kenny and Char-lie and they taught the younger players.'

The savage humour, sky-high standards and team bonding based around the pub had been passed like a torch down the generations. McDermott had embodied these ethics.

Keegan, who had once had godlike status on the Kop, was more generous than some of the crowd after the game. 'Like vintage wine, they seem to get better and better,' he said, showing all the sophistication he had picked up on the Continent.

Dalglish watched the match from his hospital bed. It was a

buoyant end to a depressing week. The FA Cup had been the one trophy to elude Paisley. It had been a decade since the trophy had resided at Anfield. For all the trips to Wembley in that time, FA Cup final day was different. Everyone wanted to bring that particular piece of silverware back to the club. Fagan's army were on the march in four competitions and the FA Cup was a clear object of desire.

Fighting on such a broad front exposes weaknesses rapidly, and Liverpool were weaker than the table suggested. The balance of the midfield had rarely been correct from the beginning of the season and, despite Souness's swagger, there was a fragility about the team that might expose itself at any time. Next up at Anfield were Wolverhampton Wanderers, who had been promoted to the top flight the previous season but who were already in free-fall. It was a perfect opportunity to continue the good mood that accompanied the rout of Newcastle. Manchester United had drawn 1–1 away to Queens Park Rangers and Liverpool had the chance to stretch the lead at the top of the table to five points.

Fagan's side had drawn at Molineux in August. That was shocking enough. Now Wolves, rock bottom of the division, came to Liverpool and earned their result of the season.

The visiting side scored within the first ten minutes through a header by Steve Mardenborough. Grobbelaar was at fault. He came for a cross when he should have stayed on his line. Despite the home team laying siege to the Wolves goal, they hung on. It was an unhappy dressing room afterwards.

Souness's prediction appeared to be coming true. Fagan was generous to Wolves and critical of his own side. 'Even though we had seventy per cent of the game, there was no way Wolves looked uncomfortable in defence,' the manager said. 'Everyone says it's easy for Liverpool but it's not. Football has changed. It has got harder for any team to win as they were once expected to.'

The cracks were showing. Fagan's excuses sounded mealy-mouthed. Even worse, the sniping had begun to seep out of the dressing room.

The press quoted an unnamed player as criticizing Grobbelaar after the match. 'He should not have come out for a ball he had no chance of getting,' the anonymous team-mate said. In the fury of the post-match debriefings, harsh words were frequently spoken in the dressing room. They rarely leaked out. In public, the club prided themselves on a unified and dignified approach. At Anfield, the recriminations were traditionally kept in-house. This was a new and unwelcome development.

There was little time for reflection. In the aftermath of the Wolves game, Rush was involved in a traffic shunt and shaken up. On Tuesday, Liverpool had to travel to Hillsborough for the quarter-final of what was turning into an epic League Cup run. To lose against Sheffield Wednesday, the leaders of the Second Division, was unthinkable. The season itself could easily turn into a car crash.

As usual in this competition, Fagan's team failed to get the job done first time. Almost 50,000 – the biggest attendance for a Liverpool game since the Charity Shield and Old Trafford – turned up on a freezing night in Yorkshire. The DJ at Hillsborough inadvertently summed up the gulf in class by proposing a 'battle of the bands'. The Beatles were matched against Sheffield's Human League and the winner judged by the crowd's applause. Even the most patriotic Yorkshireman had to admit defeat. It should have been a walkover on and off the pitch but Liverpool were again distinctly off key.

The grass was marshy to start with but Nicol, growing in stature with every game, opened the scoring. Gary Megson equalized and Wednesday went in front after the break when a charging Lawrenson deflected a Gary Bannister shot into the net. Rush, still whiplash quick on what was now a quagmire of a pitch, was then brought down in the box. Neal scored from the spot to give Liverpool the draw. Fagan was relieved that the team spirit was intact, describing it as 'one of the games of the season so far', but there was an element of wishful thinking about the statement. In reality, it meant another unwanted game. Midweeks that should have been empty and used to allow the squad to rest and recover were being filled up too often. In three days' time the side would have to go to Villa Park and try to break a run during which Liverpool had taken a mere five points from twelve in the league. It was not the sort of match anyone would look forward to on a frigid Friday night.

On a pitch that was both slick and icy, the omens looked bad when Dennis Mortimer gave Aston Villa the lead. Rush, however, was about to show his brilliance.

Without Dalglish, popular opinion had it, Rush was half the player. Certainly, it was a partnership that enhanced both men's reputations. But anyone who underestimated the Welshman's threat when he was paired with Robinson was about to receive a rude shock.

Not long after the restart, Alan Hansen pumped the ball long and Rush sprinted clear of the Villa defence to poke the ball home with casual excellence. His second goal made the first look ordinary.

Souness knocked in a cross from the right, Nicol headed aimlessly on but the striker was waiting beyond the back post and the ball dropped to him.

Only the most confident or arrogant footballer would have attempted the left-foot volley that Rush executed with a vengeance. Most who tried it would have skulked back into position having seen the effort balloon into the crowd. Here, Rush connected with a crisp viciousness that sent the ball into the far corner of the goal. It was breathtaking. It made the hat-trick goal – a deft chip that would have been almost balletic on a perfect August surface, let alone the skating rink of January – look ordinary.

'In a way Kenny's absence helped Rushie,' Kennedy said. 'Kenny was a quality player but without him Rushie grew in stature. He could work with anyone and couldn't stop scoring. His all-round game benefited. He was a better player when Kenny returned.'

The match, live on television, showed anyone who doubted it that Rush was the most feared goalscorer in the world. Europe's top clubs began to sniff round. Fagan would have preferred goals like this to have been scored on a Saturday when the cameras were elsewhere. Now everyone knew what had been clear for so long at Anfield: Rush was unstoppable.

The homesick and withdrawn youth had become one of the main men in the dressing room. He had become vocal, he drank with the best and he produced on the pitch. Bob Paisley's faith was being rewarded.

Mood swings are never more severe than in football. Two bad results or the loss of a star player plunge a fan base into depression. A spectacular victory energizes the supporters. Bipolar, thy name is soccer.

In the previous round of the League Cup, just 11,638 had shown up at Anfield, even though gate prices had been lowered to £1 for children and pensioners. Now, for the replay against Wednesday, 40,000-plus jammed into the old ground.

It was not just Rush's heroics that inspired a revival of interest and a show of devotion. On the previous night, Everton had booked their place in the semi-finals with a 4–1 replay mauling of Oxford United. The prospect of a two-legged tie against the next-door neighbours was enticing; that of being kept apart and meeting at Wembley was even more seductive.

This was a chance to make a statement, on so many levels. Nearly half the Wednesday team had played for Everton. They were led by Mick Lyons, a Scouse icon and captain during Goodison's bleak years. He was known scoffingly as 'Dainty Mick' to the Kop, a joke figure whose ball skills looked amateur in comparison with the stylish Liverpool centre backs. With a potential showdown with the Toffees looming, this was a derby by proxy. It even had the sort of atmosphere local dust-ups generate: 12,000 Yorkshiremen helped Anfield sizzle in the cold.

Wednesday created chances early, although *The Times* noted that 'their main source of danger was provided by the extraordinary antics of Grobbelaar'. The goalkeeper's concentration appeared to be lacking as he allowed himself to be distracted by the travelling fans, at times conducting them in their singing.

Rush, however, was in a zone of concentration and confidence that comes rarely to even the best athletes. He struck before half-time, a simple tap-in from a corner. Robinson made the game safe with nineteen minutes left and then the Welshman grabbed his second, another seemingly easy conversion, to send the travelling hordes back disappointed. Now Wembley – and, more importantly, Everton – were in Liverpool's sights. A mixed January was almost over. And every day brought Dalglish closer to fitness.

17.

Down and Out

January–February 1984

*Brighton and Hove Albion (a), FA Cup R4; Watford (h); Sunderland (a);
Walsall (h,a), League Cup SF; Arsenal (h); Luton Town (a);
Queens Park Rangers (h)*

For the second successive round, the FA Cup draw presented Liverpool with second-tier opposition. For the second successive year, Brighton and Hove Albion were paired with the Anfield side. On paper, it did not look particularly exacting. On the dreadful pitch at the Goldstone Ground, it looked like a dogfight.

The previous season Brighton, led by Jimmy Case, had come to Merseyside and produced an upset. Case, an iron-hard Scouser who had worn the Liver bird with pride, had galvanized the south coast side to a 2–1 victory and a run all the way to Wembley, and defeat by Manchester United after a replay.

This time the old boys were wearing red, with Mark Lawrenson and Michael Robinson returning to their previous club. The pitch went some way towards closing the gap in class between the teams. Before the game, Graeme Souness gave his usual rallying call when confronted with a poor surface. 'No football,' he warned the team. His message was simple. No fancy stuff. Grit, rather than skill, would be Liverpool's saving grace.

However, on a windy Sunday afternoon, Liverpool suffered a number of blows. The first half took a turn for the worse when Souness was injured with barely more than half an hour played. The captain relished a battle and as he cleared his lines on the left side of his own penalty area he pulled up with an anguished hop. The Scot never went down willingly but now he stayed on the floor. His loss took the steel out of the visiting side.

Robinson then fluffed two relatively simple chances against his old team. The second, when he over-ran the ball on the muddy, bobbly pitch, was embarrassing. The break was a relief for Fagan, even though Rush almost scored just before the interval. Overall, Brighton were having the best of it.

Things went from bad to worse in the second half. Tony Grealish lobbed a simple ball over the top of the Liverpool back four and caught them square with Phil Neal lagging too deep. The right back played Gerry Ryan onside and Lawrenson was left in two minds as the Brighton striker closed in on goal. Grobbelaar did his best to block the shot but to no avail. Liverpool were a goal down and the slumped shoulders of the men in red as they lined up for the kick-off showed that a blow had been landed on their morale.

The home team had their tails up. Almost from the kick-off, Steve Nicol and Alan Kennedy left the ball for each other midway inside the Brighton half. Grealish was on it in an instant and skimmed a pass across the mud into the Liverpool half. Once again, the back four were too square and too high. This time, Hansen committed himself to catching Terry Connor offside. It was the wrong decision. The little striker ran free and put the ball into the net with ease. The ground went wild.

At the final whistle, the crowd surged on to the pitch, buffeting the men in red as they raced for the corrugated-iron tunnel and the relative safety of the dressing room. They looked bewildered, these European football aristocrats, as if caught in a revolution. Without Souness, their conviction drained quickly and their confidence went with it. The prognosis for the captain was that the injury would keep him out for between three weeks and a month.

Fagan blamed his defenders. 'We were well beaten in the end,' the manager said. 'Two mistakes by our centre halves cost us dearly. We obviously missed Souness but injury is something you have to come to terms with.'

Connor, the scorer, might have spoken for all of Liverpool's upcoming opponents when he summed up how Brighton felt during the game. 'When Graeme Souness limped off, it was a sign for us,' he said.

The signs for Liverpool were getting worse by the day. No Dalglish. Now no Souness. The most crucial period of the season was looming, with vital league games and a League Cup semi-final just days away.

Any dreams of a quadruple were over. Unless Fagan could shuffle his already under-strength pack quickly, the other three trophies would be as out of reach as the FA Cup. The *Daily Express* summed up the popular view. 'Souness's absence plunges Liverpool into the unknown,' wrote John Keith, who wondered whether Fagan could harness his resources to compensate.

Inside the dressing room, the spirit that Souness and Dalglish had fostered was coming to the fore. 'No one person is bigger than the team,' Nicol said. 'We would have rather had them playing, of course. Who wouldn't want Dalglish and Souness in their team? But I looked around me and saw the quality. We just decided we'd have to do it a different way to the way we'd done it with them.'

Craig Johnston agreed, seeing it as an opportunity for the fringe players to contribute. 'The team was strong enough and we had good players waiting to get into the side and give it their own sense of energy,' he said. 'Look, there was Hansen, Lawrenson, Whelan, Lee, Nicol. Plus Rush up front. Why would we be scared?'

The senior players took the same sanguine attitude. 'No one was worried,' Kennedy said. 'Look at the replacements. They were ready to do the job. Michael Robinson and David Hodgson stepped up and were fantastic. There were options all over in midfield. We fought for everything. We were unstoppable. We got into a frame of mind where we were going to win.'

'With the quality we had, whoever played was going to do well,' Souness said. 'We expected to win, the crowd expected to win, the staff expected to win. We delivered.'

People often underestimated Sammy Lee. He was easy to overlook: his team-mates were head and shoulders taller and his blond-haired freshness made him appear to be an over-promoted schoolboy. Yet the little man's impact on the pitch was huge.

'Sammy worked and worked,' Nicol said. 'Always available, always tackling. He was the sort of player who makes the rest of the team look better. The sort who glues things together.'

Lee was a butcher's son from the Bullring: the huge, circular tenements on the edge of the city centre overlooking the approaches to Lime Street station. It is an area of Liverpool perhaps less folkloric than Scotland Road or Toxteth, but it is as tough as any place in town.

The midfielder came to the club as a schoolboy. He made his debut in 1978 and grew in influence as the 1980s went by. His most famous feat was to mark Paul Breitner in the second leg of the European Cup semi-final in 1981. Bayern Munich had drawn 0–0 in the first game at Anfield and had presumed they had already booked a place in Paris for the final. The feeling grew even stronger when Dalglish limped out of the crucial match in Bavaria before the first ten minutes were up. Breitner, Germany's finest midfield player, was expected to run the game but Bob Paisley had detailed his energetic and mobile youngster to ensure the German never had time to play. To characterize Lee's performance as a man-marking job is to understate the brilliance of his display. He did not follow Breitner slavishly. Instead, when Liverpool had the ball he switched his attention to attack. He just made sure he knew where the Bayern playmaker was and got close to him as soon as Liverpool lost possession.

There was so much to admire about Lee's game. He was not flashy but he covered acres of space and had an engine that allowed him to run for ever, despite his chunky frame. He had a marvellous passing range that was almost the equal of Souness's sublime long balls, a shuddering tackle and a powerful shot. In many ways he was ahead of his time.

Those who played alongside Lee recognized his effectiveness. 'Sammy never got the credit he deserved,' Nicol said.

Phil Neal agreed. 'If they are to get into the top three, every side needs its hard-working bees,' the full back said. 'Sammy was one of those bees. He played just in front of me and we formed a really good partnership.'

In February 1984 he was approaching his twenty-fifth birthday. He had played in teams full of leaders and had been content to take a back seat with his happy-go-lucky spirit and sharp wit. Now, for the first time, he was senior man in a midfield of Steve Nicol, Craig Johnston and Ronnie Whelan, who was still easing his way back from the hip operation of the previous summer. It was not Lee's natural forte. Despite his effervescent personality, he only really took the lead in celebrations.

He was approachable, too, still drinking around town with his mates from school. On one occasion the crowd of spectators watching a pub fight between two groups of young lads outside Ma Edgerton's at throwing-out time on Saturday night were surprised to see a diminutive and innocent-looking European Cup winner in the middle of the melee throwing devastating haymakers. Whether the fray was outside an alehouse opposite Lime Street station or in a congested midfield at Wembley Stadium, Lee would give everything. He was that kind of man and player: loyal, and the sort you would want beside you in a battle. Yet he would always rather have fun.

'He was always the one who started the singing after we had picked up a trophy, all the old Liverpool songs,' Neal said. 'We had some great singalongs. He made the mood upbeat. But he was always a very apologetic person. He always apologized for almost anything he did. He is a lovely-natured person. I love him to bits.'

As the only Scouser in the side, Lee was conscious that he carried the flag for the city. 'It wasn't exactly more pressure but things had changed since I first came into the team. Then, the dressing room was full of locals. Now I was the last man standing, passing along all the songs.'

He did not feel isolated, though. 'They all knew what was at stake and what it all meant to the crowd,' he said. 'You didn't have to tell the likes of Souness what a derby meant. They were all as committed as if they'd been born in L4. If anyone showed a sign of not understanding what you had to do, they didn't last long.'

Now, he had to fill some of the vacuum left by Dalglish and Souness. This tough little man immersed in the culture of Liverpool Football Club would not let anyone down.

Back at Anfield, playing without either Dalglish or Souness in the team for the first time in six years, Liverpool brushed aside Watford with a routine 3–0 victory. The game was over by half-time with goals from Rush, Nicol and Whelan stretching the lead at the top of the table to five points. The most remarkable thing about the afternoon was the attendance of 20,746, the smallest number of people to pay into Anfield for a league match since 1961.

A potentially difficult away match against Sunderland three days later passed off almost without incident as a 0–0 draw earned a point that was all the more satisfying for the news that Manchester United had failed to turn up the pressure. Their 0–0 draw, at home to Norwich City, was altogether less pleasing than Liverpool's result. At a time when Ron Atkinson's side should have been taking advantage of the weakened nature of Fagan's squad, they were dropping points at home. It sent Liverpool into the first leg of the League Cup semi-final in good heart. Their opponents were Walsall of the Third Division. It looked almost like a bye to the final.

Walsall had other ideas. They had beaten Arsenal at Highbury in this cup run and Alan Buckley, their manager, had taken note of Liverpool's defeat away to Brighton in the FA Cup. While most criticism focused on the role of Hansen and Lawrenson in the debacle on the south coast, Buckley homed in on Kennedy. Barney Rubble was the man in Walsall's sights.

Buckley was so convinced that he had isolated Liverpool's weak link that he left Mark Rees out of the previous match. 'He is our only wide player,' the Walsall manager explained. 'I couldn't risk losing him.'

There was a new face in the Liverpool side. Lawrenson had picked up a groin injury at Sunderland and Gary Gillespie made his debut. It added another touch of uncertainty to Fagan's team. The newcomer from Coventry – another Scot – was just the fifteenth man to play for the first XI during the season, but he found himself part of a squad that appeared to have lost its focus along with its best players.

Ronnie Whelan gave the home side the lead before the quarter-hour mark but then Liverpool imploded. Buckley's instinct was right. Kennedy was in trouble against Mark Rees.

'He was a flyer,' Kennedy said. 'He ran the legs out of me. I was so bad, he put the ball thirty yards past me and by the time I'd turned I could just see his arse. I thought: "Christ, don't cross it. Mishit it!"'

Ironically, when the mistake came down Kennedy's flank, it was not the full back's fault. Sammy Lee was boxed in near the line at the Kop end. He tried to pass along to Grobbelaar but Ally Brown intercepted the ball and knocked it goalward. Gillespie might have cleared, but he and the onrushing Neal got in each other's way, performed a camp little dance on the line, and the veteran full back had the last touch for the equalizer.

Whelan again gave the home side the lead with a header but Liverpool had another error in them. Nicol made a challenge twenty-five yards from his own goal but only knocked the ball into space behind the Liverpool back four. Kevin Summerfield accepted the invitation to chip Grobbelaar and 9,000 Walsall fans went into transports of joy.

Fagan was in the opposite mood. 'We're only an ordinary team now,' he said. 'Every one of our players were committed but it's not enough. We haven't got a player with real flair, just honest-to-goodness effort.'

It was harsh on players like Rush, Nicol and Hansen but it was typical of Fagan's psychology. Of course, there was a second leg to be played, and the manager duly obliged with the usual caveat: 'It's only half-time.' Cliché or not, however, he was determined his team would be less generous in seven days' time.

Things had not quite turned out as planned for Charlie Nicholas. He could easily have been playing every second week at Anfield. Instead, he visited the ground for the first time as an Arsenal player, with his side sitting mid-table, eighteen points behind Fagan's team. The Scottish striker had made a public claim that he had not been impressed by the Liverpool manager, rating Terry Neill more highly than Smokin' Joe. It was another error of judgement by Nicholas. Neill had been sacked in December. Don Howe was now in charge and oversaw Arsenal's 2–1 defeat. The Kop gloated heartily. Lawrenson returned to give the defence more stability, Souness was nearing recovery. Dalglish was getting fitter every day and even eating solid food. Sammy Lee broke his nose but that would not worry the midfielder. The negativity of the start of the month was evaporating by the hour.

Being on the sidelines was irritating Dalglish, who hated being out. Even he was left on the margins when not available for first-team selection. No one was immune to indignity. 'No one liked it,' he said. 'Almost every training session ended with a match against the kids on a pitch we sarcastically called "Wembley". If you weren't in the first team, you'd be with the kids playing against the staff and senior players. It was no good.'

The system was designed to make players feel this way. The losers in the practice match would be sent to buy milk and lemonade from a small grocery round the corner from Melwood. It was embarrassing to be sent shopping with the jeers of team-mates ringing in your ears. 'Everything was geared to winning,' Nicol said. 'It was set up to make sure you didn't ever want to lose. Even in training.'

If things were looking up at Anfield, there was gloom for Manchester United, Liverpool's rivals in the title race. Robert Maxwell, the media tycoon and owner of Oxford United, had launched a takeover attempt at Old Trafford. A mood of uncertainty hung around Liverpool's main challengers. Even a 5–0 victory away at Luton Town did not lift United's spirits. Jim Smith, Maxwell's manager at Oxford, was publicly denying he was interested in Ron Atkinson's job.

Even worse, newspapers in Italy were reporting that Bryan Robson had agreed to join Sampdoria for £3.5 million. The sense that this was United's year was fading by the day. A mere seven weeks after Kevin Moran had seemed to strike the decisive blow in the title race when he smashed Dalglish's cheekbone, Liverpool were in the ascendancy. Fagan had ridden out a succession of minor crises in the hard cold of winter. The chance to claim a place at Wembley was looming and a glorious spring beckoned. Yet the manager, and the Liverpool fans, would not have been quite so happy had they realized the true target of Sampdoria's transfer attentions.

Italian football was rich. The clubs had understood that television income was crucial to the game at a time when the administrators in England believed that the small screen would kill off attendances and the sport. The first wave of expatriate players had emigrated to Serie A at the beginning of the 1980s. Sampdoria, based in Genoa, had already wooed away Trevor Francis – the subject of the first £1 million domestic transfer – and Liam Brady from the English game. Kevin Keegan's move to Hamburg in 1977 had not sparked an exodus to Germany. Italy, on the other hand, was a magnet for the world's best players. Brazilians were flocking to the country. Zico had moved to Udinese, and Cerezo and Falcão were playing for Roma. The world's best talents were gathering. Karl-Heinz Rummenigge was on his way from Germany to Internazionale, and Michel Platini, France's superstar, was at Juventus alongside Zbigniew Boniek, the brilliant Pole. The rest of the Serie A clubs were canvassing around Europe looking to tie up the biggest talents. It did not always work. Luther Blissett had moved from Watford to AC Milan to become a cult figure rather than a match winner. Legend claims the Milanese thought they were buying John Barnes.

However, Souness was high on Sampdoria's wish-list. He would be thirty-one before the end of the season and was conscious that his time as a player was drawing to an end. He had one big-money move left in his career and the salary in Italy would buy a lot more champagne than his wage packet at Anfield. Preliminary approaches had already been made, though the news wasn't public and his commitment to Liverpool and Fagan remained total. He returned for the second leg of the League Cup against Walsall even more determined to finish the season with a clutch of silverware. If he was going to leave, it would be on a high.

'It was all about leadership with Charlie,' Nicol said. 'He was the ultimate leader. Apart from the fact that he was superb, brilliant.' Did Souness have a soft side? If so, it was rarely seen. There was a glimpse of it at Fellows Park, though.

Before the first leg, Buckley, the Walsall manager, had rested Rees for a wing assault on Kennedy. He did not take the same care of the winger before the second leg. Rees played for the Third Division leaders against Southend United. It was a mistake: he was carried from the field with a mere twelve minutes played and needed four stitches in a gash on the shin.

With Lawrenson and Souness back, the defence and midfield had pace and bite restored. Rush, the words of Fagan after the Anfield game still ringing in his ears, showed the attack had a sharpness to be envied, too. In the thirteenth minute he headed a David Hodgson cross into the Walsall net and the semi-final was effectively over.

The stitched-together Rees had little impact and Liverpool never looked like missing out on Wembley. It had been four years since they had lost in this competition. The run would continue.

Yet there was drama to come. Four minutes into the second half, Ronnie Whelan lashed in a vicious shot from thirty yards. Behind the goal in the cramped, packed stadium, the Liverpool supporters surged forward in excitement that quickly turned to terror. The four-foot wall behind the goal collapsed under pressure. For a thirty-yard stretch those at the front – mainly children – were pinned under a stack of bodies.

The players reacted quickly, signalling to those at the rear of the terrace who could not see the situation at the front to move back. Both teams began dragging the injured out, dusting them off and helping with the rescue. Souness, the hard man, delicately eased a youngster from the pile and gently cradled the child in his arms. Instead of passing the boy on to a St John Ambulance volunteer, the Liverpool captain carried him across to the touchline, all the while reassuring the terrified youngster. It was just about the only act of tenderness Souness ever performed on a football pitch. Yet it illustrated his character perfectly. In a crisis, you wanted Graeme Souness on your side. He knew the right things to do and the right things to say. Champagne Charlie might have been a preening egotist at times but when it came to the crunch, he did the heroic instinctively.

The referee led the players off but restarted the game after an eleven-minute stoppage when it became evident that the injuries were relatively minor. Once the competition began anew, Souness was immediately back in hit-man mode.

Afterwards, Fagan was in as pugnacious a mood as his captain. 'Wembley, here we come,' he boomed out. However, even in his excitement he had a warning for his players. 'The game is about getting goals as well as playing football and that is what we did.'

It would take more than pretty passing to win trophies. It needed a killer instinct in front of goal and a similarly ruthless approach across the pitch.

Souness would make sure there was no shortage of cold-bloodedness. Liverpool were on their way to Wembley. Nothing was going to stop them if their captain had anything to do with it.

Anfield was a happy place but there were still undercurrents of disappointment. Phil Thompson, who had been the captain and leader at the club for so long, was placed on the transfer list the day before the second leg against Walsall. He had not played since the Charity Shield in August and his relationship with Fagan had completely broken down. While Thompson skulked in the shadows, his nemesis Souness reigned supreme in the dressing room. It was a bitter time for Thompson and the latest indignity hurt the boyhood Kopite to his core.

There were others, too. Johnston remained riddled with angst about his intermittent involvement in the first team and was still demanding to leave. Hodgson also wanted first-team football. As the injured squad members returned to health, both Johnston and Hodgson knew they would be pushed to the margins again.

Now there was an extra element which sharpened the ambition and deepened the resentment of those who were not selected. A Wembley final was on the horizon and Everton were one game away from making it a Merseyside derby. No one wanted to miss out on what was potentially a historic moment. They were playing for their places as if they were playing for their lives.

Luton, the next opponents, were merely playing for pride. They had been trounced 5–0 at home to Manchester United the previous week and had horrific memories of the mauling at Anfield in October when Rush scored five goals in a 6–0 rout. This time, Luton were determined to shut up shop and a dull match at Kenilworth Road ended in a 0–0 draw.

Yet again events elsewhere turned dropped points into a good result. Nottingham Forest and Manchester United both drew and squandered their chance to close the gap at the top of the table. Each time Liverpool appeared to trip up, their rivals made a similar slip. A routine win against Queens Park Rangers rounded out the month. There had been times without Souness and Dalglish that the team had wobbled, but weakness on the pitch had not been reflected in results. Fagan's side were top of the league and in a cup final.

They needed to step up a gear, though. March would not be so forgiving. It would start off with a derby at Goodison, include a two-legged European Cup quarter-final and a chance to win the first domestic trophy of the season at Wembley. Things were about to get serious.

18

Noisy Neighbours

March 1984

Everton (a)

Everyone in the city wanted Everton to win their League Cup semi and they obliged, beating Aston Villa 2–1 on aggregate. For the first time, a Merseyside derby would take place at Wembley with a trophy at stake. The scramble for tickets reached a frenzy.

After nearly fifteen years of inferiority, Everton were beginning to believe that they could match their neighbours. Howard Kendall's team had started the season poorly and there had been growing pressure on the manager. Then, in the new year, things began to change.

Kendall had assembled a talented squad. Neville Southall was the best goalkeeper in the division. Kevin Ratcliffe and Derek Mountfield were a formidable centre-half pairing. Peter Reid anchored the midfield and former Liverpool reserve Kevin Sheedy was developing a reputation as one of the best attacking midfielders in the league. Up front Andy Gray was a menace, his physical presence a worry for any defence. His partner was Graeme Sharp, a clever striker with a robust power that belied his lean appearance. The components were there but, through a long and painful autumn, Kendall could not get them to gel.

Then the turning points began. There were so many of them that it seemed like Everton were going in circles. At Stoke City, in the third round of the FA Cup, the manager opened the windows to the dressing room and exhorted his players to listen to the 4,000 fans in the away section. Even such an experienced professional as Gray remembers its effect. 'He just said, "Listen to them. Are you going to let them down?" You could feel the hairs on the back of your neck standing on end. We went out, beat them two–nil, and just seemed to go on from there.'

Well, not quite. Against Oxford United in the League Cup, Everton were 1–0 down and on the verge of going out. Then, with minutes left, Kevin Brock mishit a back pass and Adrian Heath equalized. 'Losing that one, I think there would have been pressure on,' Kendall said sardonically. As it was, Oxford were beaten with ease in the replay. It seemed throughout that January that the Everton manager was one embarrassing defeat from the sack.

In the next round of the FA Cup, the Blues teetered on the edge again. Gillingham drew 0–0 at Goodison and, in the dying seconds of the replay, Tony Cascarino bore down on goal with only Southall to beat. 'We were bad again that night,' Gray said. 'In the last minute, Cascarino broke away, totally free. Had he scored, the whole history of what came after may have altered. He missed. Neville made a great save in a one-against-one situation. That rescued us. We went to a third game.'

Cascarino had Liverpool sympathies from childhood. 'I would have liked to have scored against them,' he said. 'I wish I'd scored.'

'Gillingham was the turning point for us,' Neville said. 'We drew nil–nil and got absolutely battered. That was a good result.'

Somehow, some way, Kendall's side survived crisis after crisis. And now they were preparing themselves for a showdown with their nemesis with a trophy on the line.

First, there was the matter of a league derby. The earlier meeting at Anfield between the teams had been a tame encounter, where Liverpool had eased to a 3–0 win. Fagan had complained that it didn't even feel like a derby. At Goodison, things were different. The *Sunday Times* called it 'ferocious, almost blood-curdling'.

Johnston summed up the feeling of taking part in a derby better than most. 'Because I wasn't one of the stars, I shit myself before games,' he said. 'It was worse before the derby. I remember being at Goodison and I was sick with worry. If you do something good, then great. But if you lose the ball, all the Blues are laughing and all the Reds are moaning. It's the most frightening place in the world.'

If the disapproval of the terraces was not bad enough, the level of savagery on the pitch concerned the hardest of players.

'If you're making mistakes, you start not wanting the ball,' Johnston said. 'If it comes to you, Reidy, Sharpy and the rest are trying to injure you. That's what derbies were like. Everyone was trying to hurt each other. You mean to do it. You tackle them and catch them and nobody notices except you and them. If you do it right, you get that feeling: "They won't come back."

'It might shock people in these politically correct times but it was true. Derbies were different to other games. They were meatier.'

The meat was blood red. 'The ball would come and you'd limp away after having had someone's studs rake your shin and leave your socks in shreds,' Johnston said. 'If you'd made a mistake and been kicked up in the air, you wouldn't want the ball. Some people want to hide.'

At Goodison, waiting to enter the cauldron, the Australian found his focus.

'The extra one per cent that makes the difference can be found in the dressing room, in the moment of quiet and reflection,' he said. 'Trying to psych myself up, I had an epiphany. I had Souness to my right, Hansen to my left. Dalglish in front of me. Rush too. I thought, "What the fuck am I worried about? Imagine I was sitting in the Everton dressing room!"'

Fagan's team started best and Johnston, no longer cowed by the pressure of the occasion, sent in a cross that allowed Rush to score.

But the home side were becoming more fearless by the day. Everton grew in confidence and stature and the match got faster and nastier as the minutes ticked on. The men in blue were getting on top and when Kennedy found himself mismatched against the powerful Gray in the area, he hung on to the striker and gave away a penalty. Sharp stepped up to equalize but fluffed his kick. Grobbelaar saved. 'There was always a hail of coins that came from the Gwladys Street end,' the goalkeeper said. 'I used to pick them up and gloat to them, "I'm getting richer." They didn't like that.'

The save seemed to be a defining moment. It appeared that

Everton's newly discovered mental strength had once again failed in the face of red dominance.

There was another twist. Alan Harper, another man who had come through the Liverpool reserve team and moved across Stanley Park to get a chance of first-team football, came on as a substitute to equalize with six minutes left. The 1–1 draw left Everton more satisfied than their neighbours, and whetted their appetite for the showdown at Wembley that was a mere three weeks away. 'It was the first result we'd had against them for a while,' Kendall said. 'It gave us confidence.'

'It was,' Johnston said, 'certain to be a bruiser at Wembley.'

If thoughts at Goodison were focused on the League Cup final, the mood was very different at Anfield. Two points had been dropped and Manchester United had pulled closer in the race for the title after a 3–0 win away to Aston Villa. Not only that, in four days' time Benfica were on Merseyside in the quarter-final of the European Cup. The players were careful to concentrate on the next challenge. If they allowed their attention to wander, they would regret it.

'It was never the Liverpool way to look any further ahead than the next game,' Ronnie Moran said. 'This had been instilled into everyone at the club since the days of Bill and Bob. It was no different under Joe.

'You can only play one match at a time, so what's the point in thinking further ahead than that? If the players mentioned a big game a couple of weeks away we used to tell them: "Don't worry about that, son. You might not be in the bloody team."'

The question of when Kenny Dalglish would be available for selection was beginning to tax Fagan's mind. On the day after the derby – his thirty-third birthday – the Scot played for the reserves, his second game back since Kevin Moran rearranged his cheekbone. It was, like the previous day's match, a derby against Everton. It was a satisfactory afternoon. Dalglish led the second-stringers to a 2–1 win and a place in the final of the Liverpool Senior Cup. The question for the Bootroom staff was whether the leap from a reserve game in Southport to a last-eight match in the European Cup was too big even for a player of Dalglish's brilliance. Ideally, it would have been preferable to nurse the veteran back to full fitness slowly and not risk injury by asking too much too soon. But that threw up another question: could Liverpool afford to go into such a big game pairing Michael Robinson with Ian Rush? The burly centre forward did not have the craft, guile or presence that would be needed to unlock the Portuguese champions. Benfica would rest more easily knowing they would not face the threat of Dalglish.

19.

Happy Returns

March 1984

Benfica (h), European Cup QF; Tottenham Hotspur (h); Southampton (a)

Benfica are one of Europe's great names. The Portuguese club had been a power in the competition in the 1960s, appearing in five European Cup finals and winning two. In those days they had been led by Eusebio, one of the great football icons and the first black superstar in Europe.

Since then their domestic dominance had not been converted into Continental success. Their last visit to Anfield, six years previously, had ended in a 4–1 defeat and an easy passage for Liverpool into the next round.

They came now in good heart. They had beaten Braga 7–0 while Liverpool were drawing with Everton and were on a long unbeaten run, during which they had dropped just two points out of forty (it was still two points for a win in Portugal). Their record compared favourably with Fagan's downbeat appraisal of Liverpool's form going into the match. 'We're not as good as I'd like,' he said. 'We were in a small crisis with Dalglish and Souness out of the side. But now we're almost out of it.'

Sven-Göran Eriksson, in charge of Benfica, was generous in his praise of the home side before the match, calling Liverpool 'the best team in Europe'. They did not look it in a first half that left the Kop worried for the team's future in the competition.

The thirty-six-year-old Swede, who had spent time at Anfield in the 1970s as part of his coaching education, set up his side in a compact, defensive formation. Like Bilbao in the previous round they were determined not to concede.

Eriksson, conscious that a scoreless draw had not been enough for the Basque side, was hopeful that his team could nick a goal and, in the first half, he nearly got his wish. Twice Benfica broke with speed and Grobbelaar had to be sharp to keep José Luis out. As feared, Robinson did not have the subtlety or movement to trouble a classy defence. At the break murmurs of discontent rippled around the stadium.

Ten minutes later, there was a different buzz around Anfield as the teams emerged for the second half. Ten Liverpool players walked on to the pitch, Robinson not among them. It was a full thirty seconds before the eleventh emerged. There, walking from the sidelines, was Kenny Dalglish. He looked gaunt following his nine-week absence. His face still showed the marks of disfigurement from the operation to set his smashed cheekbone. More than 39,000 people rose in prolonged and emotional applause. Benfica, who had achieved the classic Liverpool trick of taking the crowd out of the game in the first half, now had to start again and the volume was up two notches even before the restart.

Right away Dalglish had an impact. The ball pinged towards the Scot and he killed it dead with his first touch. Rush, running free, had escaped his marker and the crowd roared in anticipation of a slide-rule ball that would release the striker.

Instead, uncharacteristically, Dalglish tried to run at the bemused centre half, Alvaro, who appeared transfixed and frozen to the spot. The Scot ran straight into him.

The ground went silent in shock – except for a lone, appalled voice from the Kop that roared, 'You greedy little twat!'

Even the greats couldn't get away with much at Anfield. 'You could never make the slightest slip,' Nicol said with a smile. 'No one, I mean no one, would let you get away with it. No one got a free pass.'

Benfica, so comfortable for forty-five minutes, now began to get a measure of what it would take for them to get a pass into the semi-finals. And there would be no more criticism for Dalglish. The match had turned.

The Alan Kennedy–Ian Rush combination that had caused so

much mirth after the Welshman's headed goal in Bilbao, struck again. The left back crossed and Tosh headed home. It was a narrow margin but more than Liverpool had taken to the Basque Country. In the Estádio da Luz in Lisbon, Dalglish would be ready to play from the start. After watching the way his No. 7 had unnerved the Portuguese side, Fagan had a quiet confidence about him afterwards.

It was, he accepted, a 'calculated gamble' to bring his talisman back. But it worked. The psychological impact was massive. 'It wasn't so much what he did on the ball,' the manager said. 'Any world-class player will cause problems. He did particularly well and won the game for us. His presence frightened Benfica.'

The Times endorsed Fagan's viewpoint. 'As Dalglish walked on to the stage seconds before the start of the second half, the hearts of Liverpool rose as visibly as those of Benfica fell. Timed to perfection, his entrance was pure theatre.'

A Portuguese journalist was so impressed by the transformation of the team that he described Dalglish as 'the Messiah'. That caused sniggers in the dressing room, too. 'It was a relief to be back after so long out,' Dalglish said. 'Back on the winning side at "Wembley".'

It was good to have the Scot available again but, in true Anfield style, Fagan and his Bootroom boys were already looking for a player who could fill the void when age finally overtook Dalglish. Paul Walsh, of Luton Town, was a prime target. Gary Lineker, the Leicester City striker who was perhaps too similar to Rush, was also under consideration. Sentimentality could exist in the moment for emotional returns. In the long run, however, it was anathema at Anfield.

Dalglish was a long way from needing to be replaced, though. In the league, it was as if he had never been away, equalizing an early Tottenham Hotspur goal at Anfield as Liverpool kept their title challenge on course with a 3–1 victory despite the absence of Rush. Yet all Fagan's alarm bells were ringing.

'I wasn't impressed with our performance throughout, yet the spectators said it was a good game,' he wrote in his diary. 'We were too easy-osey on parts of the field, especially Sammy, Ronnie and Craig. For me, they were poor and I felt like [giving] an old-fashioned blast to all three. Good job we had Grobbelaar and the two centre backs.'

Manchester United had clawed back some points over the previous month and were now just two behind. The Maxwell takeover of Old Trafford had fallen through and Ron Atkinson's team had emerged from the uncertainty as Liverpool's only viable challengers.

Fagan's team had a chance to pull further ahead on Friday night away to Southampton at the Dell. It was another of Liverpool's bogey grounds. The day before the game, Souness suffered a personal blow when his mother died. He was absent on the south coast for the sort of game where he would have made a difference.

On a dull night, Liverpool looked like they were mourning in sympathy with their captain. Southampton kept the pressure on with high balls, their direct football never giving the visiting side a chance to get possession and play. Danny Wallace scored twice, first with a bicycle kick and then with a header. To lose 2–0 was bad enough, but Nicol and Kennedy limped out of the game as well.

'Not good enough,' Fagan said. 'We got beat and deservedly so. We had flashes of doing something, but that was all. We are not the Liverpool of old, not enough personalities, not enough good players. I'm not surprised with the result or the prospect of not winning.'

Now United had the chance to go top of the table with a home game against Arsenal. They won in emphatic style, 4–0. Old Trafford once again sensed that their great rivals from down the East Lancs Road could be overturned.

Now the pressure was ratcheted up to its highest level. In the next week, Liverpool would go to Lisbon with a slender 1–0 lead against Benfica and then return to Wembley for a League Cup final against

Everton. By the time they resumed their title challenge against Watford on the last day of March, the League Championship could be the only trophy available to Fagan's side. The next few days could come to define the season.

20.

Light Fantastic

March 1984

Benfica (a), European Cup QF; Everton, League Cup final, Wembley;
Everton, League Cup final replay, Maine Road; Watford (a)

As usual a slip brought the critics out in droves. Right from the beginning, plenty of people were ready to question Fagan's abilities and credentials for the job. Liverpool's next move gave them more grist for their argument.

On the Monday after the Southampton defeat, Liverpool paid Ipswich Town £450,000 for John Wark. The Scotland midfielder had caused his new team plenty of problems in the past but *The Times* saw 'an uncharacteristic hint of desperation' in the signing.

Wark's arrival hit Craig Johnston particularly hard. The Australian had been unhappy all season and felt Fagan had no confidence in him.

'Craig was his own worst enemy,' Dalglish said. 'He just didn't believe in his footballing abilities. When his form deserted him, Craig became depressed.'

Wark was bought to provide goals from midfield. Johnston believed he could do that job. By dipping into the transfer market, Fagan undermined the midfielder's confidence even more.

If Johnston's state of mind was in question heading to Lisbon, Souness's anguish was more understandable. He attended his mother's funeral on Monday and then almost missed the flight to Portugal the next day.

The captain had been the subject of some public criticism from Bob Paisley, who had been watching Benfica before the first tie. Paisley had noticed that the Portuguese side did not mark man-for-man but played a zonal scheme. Souness, he felt, had misused the opportunities Benfica's system gave him in an attempt to get forward and join the attack.

'I said to Graeme Souness I didn't think he'd be picked up,' Paisley said. 'He had the freedom of the park and he probably abused the space he was getting. It was probably his undoing trying to get up there instead of doing the providing.'

It looked like turmoil at Anfield. In the glare of the Stadium of Light, any weaknesses would be exposed.

Nothing was left to chance in Benfica. With 70,000 people crammed into the stadium, Fagan knew the first item on the checklist was dampening the atmosphere and killing the excitement. It was a forbidding sight. Tony Ensor, who would later become a director, was on the team coach.

'It was dark and the place was illuminated and the stadium was packed,' he said. 'It was like a seething cauldron. I remember getting great heart and a sense of confidence from the way in which Dalglish, Souness, Phil Neal, people like that, walked off the coach in that determined way, in no way overawed by the task that faced them.'

The team were in no mood to capitulate.

'Joe loved nights like this, we all did,' Dalglish said. 'It was always, "Shut the crowd up. Get on top, the [opposition] fans will get edgy and on their backs." We thought we could win anywhere.'

During the early exchanges Liverpool stopped the play as often as possible, disrupting any Benfica rhythm. They worked the offside trap, fouled when necessary and controlled the tempo. Then they took the lead.

Paisley's tactical acumen was spot-on, too. Liverpool were given room. 'They didn't press us at all and couldn't seem to work out how we were playing,' Kennedy said. 'Nobody could pick Kenny up, Ronnie Whelan kept getting forward into the box every time Rushie took the defenders wide. Everything we tried came off.'

Whelan headed Liverpool into the lead before ten minutes

were gone but Johnston rose to the challenge of Wark's arrival. First, he cleared off the line after Lawrenson misheaded the ball and then went up the other end to score from the edge of the box.

'Craig was magnificent,' Dalglish said. 'He was everywhere and always in the right place.'

It was all over by half-time. 'They were so open we couldn't believe it,' Kennedy said. 'It was so easy it was an absolute doddle.'

Benfica pulled a goal back with sixteen minutes to go but that was the signal for Rush and Whelan to score again. The 4–1 victory swept away all feelings of negativity. The mood was buoyant. Fagan grinned and Dalglish took issue with the press, who had written about his face being 'disfigured'. It would, he said, upset his surgeon.

After the match, the players went to a taverna outside the city. There, Johnston had an experience he would never forget. 'I was in the bar with Lawro, Jocky, Kenny and Charlie,' he said. 'Some supporters came in. One of them said: "Look, there's Hansen and Lawrenson." Then I heard another go: "Wow, there's Craig Johnston and Kenny Dalglish." They'd said my name in the same sentence as Kenny's. I'll never forget that.'

The Australian craved acceptance. He wanted not only to be part of the team but thought of as a regular and important contributor. After the display in Lisbon, he felt that status was warranted.

'I had a beer and a light seemed to hit it and it looked like the most beautiful thing in the world,' Johnston said. 'It tasted better than any beer I'd had in my life. I could have sworn it tasted two or three times better than their pints. You know why? I deserved it more. God had given them far more talent than me. I would run like a lunatic to get the ball and give it to them. That was my job.'

It was a boost for the Australian to be included with such peers. Like the rest of the side, he would be going into a League Cup final in good heart. The whole of Merseyside was in a state of excitement. Big games were becoming a habit.

There was barely time to take a breath. Lisbon on Wednesday, home Thursday, the European Cup semi-final draw on Friday, travel south Saturday and a Wembley final on Sunday.

The other three teams in the pot for the last four of the Continent's great competition were Roma, Dinamo Bucharest and Dundee United. The least attractive proposition was a trip to Romania. Over the previous four seasons Liverpool had lost three times behind the Iron Curtain. Dinamo Tbilisi, CSKA Sofia and Widzew Łódź had all knocked the Merseyside team out of the competition.

Of course, Bucharest were matched against Liverpool, with the first leg scheduled to take place at Anfield. At least this time the opposition were not completely unknown. Fagan's side had beaten them 3–2 in a pre-season match in Spain seven months before.

There was no time to be reflective about foreign adventures as a local difficulty loomed.

Everton were feeling increasingly upbeat about their prospects. 'We were closing the gap on them all the time,' Howard Kendall, the former player who returned to Goodison as manager in 1981, said. 'We thought we could challenge them. It felt like we were growing stronger and they were getting weaker.'

One of the main reasons for Everton's revival was the arrival of Andy Gray from Wolverhampton Wanderers earlier in the season but the robust centre forward was cup-tied for the final after playing in an early round of the competition for his former club. The physical striker was the sort of player who put Alan Hansen and Mark Lawrenson under pressure and whose presence in the box tested Bruce Grobbelaar's decision-making when coming for crosses.

Kendall was still bullish. Asked about his pre-game message to his side, he said: 'The first touch can make or break a player at Wembley. I'll be saying we don't have to pay Liverpool too much respect.

They're expected to win, but this is just one match and we did well in our last encounter.'

The Everton manager also sent a message to the fans. 'I think our players will want to please the supporters more than Liverpool's players will,' he said. The atmosphere across the city could hardly be more frenetic.

Everything stopped for football. The League Cup final even threw up a massive problem for the city council, who already had enough to worry about.

In the local elections of May 1983, the Labour Party won control of the city. The results were very much against the political trends in Britain. The Labour manifesto contained commitments to maintain jobs and build new houses despite Whitehall policy demanding massive cuts to regional budgets.

Labour was elected in a landslide and the councillors were on a collision course with the Thatcher regime. In the spring of 1984 it became clear that the council were determined to carry out their electoral promises. To do that, they would have to spend more than their allocated budget and break the law. The Labour group argued that too much government money had been withdrawn from Liverpool over the previous three years. Both sides took entrenched positions, the *Guardian* reporting that 'the air is thick with talk of rebellion, even revolution'.

And then football interrupted proceedings.

The crucial budget meeting was scheduled for 29 March, accompanied by a city-wide strike. This was four days after the League Cup final. Politicians in the city were embroiled in lengthy and exhausting talks to try to avert the crisis when a bigger problem reared its head and took the focus away from the fiscal meltdown. Negotiations were shelved and more important matters attended to.

'It was the first time the two clubs had played each other at Wembley and the plan was for both teams to go on an open-top bus tour afterwards,' Derek Hatton said. Hatton, an Evertonian, was deputy leader of the council, its most visible face and one of Thatcherite

Britain's public enemies. On Merseyside, he was one of many with twin obsessions.

'Football and politics were everywhere at the time,' he said. 'Every pub had an expert who could sort out the city's treasury and others who could whip the football clubs into shape. Both subjects were important to people.' Shankly's flawed axiom had it that the sport was more important than a matter of life and death. It is not. But it certainly edged out the politics.

'We were having huge budget battles, London was threatening to suspend the council and send in a commissioner, and the press were screaming for blood,' Hatton continued. 'Then we had a real crisis. The question was: who would go first on the open-top buses?

'We thought the winners would take the lead bus and the losers follow on. Then Howard Kendall said to me, "If you think we're going behind those red bastards if we lose, you can fuck off!" He wasn't giving an inch.

'So now we had to convince the Liverpool supporters on the council to use their influence at Anfield to stop this blowing up into a serious diplomatic incident. In the middle of the budget battle, with this massive economic turmoil, the most important item on the agenda was football. You wouldn't want to underestimate the power of the game.'

A look around the city confirmed Hatton's view. Houses everywhere were decorated with red or blue flags. Split households, and there were many, had both. A Town Hall function to celebrate the occasion summed the situation up. Hugh Dalton, the council chairman, said: 'We are facing many difficulties, particularly over unemployment, so it is a great pleasure to be able to pay tribute to the prestige and honour our clubs have brought us.'

A compromise was reached. The teams would mingle on the homecoming buses. Negotiations with the government were not fated to be resolved so easily.

Football allegiances famously split families on Merseyside but the other side of the equation is that it unites fans. The trains and coaches heading south on that last Saturday in March were not red or blue but a mix. They left a deserted city behind them and those who remained rued that they were not heading south to witness the historical event.

They flooded into London entwined and intermingled. Segregation was not an issue.

Along with pride, the thousands of Scousers brought their politics south. On the trains, young men handed out 'I Support Liverpool City Council' badges in red or blue. Ski hats were the fashion of the day and almost all were adorned with these stickers and chants of 'Merseyside' were intermingled with 'Derek Hatton, we'll support you ever more' and 'Maggie, Maggie, Maggie! Out, out, out!'

While the fans drank the West End empty and sang their songs long into the night, the Liverpool players were tucked up in bed in the West Lodge Park Hotel in Hertfordshire.

There, the spirit of friendliness was tested. 'About four thirty in the morning I was woken by someone chanting "Everton, Everton",' Souness said. 'Many of the other lads were woken up and Alan Kennedy chased the culprit as far as the lift.'

The interloper was lucky it was Kennedy. The left back's lack of pace told again. At least that was the joke around the breakfast table. It was a relaxed group that headed for Wembley for the most anticipated derby in history.

It was raining and that suited Everton. Warm weather and a perfect pitch, they believed, went in favour of Liverpool's stylists. 'I'd looked at all the Wembley cup finals and thought it would be absolutely roasting,' Neville Southall said. 'But it pissed down and I was happy with that.'

In the cold and wet, Everton went on the attack early and the defining moment of the game came after just six minutes. Graeme Sharpe, invariably successful in the air against the Liverpool defence, knocked the ball to Adrian Heath and the little striker had an opportunity against Grobbelaar. Heath chipped the onrushing goalkeeper but Alan Hansen, charging back, stopped the ball on the line. The interception seemed to involve plenty of knee and even more hand. The entire stadium thought it was a penalty. Alan Robinson, the referee, waved play on.

Seven years earlier, Everton had missed out on an FA Cup final when Clive Thomas disallowed a late Bryan Hamilton goal at Maine Road that would have given them a 3–2 win over their neighbours. Thomas had become an almost mythical hate figure in Everton legend. Now Robinson joined him on Goodison's blacklist of despised officials.

Hansen is adamant that it was not a spot-kick. 'It was never a penalty,' he said. 'The ball rebounded up off my knee and although it struck my hand it was never intentional.'

Kendall, like most in the ground and the global television audience, saw it differently. 'It was a clear handball. Who knows? If we'd have put that one away we may have gone on to win it.'

Instead, the match petered out as a 0–0 draw, amid recriminations about Liverpool's poor performance. 'We got the slating we deserved at half-time,' Souness said. 'Joe told us it looked as if only two or three of us wanted to play.'

Craig Johnston wanted to play and when he was withdrawn to be replaced by Michael Robinson in the break before extra time, the frustration that had always threatened to boil over in the six days since John Wark's signing finally came to the surface.

'Now's your chance to get Warky on,' he sneered at Fagan. Wark was cup-tied for this match but available for league games. This insubordination was too much for the Liverpool manager. Smokin' Joe exploded.

'Do you think the game's all about you, son?' he asked. 'Go on, piss off. Now.'

'I was pleading with Joe not to bring me off,' Johnston said. 'I was fitter than anyone. The longer we played, the more chances I'd get. I couldn't understand the logic.' The explosion was part of a wider issue that Johnston grappled with constantly. 'I wasn't the most naturally gifted so I felt I'd get the hook in every game I played in,' he said. 'It was as if it would be my last game. It made me more nervous and sicker than the rest.'

It was the last sour note of the afternoon. Both sides had something to take away from the draw – Liverpool had two goals disallowed to counter Everton's penalty appeal – and players and fans joined together to express a unity rare in the game. John Bailey, one of the three Scousers in the Everton squad, found the aftermath emotional. 'I can remember running around with Alan Kennedy,' he said. 'We tied our red and blue scarves together. It still brings a lump to my throat.'

It was a very different response from the usual Liverpool way. Normally, after a disappointing draw the team would keep a low profile and not risk the Bootroom's wrath by fraternizing with the opposition and cavorting around the pitch. The mood of togetherness got to everybody, though.

'That day was different,' Dalglish said. 'It was special. The game might not have been but the atmosphere and the fans were different. It was a celebration of the city. We'd be ready to battle each other again at the replay. But for that moment, it was something special. At a time when everybody saw the fans as hooligans, as violent animals who couldn't be trusted to mix, the world could see it could be different.'

Bailey agrees: 'To run round the stadium and to see everybody together, everybody in different colours, my family in different colours, strangers from all over the country, different supporters' groups together, smiling, having a good time. You come off and think, "This is what every game should be like. Why be segregated? Why not mix?" I wish we could have had a bigger stadium. We could have filled it with 200,000 Merseysiders.'

Even Fagan was remarkably phlegmatic. 'Of course, I'd have preferred it if we had won but at the end, when I looked around and listened to the fans chanting "Merseyside! Merseyside!" I thought, "At least they are all going away happy."'

Ultimately, the manager blamed the midweek exertions. 'We didn't play particularly well, no snap, no sparkle, too methodical in thought and action. We seemed to have Benfica on our minds. We tried to play the same way we played there, like a game of draughts.

But there is no way you can do that in English football. We were harried down and it could have cost us the game. English football is all about pride and passion and we did not show that in the first half.'

The *Guardian* agreed with Fagan's assessment. 'Liverpool will enjoy the luxury of a second chance because Everton could not quite muster the knock-out punch.'

There was one winner that Sunday, at least. Ian Rush won the Professional Footballers' Player of the Year award, an honour Dalglish had accepted the previous season.

This long League Cup campaign was already twelve games old and had passed through Wembley. Now it would move to Maine Road for the replay. It had been a lot of work and still the £64,000 prize for winning the trophy was up for grabs. It was another mid-week match that meant the team would get no rest. Two derbies are attritional enough for one season, never mind four. And with the Manchester weather expected to be grimmer than Wembley's and City's pitch worn and boggy after a long winter, it was a dog-fight Liverpool could have done without.

By Wednesday all the emotion of a united Merseyside was long gone. It was all about winning a football match. Fagan, never one to hold a grudge when there was a game to play, selected the same starting side as Wembley, including Johnston. It would have been easy to replace the Australian with Steve Nicol but the manager was only concerned about picking the right team.

For young Nicol, missing out on the final was a disappointment but the Scot had got into step with the Liverpool way in a manner Johnston had not. 'I was still at the stage of establishing myself,' he said. 'I just accepted Joe's decision. I didn't want to come across as big-headed. If you did, you'd be slaughtered. It didn't do to get carried away.' The down-to-earth attitude would stand him in good stead. But for now, he watched from the stands as the most ferocious of derbies took place in the Maine Road mud.

'The replay was really tough,' Alan Kennedy said. 'It was played on a dismal night. It was made for their style and they had the better chances.'

Souness had taken on board Fagan's comments after the first game. There would be no Continental prissiness on a foul northern night and the captain matched force with force. After twenty-one minutes, he hit a wobbling, bobbling left-footed shot that skimmed above the mire and beat Southall. Liverpool had the lead and, for the moment, the barrage stopped.

'It seemed to knock the stuffing out of them for a while,' Kennedy said.

Half-time brought both sides a chance to regroup. In the red dressing room, Souness was at his best. 'He used to go round every player,' Rush said, 'fist clenched, geeing us up, telling us the game was there for the taking. He pumped adrenalin into you. You used to go out thinking you couldn't lose. That was the Souness psychology.'

Across the corridor, the Everton manager was working his own mind games. 'You knew what Kendall was telling them,' Kennedy said. 'He was saying, "Get into the bastards. They don't like it. Make them battle. Turn it into a scrap." It was proper alehouse stuff in that second half.'

From then on it was all about grit. It was survival of the toughest. Souness's goal – and his performance – was the difference between the teams.

'A lot of people thought they could rough us up,' Hansen said. 'But we could scrap with the best of them. It really was blood and thunder.'

Fagan was ecstatic at winning his first trophy. 'Well, the lads did it!' he wrote in his diary. 'And well worth it. The man of the match scored the goal and didn't he play well? But let's take nothing away from the other ten – each one deserved a medal for their commitment and attitude.'

There was some relief in the dressing room, too. 'We probably didn't deserve to win it, really,' Kennedy said. 'We all said later, "Bloody hell! We were lucky there." We were happy with the result but not the performance.'

Winning the League Cup had the biggest impact on the manager. Ever since he had taken the job – reluctantly – there had been an element of doubt in his mind as to whether he could match the lofty achievements of Shankly and Paisley. The League Cup had been hard work. It had been won with graft and fortitude rather than skill and class. Yet now it nestled in Anfield's trophy room and Fagan would always have at least one honour to his name. At sixty-two, he had broken his duck.

'That win really took the pressure off and you could visibly see the change in him after that,' Grobbelaar said. 'It was as if a huge weight had been lifted from his shoulders. Any man would have been anxious following in the footsteps of Bob Paisley, and Joe, although he never showed it, was no different. Winning the Milk Cup gave everyone the belief that more could follow.'

The team celebrated the victory for most of the night. 'No milk for us,' Kennedy said. 'We should have been sponsored by lager.' Prophetic words.

With one bauble in the bag, it was time to turn back to the league. Both main contenders faced awkward away games, Liverpool at Watford and Manchester United travelling to West Bromwich Albion. United were a point clear and, with ten games to go, had their destiny in their own hands.

Fagan faced a difficult situation, too. John Wark, signed less than two weeks before, was eligible to play in the league. The Scot had a knack of scoring goals from the midfield. It was a skill long envied at Anfield. 'How many times have you heard it said that goalscoring is about being in the right place at the right time?' Bob Paisley asked. 'Most footballers know where the right place is but relatively few can sense when the time is right. John Wark has great timing. You could set your watch by him.'

Wark was twenty-six when he arrived at Anfield. The Glaswegian had signed from Ipswich Town, where he had helped the Suffolk club win the FA Cup and the Uefa Cup. He also featured in the Sylvester Stallone film *Escape to Victory*, alongside Michael

Caine, Pelé and Bobby Moore. He could casually attest to Caine's skills – 'a good player but his legs had gone' – and Pelé's ability to execute an overhead kick on the first take. After that he was never going to be overawed by a move to Liverpool and a dressing room full of stars.

He was shocked by the champions' slapdash approach to his medical examination after the transfer. It made him wonder whether the tales of Liverpool's thorough approach to the game were mere myth. The doctor was ancient and merely took Wark's blood pressure and had him touch his toes. That was the extent of the medical. The Scot had arrived from Ipswich expecting a new level of professionalism. His first impression was that 'the whole regime was a bit Dad's Army'.

That was until he got the sergeant-major treatment from Ronnie Moran. During his first training session, Wark knocked a long pass down the touchline. He stood back and admired his footwork but his sense of self-satisfaction was destroyed by a raging Moran. 'We pass and move here!' an incandescent Moran screamed. 'Don't ever stand round admiring what you've done.'

Wark's next lesson in Anfield's version of professionalism arrived rapidly before the Watford game. Fagan had a straight choice between the newcomer and Johnston. It was clear that selecting Wark would lead to a massive row between the Australian and the manager, but Fagan had no qualms.

'It is decision day regarding Wark,' Smokin' Joe wrote in his diary. 'I am going to put him in for Johnston. I think he may bring more stability to the midfield. Also, he can score goals and maybe get the ball a bit better than Craig. I am sorry to have to do it but this is part of the job and I get paid for it. It is all right winning Milk Cups but that is not all I am here for. It is to try and improve the first team. Sorry Craig.'

Compassion was confined to the diary. In the dressing room, Fagan had to be ruthless. Souness feared the manager would mis-handle the situation but had to admit his error. 'Craig was a great lad but prone to fly off the handle at times if not playing and I feared that Joe was maybe too nice to cope with it,' the captain said. 'But I should have known better because he handled it superbly.'

Against Coventry, when Johnston was dropped after a victory in the previous game, the team's performance did not back up the manager's judgement. Against Watford, it was the opposite. Wark, 'bringing another dimension to their attack', according to the *Sunday Times*, opened the scoring after fifty-eight minutes. Rush added a second with ten minutes left. United, by contrast, lost 2–0 at West Brom. It was a confident Fagan who joked afterwards about his team talk. 'It was one of our longer meetings,' he said. 'All of sixty seconds. We decided to forget the Milk Cup and be aggressive.'

Wark was surprised to be picked but he would now go on to play a decisive role in the title race. Johnston remained resentful but at least his day ended with a smile. 'Being dropped was a blow,' he said. 'After the League Cup final everyone was saying "you can't be dropped". Then Fagan left me on the bench. I told him he couldn't change the rules when it suited him. If you keep saying you can't change a winning team, then you shouldn't.'

If the demotion was painful, insult was soon to be added to injury. 'I was friendly with Stan Boardman, the comedian,' Johnston said. 'He asked me to get tickets for him for Watford. I got them and was expecting to play.'

In the second half, Fagan told his substitute to warm up. 'I was running down the touchline and started getting abuse from the crowd,' the Australian said. '"F— off back to Oz, you long-haired bastard." I'm not very happy. I went and sat down and Fagan tells me to warm up again. I didn't want to but I didn't want to tell Joe, Ronnie and Roy it was because of the stick.'

Growing angrier, Johnston ran the gauntlet again. 'I was stretching and it starts: "Kangaroo shagger." I looked at the bench and Joe, Ronnie and Roy were laughing at me. I turned to the crowd to see who was shouting and to give a bit back and it was Stan Boardman. It gave me a laugh on a bad day.'

Even if he was laughing through gritted teeth after Watford,

Liverpool were back on top of the league with the first leg of a potential treble in the bag. The squad had been strengthened and confidence was booming. There weren't too many unhappy faces around Anfield.

21.

Packing a Punch

April 1984

West Ham United (h); Dinamo Bucharest (h), European Cup SF; Stoke City (a); Leicester City (a); West Bromwich Albion (h)

The scouts from Dinamo Bucharest were not smiling. Mircea Lucescu, the Romania coach, had been co-opted to watch Liverpool's match against West Ham United, who were sitting in fourth place in the table. It should have been a serious test of the champions' credentials. Lucescu did not like what he saw.

The afternoon opened with a show of triumphalism as the League Cup was paraded in front of the Kop. The mood of superiority continued as the day wore on.

This was a team brimming with confidence. They swarmed all over their opponents. Within six minutes, Liverpool were in the lead; by half-time it was four. The final score, 6–0, could have been doubled.

The visiting fans had written the game off early. They entertained themselves by performing a conga around the Anfield Road terrace and celebrating wildly when their team won a corner.

Liverpool's weapons were obvious to the Romanian spy. Rush scored two and Souness matched him with a brace. Dalglish, back at the very top of his game, orchestrated the display, and the midfield that had worried Fagan for so much of the season now purred like a precision engine. Wark added the attacking dimension the manager had yearned for.

The newcomer's presence allowed Dalglish to play further up the pitch and Wark's more disciplined approach gave Souness extra freedom. This left Johnston feeling even more isolated. The unforgiving cycle of build-up and let-down had left him angry and disappointed. Now he became the leader of the disaffected group within the squad. He became the founder member and chairman of the SGG – the Sour Grapes Gang. It was partly an outlet for the outsiders to let off steam, partly a humorous attempt at self-parody.

'Whatever I did, it was not enough to get into the first team,' he said. 'In the reserves, you're disenfranchised. If you took it personally, you'd implode. Then, when you got your chance, you tried too hard. So I started the SGG and we used to have meetings and blame everyone else. We'd get together in pubs on the Wirral. We all seemed to live there and the elite group lived in Southport. As chairman, I had to be on call for the other members. It made the dressing room more buoyant. Everyone heard about it and it became a big joke.'

At least the Australian would be back for the European tie. Yet the new formation that had swept away West Ham had been counterproductive in some ways. After the Romanians had witnessed such a powerful performance, there was no doubt that Dinamo would come to defend.

Fagan was expecting similar treatment to the Bilbao and Benfica games. Liverpool had pioneered the tactic of going to a foreign stadium and killing the match. Now, they were ready for a taste of their own medicine. 'We mastered that system early but things have levelled off now,' the manager said. 'There are others who are as good as we are now.'

Even after winning the League Cup, there were still questions about Fagan's ability to lead his team to European glory. On the day of the game, David Miller in *The Times* queried the manager's credentials: 'One of the most telling factors in the outcome of this semi-final could be the relationship between Joe Fagan, in his first season as manager, and his players: can he encourage them sufficiently to lift their game for the occasion after many peaks of the past, even if players such as Lee, Lawrenson, Whelan and Rush have fewer honours than some of the older hands? I am not one to elevate the manager above the players, but this is an instance where Fagan's ability could matter.'

The unhappy Johnston was back in the team for what turned into a rancorous and vicious night. Dinamo packed their defence and resorted to every trick in football to break the home side's rhythm. The unpleasantness started early and mushroomed as the march went on. 'They were completely cynical,' Kennedy said.

'They hacked, kicked and battered their way through us,' Rush agreed.

'It was horrible. The Butcher of Bilbao had nothing on these boys,' Dalglish said.

Rush had a goal disallowed for offside early but there was danger at the other end, too. For all their violent approach, Dinamo had the skill to trouble any side. Ionel Augustin broke from the halfway line and hit the post with a shot from the edge of the box. As the fury of the opening minutes subsided, the calls of the players echoed around the empty areas in the ground. A mere 36,941 had come to Anfield for this European Cup semi-final. Only the Kop was full, and its roar was quieted.

Then, after twenty-five minutes, Johnston broke down the left and was brought down near the Main Stand touchline. Kennedy came up to take the free kick and swung in a cross as the referee was still backing the Dinamo wall away. No one seemed ready in the middle, either, as Sammy Lee, the smallest man on the pitch, came charging between two defenders to power home a bullet header. Now Liverpool had a margin but the goal, if anything, magnified the ill will.

There were running battles across the pitch. Alexandru Nicolae kicked out at Rush, provoking a shoving match on the sidelines; Ioan Andone was the nastiest of a four-man Romanian hit squad directed towards stopping Dalglish; and Souness, who was never shy of a feud, had become embroiled in an ongoing battle with Lică Movilă, the Dinamo captain.

Lee had the ball in the net again but the goal was called back for offside. Then, as the game ground on to its spiteful conclusion, Souness changed the complexion of the entire tie.

As another attack broke down in front of the Kop, the Dinamo defence rushed forward to catch any lingerers offside and Liverpool dropped back to cover any potential breaks. Left behind on the edge of the area, lying alone, was Movilă, clutching his face.

Nearly everyone in the ground had been watching the ball and had not seen what caused the Dinamo captain's injury. The referee summoned the Romanian trainer and various players milled around. Movilă appeared to be suggesting he had been punched. Souness stood, some distance away, hands on hips, a picture of innocence.

Steve Nicol was on the bench and, as a defender still learning his trade, had less focus on the ball than most. He was studying the back four's movement. 'The ball got cleared and almost everyone followed the ball,' Nicol said. 'I was watching the middle and just saw a red blur, an arm swing and the Romanian go down. You couldn't see it completely clearly but I'd seen enough. There was a punch. It was a beauty.'

The youngster was experienced enough to know exactly who was responsible. 'It was a classic Souness moment,' he said.

There were still twenty minutes to go. If things had been tense so far Souness – in Cold War terms – had just made them go nuclear. Movilă walked to the sidelines clutching his jaw. It was broken in two places. Souness, who had been so enraged when Kevin Moran had smashed Dalglish's cheek, had just pulled a similar stunt. And he was proud of it.

'Movilă was the worst of the lot,' he would later say. 'He kicked everything that moved and three times caught me with punches off the ball. I went completely crazy when he came in late and high yet again and as he half turned I let loose with the best punch I have delivered in my life.'

'I heard it more than I saw it,' Kennedy said. 'A thud. I just saw a red blur and heard a boom. He turned into Souness, too, which probably made it worse.'

The left back could not believe that Souness had escaped unpunished. 'How the ref didn't see it I'll never know,' Kennedy said.

Dalglish was a matter of yards away from his team-mate when

the blow was landed. 'Oh, I saw it,' he said. Was it as good a punch as legend has it? 'Oh yeah.'

The incident had been brewing for some time. 'Movilă was warned,' Dalglish said. 'Graeme told him if he pulled his shirt again he'd get it. He got it.'

Even some of Souness's team-mates thought that their captain had overstepped the mark. 'I'm not saying it was a bit naughty but it was . . . well, a bit . . . let's just say Movilă wasn't happy,' Kennedy said.

No one in the Dinamo camp was. If Souness had not been a marked man before, he was now. In the final minute, he went into a challenge with Gheorghe Mulţescu. The Romanian did not even try to disguise his kick towards his rival's groin. This was even before the full scale of Movilă's injury was apparent.

As they left the pitch at the end of the game, Souness passed the injured party. 'He was standing at the mouth of the tunnel with a towel around his head and his face packed with ice,' the Scot said. 'There were two big fellas, one either side of him. They looked like cops. They were scowling at me.' The Liverpool captain was not intimidated. 'It was all a bit of a laugh,' he said, before adding reflectively, 'Well . . . not for him.'

Kennedy says that Souness was dismissive afterwards. 'Listen, whatever he got, he deserved. End of story,' the left back remembers the captain saying. It was, however, far from the end of the story. As Brian Glanville wrote a few days later: 'I don't think I would like to be Graeme Souness in Bucharest.'

Asked was he worried about the second leg, Fagan said, 'Not one little bit. At this stage of the tournament you have to have faith in the referee.' He accompanied the statement with a theatrical swig of strong liquor.

It was an eventful night in the European Cup. The other semi-final, between Dundee United and Roma, had a surprising outcome. The Italian side were the favourites to reach the final, which would take place in their own Stadio Olimpico. On a thrilling night at

Tannadice, the Scots seriously damaged Roma's hopes of winning the trophy in their own backyard.

Roma came to Scotland with a similar plan to Dinamo's but had been stunned by the home side's high-tempo game. The 2–0 victory gave Jim McLean's team a bigger cushion than Liverpool's and the United manager was confident. 'I am convinced now that we will give the Italians a run for their money and perhaps even score over there,' McLean said.

No one from the away team was hospitalized at Tannadice but the bad feeling between the two clubs was as bitter as that which had developed at Anfield. The Roma players claimed McLean called them 'Italian bastards'. It would not have been a surprise. The forty-five-year-old was renowned for abusing his own players. Early in the match against Roma, one of the United players took a short throw-in against McLean's instructions to bomb the ball into the Italian side's area. 'You're a fucking ignorant cunt!' the manager bawled.

'The spectators behind my dugout are the ones who get the most entertainment,' he said afterwards.

The Italian press were not amused by McLean and seized upon an inappropriate quip to stir up a frenzy of hatred. 'One of their reporters had asked if we were on drugs after our two–nil win,' McLean said. 'I joked that if we were I hoped we were still on them for the next game. That translated in the Italian press that we were using drugs and only added to the hostility.'

It would be hard to imagine two more potentially rancorous second legs in the history of the European Cup semi-finals. They would not disappoint.

With the European Cup hopes hanging in the balance, it was back to the league and the Victoria Ground to face Stoke City on a sunny spring afternoon. After the victory over Benfica in the previous round of the European Cup, Fagan had been disappointed by his side's approach and attitude in the next game against Everton in the League Cup final.

Against Stoke, the pattern was repeated. This time Liverpool did not escape with a draw. The tension was showing. Fagan's team conceded a goal in each half of the 2–0 defeat and Souness was booked, earning him a one-game suspension.

There were recriminations afterwards and the captain, in fury, punched a door. Unfortunately it was glass and there was a substantial amount of blood from Souness's cut hand to go with the thunder of an angry dressing room. Earlier in the week, the Liverpool captain had escaped punishment for his jaw-breaking punch on Movilă. He did not get away with it at the Victoria Ground.

'There was a secretary in the room and the club made me write a letter of apology,' a rueful Souness said. 'It was embarrassing.'

Liverpool's anger and embarrassment were eased a little when news came through that Manchester United had been beaten, too, 1–0 away to lowly Notts County. It was a bonus. 'United seemed to fall short,' the Liverpool captain said. 'They had talent but slipped up when they were playing lesser teams.'

That result kept Liverpool at the top of the table and the gap at two points but, with just seven games to play, margins were tight. It would be a mistake to rely on rivals tripping up.

'Too many players had no legs and no zip to carry us through,' reflected Fagan. No wonder. They were fifty-eight games into the season and had used a mere fifteen players. Dalglish, in particular, was feeling the pace. 'He looked thoroughly bored and out of touch,' Fagan observed in his diary.

United could still not turn up the pressure. The next Tuesday, Ron Atkinson's side went to Watford, where Liverpool had won 2–0. United could only draw 0–0 and, instead of going top, they remained in second.

The scale of the missed opportunity became clear to Old Trafford twenty-four hours later when the league leaders struggled to a 3–3 draw away to Leicester City. After taking an early lead, they were behind twice and needed Wark to score a late equalizer to secure a point.

A routine 3–0 win over West Bromwich Albion provided a relatively easy warm-up for the second leg against Bucharest. While the Midlands side were dispatched at Anfield, United again kept pace. But games were running out. Liverpool, despite another wobble, were closing in on the title.

22

Iron Will

April–May 1984

Dinamo Bucharest (a), European Cup SF; Ipswich Town (h);
Birmingham City (a)

Relatively few Westerners travelled behind the Iron Curtain in 1984. When they did, they found a very different culture and very different attitudes. 'Bucharest and around the ground were very grey and full of grey people,' Kennedy said. 'There were lots of military personnel standing round, people in uniform. You never felt entirely welcome.'

Graeme Souness was certainly unwelcome. 'There were some dark, unfriendly Balkan faces peering at Joe Fagan's team when they arrived at the airport,' *The Times* reported. 'The air hangs heavy with retribution.'

'The atmosphere was decidedly chilly,' Grobbelaar observed. The goalkeeper had been in dangerous situations during his time in the Rhodesian army and was not easily intimidated.

'Everyone was waiting for Charlie,' Nicol said. 'At the airport, people were screaming at us. It took us a little while to realize it was all about Souness.'

It was a time for pulling together, rallying round the captain. Yet typically, the rest of the squad saw the situation as an opportunity to have a laugh at Champagne Charlie's expense.

'Once we twigged it was all about him, that was it,' Nicol said. 'We got on the coach and we were all pointing at him, directing the angry mob to where he was sitting so they could bang on the window. We were all laughing at him and pointing. It went on the whole trip.'

If anyone could cope with the harsh intensity of Bucharest, it was Souness. But his team-mates were relishing his discomfort and keen to keep the pressure up.

'They were banging on the coach,' Souness said. 'I was sitting there and suddenly this fella came up to the window and his face was level with mine. That must have made him about seven foot tall. He was a giant. He was making gestures like he was gouging out eyes.'

Lesser men might have moved to another seat but the Scot quickly formed a strategy. 'I looked around and pointed to Alan Kennedy,' Souness said. 'He had a moustache and curly hair and was about my size. He could easily have been mistaken for me if you didn't know. "That's Souness," I was saying to the giant, shaking my head and directing him to Alan. "Not me, him."'

The baiting continued throughout the trip. 'When we went downstairs in the hotel, there'd be people waiting around and we'd all point at Charlie,' Nicol said. '"Here he is, here he is!" We were loving it!'

So was Souness. 'He was made for situations like this,' Dalglish said. 'He was going to confront it head on.'

It was the same at the stadium. 'We were warming up on the pitch and every time a ball was passed to him, the crowd went mad, booing,' Nicol said. 'Pass to any of us, silence. Pass to him, frenzy. We were warming up with about five balls and every time he got rid of one, we'd knock another to him. Five balls were pinging towards him and the crowd were going mental. He was stepping over them, launching them long, anything to stop them going wild. We were all laughing, trying to make it worse.'

The man in the spotlight remembers it well. 'There were all these daft banners saying what they were going to do to me,' Souness said. 'Then Alan Hansen worked out that when the ball came to me in the warm-up they'd boo, so they started passing every ball to me. Every time it arrived at my feet there was a crescendo of noise.'

As the anger turned up a notch, so did the piss-taking. 'You could feel the tension rising,' Kennedy said. 'We were all going: "Oh, Graeme, please, there are sixty thousand lunatics here and the police are all against us. They'll be on the pitch in a minute! Souey, of course, couldn't give a shit. He was absolutely loving it. Loving it.'

There was never any doubt that Souness would play. Fagan knew he needed his midfield general. 'Joe had no problem playing him even though it was very hostile,' Kennedy said.

Nevertheless, the manager made sure his captain knew what was expected of him: 'Don't get too involved. Deal with it if they come looking for you but just play your football and don't get sent off.'

It was another awful night. The rain bucketed down and in the sunken bowl Liverpool battled both the howling wind and the hatred. 'It was a formidable stadium,' Kennedy said. 'We had to keep the crowd quiet.'

The Romanian side made their intentions clear before the kick-off. 'Their captain had played up front at Anfield,' Souness said. 'He was of a similar shape and size to me and had curly hair. He was aggressive during the coin-toss and then dropped deep to play in midfield. He pointed to himself and then to me, as if to say, "It's between us now."' It was a challenge Champagne Charlie would not let go unanswered. 'I gave him the thumbs-up,' he said.

Within seconds, the assault on Souness began. 'A couple of their players had a pop at him,' Kennedy said. 'But he got a couple of them back, too. He was good at doing his little bits and pieces off the ball when he needed to. It was pretty fierce. Every time Graeme got the ball, their whole team were out to get him. But he was just too good for them. They couldn't close him down.'

On the sort of pitch that was made for fighters and not the flighty, Souness imposed himself. 'He rode everything they threw at him,' Dalglish said. 'Lesser men would have folded.'

Before the game, Souness's colleagues were happy to let the captain be singled out. Now they worked hard to take the strain off him. 'He understood the pressure and coped with it,' Kennedy said. 'He needed his team-mates, though. We made sure he always had an option so he never got caught in possession.'

As usual, Fagan's plan was to take the crowd out of the game. In such hostile circumstances, it needed more than a spell of posses-sion and judicious fouling. In this maelstrom, it needed something special. Souness and Rush provided it.

A Sammy Lee corner was cleared but dropped only as far as the Liverpool captain some twenty-five yards out. For once, there was no Romanian nearby to rake his studs down Souness's leg. The Scot dinked the most delicate ball into the area along the inside-left channel. Its perfect weight and pace made a beautiful counterpoint to the physical ugliness of the game so far. The ball dropped to Rush, who expertly dribbled past the left back and shot instantly from an angle. The wet net rippled and the crowd groaned. With just eleven minutes gone it was 1–0, Liverpool were two up on aggregate and the tie was over. The goal was Rush's hundredth for Liverpool and few had been so important. 'I couldn't have picked a better occasion,' Rush said. 'But when everything is against you, as it seemed here, Liverpool have a habit of rising to the occasion.'

The only question left was whether Souness would emerge from this bear pit intact. Dinamo's sole cause now was to inflict punish-ment on the Scot – or any Liverpool player they could get near. 'Some of the tackles were horrible,' Kennedy said. 'This guy took me out near the touchline and I ended up about ten yards off the pitch when I landed. I thought, "I'm not getting caught by these again!" We were all under pressure.'

It was important Liverpool held their nerve. Even with the Roma-nians now requiring three goals to progress, the team were conscious how quickly things could turn. 'Every match has psychological turning points,' Johnston said. 'They can go one way or the other. If someone jumps out of a tackle it affects the subconscious of the team. The rest of you think, "If he didn't want to risk getting injured why should I?" It works the other way, too. When you see someone going in brave into a dangerous tackle, you're going to do the same thing.'

Costel Orac pulled a goal back before half-time but Dinamo still needed two goals to win. With Souness dictating the pace of the game, it never looked feasible. Rush added a second with six minutes left to earn a stunning victory.

Souness had run the gauntlet: his socks had been shredded by Romanian studs and policemen were making throat-slitting gestures at him as he headed for the dressing room. It didn't matter. Liverpool had won. Kennedy summed up his triumphant captain: 'They were never going to get him,' the left back said. 'Far too clever for them all.'

In the safety of the changing room, they found Fagan in an unusual mood.

The manager shouted for silence. 'All of you shut up and sit down!' he said, cutting the celebrations short. The players looked warily at each other, expecting the usual mantra: don't get overexcited, focus on Saturday, the league still needs to be won . . .

But Smokin' Joe shocked them again. 'You fucking beauties!' he bawled. The place erupted.

Fagan was even more bullish to the press. 'I am thinking at this moment of the treble of the league and two cups,' he crowed. 'I am elated for the whole squad after this performance. Dinamo met us on a day when everybody in the Liverpool side was on top song. It was quite a remarkable performance. The players did not seem to have any nerves. I had them for all of us.'

Meanwhile, Roma had managed to overturn the deficit against Dundee United and for once the manager was willing to look ahead and issue a clarion call. 'We don't mind playing Roma on their own pitch in the final. Our chaps grow bigger when the atmosphere is there. It will not worry me meeting them on their own ground.'

If Fagan had known the full story of what had happened to Britain's other semi-finalists, he might not have been so optimistic.

If Souness had been the target in Bucharest, even Caligula would have been awed by the contempt Jim McLean had generated in the Eternal City. The Roma president, Dino Viola, seized upon the Dundee United manager's comments about hoping his players were taking the same drugs for the second leg and treated them literally.

Roma, he told everyone who listened, were facing a team who admitted having an unfair and illegal advantage.

The Curva Sud section of the ground was draped with banners that illustrated the fury: 'God Hates Dundee United'; 'Rome Hates McLean'; and 'McLean Fuck Off'. This was where the ultras gathered. They were obsessive, fanatical and the object of some contempt from the more patrician Romans. 'Gente del Terzo Mondo', was a derisive description that was commonplace – Third World People.

They produced a level of hostility that went beyond the pale. Roma would not be denied their place in the final, or the European Cup they had come to see as their destiny.

They took no chances, either. An intermediary paid Michel Vautrot, the French referee, in the region of £50,000 before the game. Riccardo Viola, the son of the Roma president, later told the story. 'Roma gave a middleman one hundred million lire destined for referee Vautrot,' Viola said. 'That is true and a shameful fact.'

Senior figures in Italian football were involved to make sure Dundee United would not go through.

'Spartaco Landini, the director of football at Genoa, came to see my father,' Viola continued. 'He told him Vautrot was a friend of his and that we could get at him via another friend. He said a dinner would be organized with the referee on the eve of the game and a signal to show the deal had been done would be demanded. During the dinner a waiter went up to the referee saying, "Telephone call for Mr Vautrot." That was the prearranged signal.

'Vautrot left the table and when he returned said, "My friend Paolo rang and he sends you his best wishes." Then I got up, rang my father and told him, "Message received." All this was done because we had a difficult game ahead of us against Dundee United. Going out of the competition would have had serious repercussions.'

Roma might have kept their money because it was a different United team in the second leg from the one that shocked Tannadice. It was as if they had taken sedatives. The pressure had got to

McLean's side and the Italians came storming out of the blocks on a baking-hot afternoon.

Roberto Pruzzo scored twice in a first half during which the Scottish side wilted in the face of Roma's onslaught. Vautrot was fastidious and quick to clamp down on the physical side of United's game but his decisions were difficult to dispute. The winning goal came in the second half, when Hamish McAlpine, the United goalkeeper, pulled down Pruzzo. Any referee would have given the spot-kick and Agostino Di Bartolomei sealed Roma's place in the final.

What happened afterwards was more disturbing. The Roma players and staff surrounded McLean and the Scottish bench and abused and spat at them. Punches were thrown and what should have been a time of celebration for the home side turned into a sour, vindictive scene.

'We must thank Signor McLean for having given us such a charge,' Di Bartolomei said facetiously. 'Thanks to him, we've got to the final. In every one of us there was a thirst for revenge and we showed it to him.'

This was a mere semi-final and Roma had won. What would be their approach to the final? And how would they react if, God forbid, they lost? Liverpool had won in Bilbao, Lisbon and Bucharest in increasingly hostile circumstances. This would be a challenge of a completely different order.

As usual, Souness embraced it. Before the second legs, Michael Robinson had expressed the hope that Dundee United would win in the belief that it would be the easier option in the final. Souness looked at him as if he were mad. 'We're the best in the world,' Robinson remembers his captain snarling. 'Nobody can fucking beat us. It's impossible we'll go to Rome and get beaten.'

Joe Fagan and his team knew nothing about what had happened to McLean and United as they flew back from Bucharest. Champagne flowed and songs resounded about the aircraft as the manager reiterated his lack of fear at the prospect of playing Roma on their home ground. 'It doesn't mean a thing,' he said. 'We take everything in our stride as it comes along and always have done.'

Peter Robinson, the general secretary at Anfield, was asked whether Liverpool would complain to Uefa about the venue. 'It's not our style,' he said.

There had been too many disappointing domestic results after a big European night. Once again, the pattern repeated itself.

The weather at Anfield could not have been more different from that in Bucharest three days earlier as warm sunshine illuminated the pitch. Liverpool's display against Ipswich Town left no one feeling bright, though. Eric Gates gave the visiting side the lead but Alan Kennedy pulled things level with one of his classic, thirty-five-yard left-foot blasts. When Rush gave Liverpool the lead before half-time, it looked like Fagan's side would cruise away. For the opening exchanges of the second period Liverpool played like champions. Then, out of nowhere, Gates struck again and nervousness took over the home team. Despite having all the possession and the frantic urging of the 32,000 crowd, Liverpool were unable to break the deadlock. Two more points had been dropped at a critical moment in the season.

The good news came in the dressing room. Manchester United had once again drawn, 0–0 at home to the West Ham side Liverpool had smashed six goals past just three weeks before. It looked like Fagan's team were doing their best to lose the league but their great rivals refused to take advantage.

The Liverpool manager later claimed that he hadn't been worried about Ron Atkinson's team. 'You could always read the script with United,' he said. 'I felt there was something predictable about them. I felt that even if we slipped up they wouldn't win it. I felt we could read them more than either Southampton or QPR.'

The pressure built at Old Trafford every season. United's last title had been won in 1967. With the chance to end that woeful run Bryan Robson and his team lost their nerve. 'These days both teams seem to be riding a curious tandem: Liverpool and United win, lose and draw together,' the *Sunday Times* said.

The cycle continued the next Saturday. Liverpool were at St Andrew's to face Birmingham City and United travelled to Goodison Park to play Everton. Fagan's team could not score in a match enlivened by the schizophrenic Grobbelaar. Early on, he fumbled the ball and Birmingham nearly scored. Later in the game, he was quick off his line to smother an attack that had beaten the offside trap. Next, he made a remarkable double save, stopping goalward-bound shots by first Kevin Rogers and then Robert Hopkins. Finally, in the last minute, with the point seemingly secure, he fumbled a back pass from Phil Neal out of play and then flapped at the subsequent corner to give Birmingham a golden opportunity to score that was spurned by Mick Hartford.

Roma's spy at the match was Luciano Tessari, a goalkeeper himself. He was noncommittal, describing Liverpool's performance as '*regolare*' or ordinary. However, it was clear to the Italian that Grobbelaar would be a key target for his team in twenty-five days.

The goalkeeper always laughed off his mistakes. In public, he presented a happy-go-lucky figure, revelling in the clownish antics that drew the cameras before and after games.

In a remarkable interview with Simon Barnes in *The Times*, the former Rhodesian soldier outlined his philosophy. Barnes rang the club, asked for an interview with the goalkeeper and was told Grobbelaar would ring back. He did. 'I said I'd take him to lunch,' Barnes remembers, 'and he said, "Let's skip the eating and go straight to the drinking." So we went out for a beer.'

The writer found his subject a compelling character. 'He was fantastic company. He'd been around before becoming a footballer and had seen – and been involved in – things that don't bear thinking about. He knew that football wasn't everything. He was not going to get upset about dropping a ball or conceding a goal. He knew there are more important things in life.'

The interview gave an insight into one side of Grobbelaar's character. Recalling his performance the previous season that led to Liverpool being knocked out of the European Cup, the goalkeeper compared it favourably to some of his other displays.

'You thought I was bad against Widzew Łódź? You should have seen me against Nottingham Forest last time,' he said, recalling the league game back on New Year's Eve. 'I was even worse. I didn't do one thing right. Every cross, I dropped it. Every shot, I fumbled. The ball was a bar of soap, my hands were covered in lather. They didn't score – but I don't know how.'

Much of the criticism, Grobbelaar suggested, was because people did not understand his role. 'A Liverpool goalkeeper needs to be a sweeper as well as a goalkeeper,' he said. 'When the Liverpool defence gets caught I have to come off my line. The fault is not that I go for the ball when it beats the defence. The fault is the occasional split-second hesitation.'

This did not mean he was unaware of his own shortcomings. However, criticism was frustrating. 'A goalkeeper must learn to be critical of his own performance, he must know when he is in the wrong,' he said. 'But I hate it when I've had a moderate day and the press tell me I've had a stinker. Journalists don't think I'm good because I'm flashy. But I don't think they would treat an English player in the same way.'

Ultimately, his philosophy was simple: 'I just thank my lucky stars I'm still here. I came out of the army knowing I was good enough to do anything I desired.'

There was another, less secure side to Grobbelaar. The goalkeeper was the subject of a regular correspondence on the letters page of the *Echo*. The critic repeatedly condemned the player's performances and signed off his missives with the address 'The Yankee Bar'.

This pub on Lime Street – its real name was the American Bar – was a well-known haunt of Liverpool's hard-core support. It was where the travelling fans drank before and after away matches and had the reputation of being one of the rougher drinking holes in the city.

Grobbelaar, his anger clearly fuelled by a boozing session of his own, would occasionally turn up at the Yankee demanding 'a straightener' with the letter-writer. He would stagger around the bar, ferociously asking the Scally clientele to point out his critic. He would offer to fight anyone who slated him to his face.

It took some nerve. Drinkers here were not to be intimidated. Fist-fights were not unusual in this establishment.

He drew some scornful looks but most customers smiled. It did Grobbelaar's reputation no harm. The hardest of the hard core admired him for fronting up and saw him as one of their own. The sporadic visits to the Yankee were the talk of the trains and the terraces when the chatter might have been about his fumbles and faults. Almost everyone saw him as a liability but they recognized his ability, athleticism and commitment. And his visits to the Yankee proved he cared, despite the impression he sometimes gave in public.

The game away to Birmingham was a turning point for Grobbelaar's room-mate. Craig Johnston reached his lowest ebb of the season. John Wark was picked in front of him again and the Australian was in deep despair as the 0–0 draw played itself out. 'At half-time, you realize you're not getting on,' he said. 'You've got all that unspent energy.' That night, the energy turned destructive.

'After Birmingham away, I didn't want to go out with the boys,' Johnston said. 'It was building up on the coach home. I was saying, "I'm not going out, I'm not going out."'

He longed to be with the team for the night's drinking session but hated waking up in the morning as an outsider. While the first-teamers slept, Johnston would have the humiliating experience of working off his hangover in training at Melwood.

'I got home and my wife asked me how I was,' he said. 'I flipped. I started ripping my suit off, screaming and shouting, "I'm good enough for this team!"'

With no other focus for his fury, Johnston continued to tear at his clothes.

'The suit was all ripped, my fingernails were bloody and I was standing there screaming,' he said. 'But that was the turning point. I said, "I'm going to prove this fucker wrong."'

The Australian was the envy of millions. He played for the best team in the world and it seemed like a dream life. Yet here he was having a breakdown.

The anger became a massive spur, and Johnston had another factor in his favour – his willingness to learn and work.

'I got hold of the keys to Melwood and had my own set cut,' he said. 'After that, if I didn't play, I'd go back to Melwood and get in Shankly's sweat box and work on my skills. Then I'd run around the perimeter knocking the ball against the wall with my left foot and turn around and do it again with my right foot, all the time saying, "Fagan's right" to myself.

'All the bitching wasn't me. I was determined to stay in the team the next time I got the opportunity.'

Johnston wanted to contribute on the run-in and be part of the chase for glory. He would have a huge influence, but could not imagine the form it would take.

23

Three Times the Charm

May 1984

Coventry City (h); Notts County (a); Norwich City (h)

There was a score to settle on Bank Holiday Monday. Coventry City were at Anfield and, after the stuttering draws of the previous two Saturdays, Liverpool needed a win. They could not expect United to slip up again.

There was also the little matter of the 4–0 defeat at Highfield Road in December. It had already become the stuff of legend in the East Midlands. To Fagan and his squad, it was a painful memory.

Coventry fought with all their might to avoid humiliation. They hung on until almost half-time. The pressure on Liverpool was mounting and the crowd of over 33,000 were growing ever-more restless. Then, two minutes before the break, Rush struck. It was his forty-third goal of the campaign. It meant the striker had passed Roger Hunt's club record of forty-two in a season. And he did not stop there. On his own, the Wales striker matched the four goals that Coventry had scored in December. His third made him the first player to score thirty league goals in a season since Everton's Bob Latchford in 1978. Latchford had been a hero to the boyhood Evertonian.

Now Rush, at twenty-three, was already a Liverpool legend. And this was his day. He even set up Alan Hansen to score the fifth.

Rush left the pitch with the match ball and the Kop's applause ringing in his ears. All the Coventry players got was a mouthful of abuse from Hansen, who loudly reminded them that 5–0 outstripped the four they had scored at Highfield Road.

The mood was even more upbeat when the news came through that, this time, United had got off the tandem. They had been beaten 2–1 by Ipswich at Old Trafford. Liverpool were now five points clear with two games left and with an almost unassailable advantage in goal difference. A single point at Meadow Lane against Notts County would effectively seal the title. The second leg of the treble was so close that they could taste it.

How great an achievement would winning the title be? It would be Liverpool's third consecutive First Division win. Only two teams had managed this feat in the English game's history: Huddersfield Town in the 1920s and Arsenal in the 1930s.

Throughout the season, the naysayers had scoffed at Liverpool's chances of retaining the League Championship. There had been doubts about Fagan, concerns about the standard of players coming to Anfield and worries that age was catching up with the stars of the squad. 'It is curious how regularly the vultures have gathered . . . to search for some hidden frailty in the Merseysiders,' *The Times* noted.

They now gathered at Meadow Lane to place Fagan and his team with the greats. On a windy day in Nottingham, the team ran out to take their place in history.

Few will remember the game. The players recall only Alan Kennedy's fashion faux pas. The left back turned up to travel to the Midlands in a pair of red leather trousers.

'Davie Hodgson was the fashion guru of the team,' Kennedy said. 'He said to me: "Get yourself a pair of red kecks. Leather ones." I thought they'd look good on me.'

It was a serious mistake that caused hilarity among the squad. The captain was particularly scathing.

Kennedy explains: 'Graeme Souness said to me, "You look like a right prat. Who told you to wear them? Get them off."' It was the end of a short-lived experiment: 'I hung them up in the dressing room in Meadow Lane. That was it. I left them there.'

Sartorial style was not the left back's strongest point. 'I was trying to move from the 1970s look to the modern world,' he said. 'But I was clueless. When I got a new suit and the pockets were sewn up, I thought that's how it was meant to be worn. I didn't realize you had to cut the stitches to open up the pockets. I walked around with nowhere to put pens and stuff. All the lads thought it was hysterical.'

Fortunately, Kennedy's wardrobe was the only place in which disaster struck that day. On the pitch, the 0–0 draw was almost chanceless. John Chiedozie, the County winger, gave both full backs some awkward moments but it appeared that Liverpool were already practising for Rome. They played as if they were set up to stifle European opposition, giving nothing away and looking to break quickly. Their determination not to concede was clear.

At the final whistle, thousands of Liverpool fans poured on to the pitch but it was not a frenzied, joyous celebration. There was a sense that the job was only two-thirds done.

Winning the league was always the 'bread and butter' of the club's aims. The low-key finale illustrated this. Most of the attention focused on Rush. Fagan, though, knew where to direct praise.

'We needed Rush's goals and the performances from everyone else but in the end I have to choose Graeme as my Liverpool man of the season for his leadership, attitude and total commitment,' the manager said. 'There were a few times that we faltered and it was then he responded.'

The captain was not ready to go overboard with his celebrations. Souness, like many observers, believed Liverpool's rivals had made things easy for them. 'Perhaps we did not deserve the title this season,' the Scot said. 'We have slipped a bit by our standards.'

If the comments seemed unreasonably churlish, Souness knew that there were still two games to go. One would be a meaningless league match at home to Norwich City that would be little more than a party. The other would be different.

The final game of the season in Rome would determine whether this team would be listed with the sport's greats. Souness wanted his team-mates on the top of their game for this one.

Fagan's post-mortem on the season the next Monday confirmed Souness's reservations. 'It finished up the right way in the end but it's been a nerve-racking time,' he reflected. 'It's just beginning to sink in and I am glad the issue has been settled now. I thought it would go to the final game. I was nearly right but thank God I was wrong.

'I have had quite enough of the anxiety and tension. There were plenty of times, especially during April, when I wondered if we were going to make it. We never got really ahead. It may have looked as though we were quite relaxed but I can tell you the tension was there. This season we have played good football but it has been a battle all the way through. Injuries to important players upset us a little along the way but we fought through those times and showed a lot of character.'

Fagan was immediately thinking of next season. He and Peter Robinson, the club secretary, were in London to seal an £800,000 deal for Paul Walsh, the Luton Town forward.

Then it was back to Anfield to close out the season with a 1–1 draw against Norwich and Souness received the Championship trophy from the Football League's president. This time, he did not throw it to anyone.

The Tuesday-night crowd were in party mood. They refused to leave the ground until the players made repeated curtain calls. They acclaimed Rush, Souness and Dalglish in particular but hailed the manager so many of them had doubted just a year before. The acclaim touched Fagan, a man more accustomed to watching applause from the shadows. 'That was very emotional and something I did not expect,' he said afterwards. Characteristically, he looked to spread the plaudits. 'But tonight is not about me, it is about the players, the lads downstairs, the directors and the fans.'

That night, it was about the drinking, as everyone hit the town to celebrate the conclusion of a long, successful domestic season.

It was about the fans that week in Rome, too. Thousands queued overnight when the tickets for the final were released. Only three windows were open at the Stadio Olimpico and 8,000 people crushed towards the sales points, desperate to get hold of the precious tickets. It soon turned into a riot.

Police had to use helicopters and fire tear gas to calm the crowd and twelve people were injured as a result of the trouble. Cars were overturned in the melee as law and order broke down. While Merseyside was basking in success and relaxing in advance of the final, Rome was in a ferment.

Liverpool were guaranteed 16,000 tickets for the game but Roma allocated an extra 1,200. By contrast with the Italian capital, sales on Merseyside were slow. The scenes of tear gas and bloodshed were doing little to advertise the delights of the Eternal City.

24.

Riotous Behaviour

May 1984

Israel (a), friendly, Bloomfield Stadium, Tel Aviv

The team woke up with their hangovers the morning after the Norwich game with two weeks to go until their showdown with destiny. That day, Nils Liedholm, Roma's Swedish coach, took his squad into the mountains for an isolated training camp. He wanted his players in perfect shape for the biggest match in the club's history. Nothing would be left to chance.

Fagan was getting ready to take his men away, too. On the Friday before the FA Cup final, they flew to Israel. A local journalist turned football agent, Pini Zahavi, had arranged the trip. It was perfectly timed. The warm late-spring weather in Tel Aviv would be good for acclimatization for the conditions in Rome. Liverpool, however, did not take quite the rigorous approach to preparation that characterized their Italian rivals.

Zahavi had bumped into Peter Robinson at an airport in 1979 and recommended Avi Cohen, a Maccabi Tel Aviv defender, to the Liverpool secretary. The club's scouts liked what they saw and Cohen moved to Anfield for £200,000. The club paid the journalist an introduction fee and set him on the path to becoming the first 'super-agent'.

The Israeli maintained an amicable relationship with the Anfield hierarchy. He set up a friendly match against Israel in Tel Aviv but that was the least important aspect of the expedition. This jaunt was about relaxation rather than preparation. And the squad approached the idea with gusto. Instead of sitting at home with the pressure building it was a chance to get away for ten days.

'It was a long time to dwell on things and be at home,' Gary

Gillespie said. 'All you do is monotonous day-to-day training. It was suggested we go to Israel for the week and it was a real blow-out, a real blast. It was all about camaraderie.'

Nothing was off limits. 'It summed up just how much he treated us as adults,' Souness said. 'Joe imposed no curfews or restrictions. We were allowed to relax, enjoy the sun and have a few drinks.'

'A few' turned out to be the understatement of the season. John Wark, the new addition to the squad, had fitted in nicely on the pitch but he was even more at home at the bar. 'If there had been a League Championship for drinking in the seventies and eighties, Ipswich Town would have been one of the major contenders,' the Scot said. 'I found absolutely no difference when I was transferred to Liverpool.' The boozing ratcheted up a notch.

'It was brilliant,' Johnston said. 'We hit the bottle as soon as we got there. It was a wild few days. I'd like to say we were model professionals.' He laughs. 'It was about as professional a trip as there could ever be with a bunch of testosterone-filled men with big thirsts and the freedom to have fun.'

There was no attempt to hide the alcohol-fuelled boisterousness. 'We were drinking in the open, out in the square,' Kennedy said. 'Frankie Goes to Hollywood were big at the time and we were all singing "Relax". And relax we did. Joe said chill and we did. That was our style.'

The British press were used to covering these sort of adventures and thought nothing of it. There were incidents of drunkenness and brawling on almost every pre-season tour. These sort of antics rarely made the papers. The two Italian reporters shadowing Liverpool, on the other hand, were appalled at what they saw. 'The Italian press people couldn't believe it,' Kennedy said. They could hardly comprehend that this team had reached the final, let alone that they could win it in hostile territory.

'We'd had a hard season and we were relaxing,' Souness said. 'I'd try to get the Italian journalists in the bar and have a drink with them and keep them onside but they were shell-shocked.'

And that was before things in Israel turned antagonistic.

The players met the press on the beach in the morning, sustained by a bin filled with ice and cans of beer. After their PR duties were finished, the squad gathered for the usual bonding session.

'We'd meet in the bar about seven thirty and have dinner together and then have a drink in the square,' Souness said. 'It wasn't optional. It was a must. Eat together, drink together, laugh together, win together. We did it all the time.'

On this occasion, the older players went back to the hotel before it got too riotous. 'Kenny and Charlie left after a couple of beers,' Nicol said. 'They were roomies so they got off.' Without the elder statesmen, a new edge of wildness crept into proceedings. 'We were playing Buzz. It all got out of hand. Next minute we were all fighting.'

The game involves a circle of drinkers shouting out numbers until they reach one that has been assigned the word 'buzz'. If the number gets shouted out rather than 'buzz', the entire group has to drink an alcoholic forfeit. Done at speed, it quickly leads to an inability to distinguish between the right and wrong call. It turned haywire in the square.

There are different versions of what happened – hardly a surprise, given the volume of alcohol consumed – but David Hodgson was at the centre of events. Alan Kennedy remembers the reserve striker urinating under the table on his team-mates' legs. It quickly escalated into a brawl. 'Things got said and a fight started,' Hodgson said. 'Me and Rushie were quite close so it's us back to back against everybody else.'

There are various accounts of what sparked the melee. Dalglish thinks it was all a misunderstanding. 'Rushie stumbled and they thought someone had hit him,' he said. 'It was all a bit daft.'

John McGregor, the reserve centre half who had not had an opportunity to play yet, piled in and landed a punch flush on Kennedy's eye, leaving him with a shiner. Rush's nose was bloodied. Even Alan Hansen was caught up in the uproar. To outsiders it appeared that the team spirit that had driven Liverpool through sixty-six matches so far in the season had finally fractured.

Word of the brawl was spreading. Sydney Moss, a club director, was told there was trouble in the square and assumed it was fans. He went to assess the damage. He arrived on the scene and began shouting 'Lock the hooligans up!' until someone pointed out it was the players involved and not supporters.

'Somehow it calmed down and I went to the hotel with Rushie and Alan Kennedy, who fell on the ground and couldn't get up,' Hodgson said. 'The old Liverpool director Mr Moss was coming out of the hotel just at that moment. So I've got down to pick up Alan Kennedy and I couldn't get up either. And Mr Moss is stood above us frowning. He says, "Gentlemen, this is Liverpool Football Club." So I grabbed hold of his trousers and pulled myself up his body. And I put my arm around him and said, "Mossy, you old bugger, you might be a director but I think you're a great fella."'

It was now clear what was happening. Moss then took control.

'Sydney Moss was fantastic,' Nicol said. 'He'd heard there'd been trouble in the square and came down. He got everybody back to the hotel.'

Back safe from widespread public gaze, the players were packed into the hotel lift and told to go to their rooms.

By then, news of the fracas had reached the two senior team members. 'Hansen comes banging on the door, shouting: "You've got to get up! All hell's breaking loose,"' Souness said. 'Me and Kenny come out and the lift was stuck between floors with them all in it.'

The mood had switched from anger to togetherness in a matter of minutes. 'They're all singing the song from the television series *M*A*S*H*, which was popular at the time,' Souness said. 'You had to laugh.'

As the sound of the throaty choir echoed around the lift shaft, the 'Suicide is painless . . .' lyric must have appeared appropriate to the Italian journalists. It appeared this was a team with a death wish.

'We got them all into their bedrooms and settled everyone down,' Souness said. 'Until about fifteen minutes later when there's all kinds of commotion. They're all out in the corridors arguing again.'

In the harsh, hungover light of day the guilty parties gathered in a function room at the hotel and prepared to be read the riot act. 'There was a meeting next morning,' Nicol said. 'Big Al had stayed when Kenny and Charlie left. He was sitting there with the rest of us. Fagan looked at us all and shook his head. "Al, I thought you knew better," he said. You could hear the disappointment in his voice. You should have seen the look on Hansen's face.'

The centre half usually had the good sense to avoid these situations – or at least to avoid getting caught. The classy Hansen rarely suffered such discomfort, on or off the pitch. Those lower down the pecking order enjoyed the moment of Hansen's shame even as they prepared for a roasting themselves.

Smokin' Joe wasn't about to blow his top, though. Moss spoke to the miscreants first. 'There's Bob, Joe Fagan, Moran, Evo and Mr Moss, who stands up,' Hodgson recalls. 'He says, "I've been at this club for over twenty years and I've never witnessed anything like last night in my life."' The director paused before addressing the reserve striker. 'I thought I was in for it,' Hodgson said. Moss went on, 'I've had many accolades passed on to me, but never have I received one so touching than from David Hodgson.'

Then the Liverpool management shocked the players. 'They lifted the tablecloth and underneath it's piled high with beer,' Hodgson said. 'After that meeting, Bob Paisley turned to me and said, "You're a good Geordie, son. That's what you are."'

The psychology worked. 'No one fell out over it,' Nicol said. 'Shit happens. You all get together and get through it.'

It was always the way. Dalglish had been at Anfield long enough to see a pattern. 'Relaxation was done at the proper time,' he said. 'The staff always knew about it. They got it right.'

Almost to a man, the squad remember the trip with fondness. 'It was one hell of a bonding session,' Ronnie Whelan said. 'It was complete relaxation, a good laugh, a few drinks and some late nights.'

Rush flew out on international duty with Wales and the rest of the team beat Israel 4–1. The Welsh striker's verdict on the Tel Aviv trip was simple: 'It was a stroke of genius that would never be allowed to happen now.'

The game was insignificant and there was no semblance of professionalism even for the match. Robinson remembers drinking a bottle of beer less than half an hour before kick-off. It had a positive effect: the big striker scored.

'The whole run-up to the final was almost a drink-fest,' Johnston said. 'We needed to be let down after the season and then built back up for the game. It worked.'

The Italian journalists shook their heads and filed their reports. Beating a low-calibre international side was one thing but it was inconceivable that this boozy bunch of reprobates could match the professionalism and skill of Liedholm's side. Roma, holed up in their training camp in the Dolomites, were treating the build-up far more seriously. How could Liverpool beat them? Falcão and Cerezo, the Brazilians, had a global reputation. Bruno Conti and Francesco Graziani had been in Italy's World Cup-winning side just two summers earlier. Roberto Pruzzo had terrorized Dundee United and Agostino Di Bartolomei's Roman pride was as ferocious as Souness's will to win. Di Bartolomei was the hero of the Curva Sud and embodied many of the menacing attributes of the 'Gente del Terzo Mondo'. During his prime, in the dangerous days of the 1970s and 1980s when kidnapping was a real possibility for high-profile Italians, he was said to carry a gun everywhere in a small man-bag. The Roma captain's reputation was even more fearsome than Champagne Charlie's.

Getting drunk in Tel Aviv was no way to prepare for a confrontation like this, surely?

25.

Into the Cauldron

May 1984

Melwood and Rome

In between arriving back from Israel and leaving for Italy, Fagan and his Bootroom team concentrated on getting their squad back to match sharpness. After the party atmosphere of Tel Aviv, a more rigorous approach was called for. Attitudes had changed. The players were now ready for a different sort of battle and the challenge for the coaching staff was to keep them restrained. 'I remember being in earshot of a conversation between Joe and Ronnie Moran just a few days before we flew to Rome,' Mark Lawrenson said. 'I overheard him saying that training would have to be toned down. Everybody was so up for the game that the coaches were ordered to hold us back in case we peaked too soon.'

Two days before the final, just before departing for Rome, the players gathered at Melwood for light training. Almost as an afterthought, the team practised penalties. No European Cup final had been decided by a shoot-out. The previous week the Uefa Cup final between Tottenham Hotspur and Anderlecht had ended level after 1–1 draws in each leg. The game was determined by penalties. Spurs won 4–3. It was a warning.

In the Rotterdam tournament the previous summer, Liverpool had lost penalty shoot-outs against Hamburg and Feyenoord. They were only friendly matches and not taken seriously at the time, but they pointed to a lack of expertise from twelve yards. Having relied on Phil Neal for so long to take spot-kicks, there was a need to find another four penalty-takers. Rush, Souness and Dalglish could surely be relied on but the rest of the team would not inspire much confidence.

The session did not go as well as Fagan would have liked. 'We took penalties against a young goalkeeper and were so bad at taking them Joe Fagan abandoned the session,' Kennedy said.

They had been matched against a youth team, whose members had no problem slotting the spot-kicks against Grobbelaar. There are different accounts of how well the first XI did but everyone accepts they lost the shoot-out and even the most bullish memories only recall the first-teamers scoring two. 'I remember Ronnie Whelan saying to me, "The final better not come down to penalties,"' Kennedy said. And on that grim point, the team embarked for Italy.

In the time of the Caesars, Rome would celebrate a victory in war with a Triumph. The city would take on a holiday atmosphere and the successful general would lead his legions through the streets to acclaim from the populace, followed by prisoners, hostages and booty. The procession would end with a night of revelry that frequently turned into an orgy of drunken violence. The Italian capital was prepared for a modern-day version of this day of conquest and excess.

The warlike analogy is warranted. 'The Barbarians are Coming', screamed the headlines, readily demonizing the travelling supporters. The Eternal City was in its least welcoming mood.

Seven years before, in the glorious May of 1977, 26,000 or more Liverpool fans had come to Rome for the club's first European Cup final against Borussia Mönchengladbach. The day had become part of the folklore of Liverpool. It had been a joyous event. Rome was an amiable host and the red hordes were delightful visitors. There was no evidence of the hooliganism that often accompanied English teams on the Continent and Scousers outnumbered and out-partied their German rivals. The chequered red and white flags that were bought in their thousands in 1977 still appeared on the Kop, evoking glorious memories.

As a club and a city, Liverpool felt well disposed to Rome. The affection was mutual. Until their teams were due to face off in Europe's biggest game, that is.

It seemed that every tower block, every house, every window across the Italian capital was decorated with the maroon and yellow colours of Roma. Youths traversed the streets on scooters waving flags. Cars had been repainted in the team's colours and the European Cup was everywhere, spray-painted on walls, stencilled on to the bonnets of Fiats and embroidered into massive flags. There was an air of triumph by the Tiber. The game seemed almost an afterthought.

In public Liverpool were sanguine about playing a European Cup final in their opponents' stadium. Privately, they were unhappy. Aside from Roma having home advantage, there were security issues to consider. There had been few problems with Liverpool fans in Europe over the years but this match had the potential to be far more combustible. The rush for tickets at Anfield that usually characterized cup finals of any description was conspicuously absent. By the eve of the game, the club had sold just 10,000 of their 17,000 allocation. The unsold tickets were returned to Italy, where the demand was massive, but Liverpool asked for them not to be made available for fear they would compromise segregation.

The request would cost Liverpool £30,000 from their share of gate receipts but it was worth it. The scenes after the Dundee United semi-final showed how explosive events could be at the Stadio Olimpico. And that was after a Roma victory.

Fagan and the team flew out on Monday, forty-eight hours before the game. They were taken to a luxury hotel in the centre of the city, where an entire floor had been allocated to the club. Security guards ensured that there would be no repeat of the early-hours wake-up call before the League Cup final. Nils Liedholm's team had been sequestered in the mountains for the best part of ten days. Liverpool did not retreat into seclusion until close to the game. It was not isolation but insulation.

In the hotel, the players acted as normally as possible. 'How do you tell somebody how to relax when they have a massive game coming up?' Kennedy said. 'I roomed with Alan Hansen and we just chilled out and tried to get some sleep.'

'We had no sense of all the madness that was going on outside,' Steve Nicol said. 'It was a case of doing what we always did.'

Despite the security precautions, some of the players were kept awake by noises in the night. 'Me and Kenny roomed together,' Souness said. 'We could hear a radio or TV in the next room blaring out. We banged on the wall to get them to shut up but it carried on and we had to phone reception. After a few minutes it stopped.'

The next morning, the captain was keen to find out who had been so inconsiderate. 'It was Fagan's room,' Souness said. 'He'd fallen asleep and left his telly on.'

It was a good message to send out to the team. The manager was not losing any sleep over the challenges that lay ahead. He was not burning the midnight oil worrying about the Italian side. One of the basic tenets of the Bootroom was to avoid thinking too much about the opposition's strengths. Fagan detailed his thinking in his diary: 'If I go through all this [Roma's strengths], I will feel like we can't play. Too much can bog your own team down and make you forget to let them [Roma] worry about you.'

The Liverpool manager had seen the Italian side play just once, against Fiorentina, the weekend after the semi-final. Tom Saunders was given the job of taking a more forensic look at Roma. His verdict was worrying: 'They perform better on their own pitch. If Falcão and Di Bartolomei perform as they can do, the battle will be won in midfield.'

The other concern was whether the game would be turned by a third party. With suspicions over the refereeing of the Dundee United match still fresh – the Scottish Football Association approached Uefa and asked it to investigate, to no avail – attention focused on Erik Fredriksson, the Swedish official who would take charge at the Stadio Olimpico. The referee had been at a Uefa function along with delegations from both clubs and was foolish enough to give an opinion when asked who he thought would triumph. 'Roma have to be favourites,' Fredriksson said. The comment did not go down well inside the Liverpool camp. 'You know you've been written off when not even the referee thinks you can win,' Souness said.

The night before the match, Fagan took his team to the empty stadium to train on the pitch. It was another light session, designed to give them a feeling for the turf. The staff and players also faced the media. Fagan ran through his usual semi-detached routine, appearing slightly unprofessional and definitely underprepared. The manager said nothing that could be misinterpreted and used by Roma to ramp up the hatred. He was too wily to walk into the traps that had been sprung on Jim McLean. Instead, he praised Roma, giving the journalists enough to write their stories but nothing that could generate hysterical headlines. It was an old Liverpool tactic, perfected by Paisley, who liked to 'give them a bit of toffee'. Fagan certainly gave them something sweet to chew over.

'Roma are a very, very good team,' he said. 'So are we and I just hope that between us we can give Europe a game to remember with pride. I think we have a reputation for sportsmanship and skilful play and that we have earned respect wherever we go.'

Everything was designed to build the pressure on Roma and ease it on Liverpool. While Fagan was clowning about team talks, Liedholm was on the defensive. 'I would ask the fans to be patient,' he said. His team's build-up, he commented, had been 'measured and elaborate'.

Fagan was happy to play the buffoon. 'Our team talk will be longer than usual for this one,' the manager said, laughing all the time. 'About five minutes.'

Neal seemed to endorse the slapdash approach. 'We haven't even discussed Roma yet,' he said. 'We'll probably have a word or two about them before our afternoon nap but we are more concerned with our own performance.'

Contrast Neal's approach with Falcão's. The Brazilian had clearly spent a lot of time studying the opposition's methodology. 'Liverpool,' Falcão said, 'have two faces. They are a typically English team by temperament, character, commitment. Also for their technical qualities. But they are equally a European team, in some ways similar to Roma. They know more than the usual cross and attack down the middle. They know how to hold on to the ball and look for triangular moves. They have very good ball-playing midfielders, able to slow down and speed up the play.'

The Italians ate all this up. It was further evidence that Liverpool did not have a chance. Yet Fagan's haphazard preparation was not just cute psychology. There was an element of method about his madness.

'We were shown no video tapes of them,' Souness said. 'No one spoke to us about their set-piece routines and we were unaware of what formation Roma played. That's just the way it was at Liverpool back then and it didn't do us any harm.'

Kennedy has similar memories. 'There were no tactics,' he said. 'It was just a case of beat the opposition. We never talked about them too much. It was a case of going out and trying to score.'

The belief inside Fagan's team was so strong that they were unworried by any rivals. 'Look, winning is what we did, what we expected to do,' Nicol said. 'There was no expectation of defeat. None.'

'Our preparation couldn't have been any more different to Roma's,' Souness said. 'But we were totally relaxed and that gave us a belief that we wouldn't be beaten.'

In their plush hotel, Fagan and his players settled down for the night. Cloistered at last, they were ready for the challenge.

Outside on the streets, things were taking an ugly turn. The mounting hostility was manifesting itself. Liverpool fans wandering around the tourist sites began to be targeted by groups of ultras. A common method of attack was to approach from behind on a scooter and slash at the victim. The aim was to stab rival fans in the backside. The practice has its own name: in Roman slang, it is known as '*puncicate*'.

Apologists for buttock-stabbing claim it has cultural significance. Slashing an opponent's gluteus was an act of supreme skill in medieval duelling, they argue. It is, the theory goes, particularly humiliating for those on the receiving end. A more realistic explanation is that a wound to this fleshy area is unlikely to cause a serious or fatal injury and the knifeman has a better chance to escape unpunished.

For all the faux historical justification, there were few duels in Rome, just a series of unprovoked and cowardly attacks. The local police appeared disinclined to intervene.

There was madness in the air in the Italian capital. The team were tucked up safely in bed and the mounting violence would not directly affect them, but it hinted at the intensity of feeling that would greet the players in the Stadio Olimpico. They may have played regularly in front of the Kop in one of football's great arenas, but Liverpool's team would never have encountered an atmosphere this ferocious. Bucharest had been unpleasant enough. Rome would be in a different category altogether.

On the morning of the game, Fagan gathered his men for a last session of light training. They were directed to a pitch on the outskirts of town where they could go through their final preparations away from the hurly-burly of the city. When they arrived, it was clear that their Italian hosts had not been at their most accommodating. The playing area was rutted and dangerous. 'You wouldn't play Sunday league on it,' Nicol said. Mark Lawrenson went further: 'I wouldn't have taken my dog for a walk on it,' he said.

If the ploy was deliberate, it was counterproductive. 'The dirty tricks had started,' Lawrenson said. 'Some of the lads thought there and then, "Right, we're going to have these."'

Belief had always been present, but there was now a hardening of will in the team. Ever since Roma had reached the final, a phrase had been repeated around Anfield: they don't want us to win this. Now, in Rome, it was becoming a mantra.

The team returned to the hotel and went through their usual routines: food, sleep and then gather to leave for the stadium. Before they ate, Fagan provided a few official instructions, explaining to his players a Uefa directive that warned them not to run towards the crowd if they scored. 'Joe changed it to "when we score a goal" and not "if",' Souness said. 'Then he went on, "When we score our goals do what Uefa say for the first two but do what you like if we get any more." It was always about emphasizing that we were going to win. It gives you confidence.'

One player's mood was dark, though. A squad of seventeen had travelled to Rome. Aside from the eleven who would start the match, there was space for five substitutes. Someone would miss out. Phil Thompson, who had lifted the European Cup as captain, had a bad feeling about the situation. He had been marginalized since the Charity Shield in August, placed on the transfer list in April and his relationship with Fagan was irreparable. 'Dave Hodgson had had knee injuries and groin injuries,' Thompson said. 'He could hardly train.' The glimmer of hope evaporated quickly. 'When the team was picked and the subs were picked I was the seventeenth man so I wasn't going to be involved. I was extremely disappointed.' It was not the final indignity.

The others were sent off to their afternoon sleep with a word from Fagan. 'Just after we'd finished our meal, Joe stood up in the dining room and asked the waiters to leave the room because he wanted to speak to us in private,' Souness said. 'It was unusual for Joe to give a speech. We're all looking at each other, thinking "this is a first", but then he sort of started mumbling to himself about Roma and how they must be a good team because they'd reached the European Cup final. Everyone was glued to what he was saying and expecting this big impassioned speech but then he just turns round and says, "But they're not as good as us. Now the bus leaves at so and so time so make sure you get plenty of rest and don't be late." All he wanted to do was remind us how good we were. It put everyone at ease.'

Almost everyone. When the players came down to leave for the stadium, Thompson's humiliation was complete. 'As I stepped on to the stairs to get on the bus Joe Fagan put his arm around me and said, "You can't come on the bus." I was absolutely devastated,' the former captain said. 'I had a lump in my throat. I was on the verge of crying. I had to walk along the side of the bus and all the players were looking at me, wondering what's going on. "Where are you going?" I had to go on the other bus and sit next to Paul Walsh who had been signed four days before. My wife was asking what had happened. I couldn't even speak. I was so upset. I could never forgive Joe. He had to make a decision to leave me out. No problem, I have plenty of time for that, but that showed a lack of respect. I was the senior member of the squad. The players were furious.'

It was a crushing blow. But the doubts about Fagan's ruthlessness that had lingered all season were finally put to bed.

26.

Raised Voices

May 1984

Stadio Olimpico

By the time the players boarded the bus to the stadium, the terraces of the Curva Sud were already packed with ultras. The streets outside the Stadio Olimpico were largely deserted apart from police and a few disoriented Liverpool supporters arriving early. There was an eerie, portentous feeling about the hazy spring night. The visiting fans were used to crowded streets around stadiums, people hustling to get to their entrances with both sets of supporters mingling together. It felt like Roma's backers had not turned up. They had actually been waiting inside the ground for hours, working themselves into a frenzy.

The team coach still came under attack from stone-throwers, though not so violently as to worry the players. The empty streets were more unnerving.

Once inside the stadium, Fagan named his side. It was as expected. Grobbelaar in goal, the usual back four of Neal, Hansen, Lawrenson and Kennedy. Johnston was in the midfield, alongside Lee, Souness and Whelan. The strikers picked themselves, too: Dalglish and Rush. Gillespie, Nicol, Robinson and Hodgson were on the bench, along with reserve keeper Bob Bolder. It was one of those occasions where Fagan did not have to ponder his selection for too long.

'One or two players were carrying little knocks but the team was as predicted,' Kennedy said. 'By then we were very relaxed. You wouldn't say it was just like any other game but we knew what job we had to do. It was an experienced team. Bruce, Phil, Alan and Mark had played in big games before and we knew how to handle it. We had a good state of mind.'

After that, the staff began to prepare the kit and the dressing room and the players took a walk on to the pitch. It was then the enormity of the situation hit them. The huge Curva Sud let forth a grunt, a sickening thud of noise, and then erupted into a hurricane of catcalls. There was a boys' game on the pitch and the youngsters flinched as 60,000 voices howled with fury.

'I've got to be honest with you, it was the most intimidating sight I've ever seen in my life,' Hansen said. 'It frightened me how much those fans wanted Roma to win the match.'

This was Souness territory. Here, Champagne Charlie came into his own. 'Nothing scared Charlie,' Nicol said. 'He looked at them straight in the eye.'

Some men would have stuck to the middle of the pitch, taken a quick look around and then retired to the safety of the dressing room. Souness, on the other hand, was eager to walk into the teeth of the abuse. Lawrenson remembers the scene: 'We stood at the side watching for a few minutes, then Souey said, "Come on, let's walk right round and wind them up by showing them we're not scared." As we made our way round, their fans were slaughtering us and the noise was unbelievable.'

The atmosphere that had caused Dundee United to shrink had the opposite effect on Souness. 'He had huge charisma. He was made for moments like this,' Dalglish said. 'He radiated power and confidence.'

Johnston, a keen photographer, had taken his camera out on to the pitch and was snapping away. 'I took a photograph of Charlie strolling along towards them without a care in the world,' he said. 'He looked just like an Italian male model. Full of style and arrogance.'

Souness's rationale for facing down the Roma fans was simple. 'I wanted to test their anger,' he said.

The walk to the Curva Sud gave everyone a boost. 'We went out to see our supporters and our families and we've waved up at them and the quickest way back would have been just to have gone back into the dressing room,' Sammy Lee said. 'But Graeme said, "No, come on." He took every single one of us and made us walk round the running track in front of their supporters. It was a great psychological boost. They couldn't believe that we had the audacity to walk in front of them. We were actually walking alongside them, looking at them, no problem, and it was an eerie feeling.'

Events were about to take an even stranger turn. As they drifted back down the tunnel, David Hodgson began to sing. The striker was one of the trendier members of the squad. 'When I think of Davie, I think leather pants,' Nicol said. The back-up striker now began to sing a pop song introduced to the team by Craig Johnston.

'I was always in charge of the music on the bus,' Johnston said. 'I had an eclectic mix of music. I played Aussie bands and local Liverpool groups like the Icicle Works and Echo and The Bunnymen. The boys loved them. Having been in Middlesbrough, I knew about Chris Rea. Not many did. David Hodgson was from Middlesbrough and he liked Chris, too. "I Don't Know What It Is But I Love It" got hammered on the team bus in Israel. It had become one of the team's anthems.

'One of us would sing a verse and the rest would come in at the chorus, clapping and chanting, evoking all those images of unity and victory. So as we're going back down the tunnel Davie breaks into a solo rendition of the opening verse. One or two joined in and by the time we drew abreast of the Roma dressing room every one of us is singing "I Don't Know What It Is But I Love It".'

Now, in the corridors of the Stadio Olimpico, the team belted out a chorus of Rea's song. The sound of the Liverpool players bouncing down the tunnel singing had a profound effect.

Nils Liedholm's preparation was stopped short. Instead of listening to their coach, the Roma players were fixated on the chanting opponents outside their door. 'There he was, trying to give his team talk, while we were outside singing as if we didn't have a care,' Lawrenson said. 'Apparently, when his players heard us the colour drained from their faces. We had psyched them out without knowing it.'

Johnston's record collection was brimming with cutting-edge albums by bands whose credibility was sky-high in the trendy world of music. But the players latched on to a middle-of-the-road track by a then obscure and husky-voiced half-Italian singer-songwriter.

'The Chris Rea thing started in Israel. It was the song for that trip,' Nicol said. The drunken, wild week in Tel Aviv was still paying dividends. While the Roma players sat taut with anxiety waiting for the biggest game of their lives, their opponents appeared ludicrously relaxed and united in purpose.

In the Italian press and the Roma dressing room, the supposedly lax preparation of Fagan's side had been misinterpreted. 'This was the super-relaxed Liverpool they'd heard about,' Johnston said. Now, perhaps for the first time, the Italian side realized the full extent of the challenge facing them.

If the tension was growing among Liedholm's players, Fagan had to bring his side's minds back to the game. 'Alan Hansen was a great storyteller,' Souness said. 'I can't even remember what it was about. We'd heard them all before but he'd give a different twist every time. With about half an hour to go, Joe had to interrupt us and say, "Any danger of getting changed? We've got a game tonight, you know." We were still in our suits and ties.'

Not everyone was quite as nerveless as Souness. 'Ronnie Moran was scurrying around busying himself and trying to calm people but was mislaying things and getting in the way, making things worse,' Kennedy said. 'You get to the point you want to get it over with.'

Kennedy was one of the senior members of the side. Others, less experienced, were feeling the pressure even more acutely. 'It was easily the biggest game of our lives for a few of us,' Johnston said. 'There were a lot of genuine nerves there.'

Now, Fagan drew on all his experience and gave his short team talk on Roma's strengths and weaknesses. The strengths were not dwelt on.

The instructions were simple: (1) Don't let Falcão and Bruno Conti dictate the tempo; (2) Shoot on sight; (3) Keep hold of the ball.

When the bell rang to summon the teams, Smokin' Joe left his men with a last thought: Roma deserve our respect, but Liverpool are going to win here. 'From that moment we grew in stature and it just built up from there,' Grobbelaar said. 'We were so pumped up it was untrue.' Now Liverpool filed into the tunnel, ready to do battle.

In the concrete underbelly of the Stadio Olimpico, Liverpool waited for Roma. And waited. And waited. 'The cheeky Italian bastards,' Grobbelaar said. 'They were trying to pull another fast one by keeping us waiting but it didn't work.'

In the gloom, the Liverpool players made their own entertainment. 'It was a long, dark tunnel and we're waiting there,' Johnston said. 'Everyone knows we've been on the piss, everybody knows about the fights. Everyone had written us off. We were waiting there for Roma and we could hear them going through their exercises. You could hear the click of studs on the concrete floor and it had a sort of rhythm as they warmed up together. We picked up on the beat and started singing again.'

Chris Rea's words echoed off the concrete walls: the most celebrated sing-song in football history was under way. 'There was no plan to sing it in the tunnel,' Nicol said. 'We were just standing there and Sammy started singing. Then we all joined in. We thought it was great.'

The longer they waited, the louder the singing got. 'One by one all the lads joined in,' Grobbelaar said. 'It wasn't long before the entire team were belting it out once more at the top of their voices. Every time we got to the chorus I would start banging on the door of the Roma dressing room as if I was playing the drums.'

When the Italian side eventually came out, things didn't get any calmer. 'Souey looked each and every one of them in the eye and continued to sing in their faces,' Grobbelaar said. 'As they went past one by one the volume got higher and higher until it was so loud we couldn't even hear the noise of the crowd outside.'

'We were all marching on the spot,' Johnston said. 'Nobody had ever done that before or has done it since.'

'It was a way of breaking our nerves,' Kennedy said. 'Putting the wind up them. The Roma players were gobsmacked. They must have thought we were lunatics. All these cool, international foot-ballers. Now they all just looked scared shitless.'

'The boys were singing their heads off,' Dalglish agreed. 'Roma must have thought we were insane.'

Souness eyed his opponents closely. 'You should have seen the fear on their faces. We were all singing and acting like village idiots. They were frozen with fear.'

Liverpool were ahead in the psychological war. Now they just had a game to win.

27

The Game of Their Lives

30 May 1984

Roma, European Cup final, Stadio Olimpico

The stadium exploded as the teams walked out together, Liverpool in their grey tracksuit tops, Roma in all white. Flares, smoke bombs and fireworks obscured the Curva Sud while the travelling fans at the other end waved their red and white chequered flags and tried to make their voices heard above the wall of Italian noise. Never was Fagan's exhortation to silence the crowd more appropriate. And never would it be more difficult.

Roma kicked off and tried an extravagant tactic. Falcão tried to emulate Pelé, his countryman, by scoring straight from the kick-off. It was a simple take for Grobbelaar and played into Liverpool's hands: give the goalkeeper an early touch and get the ball and keep it.

No one was trying anything special. Get possession, make the opposition work, hold the ball. If nothing was on looking forward, go backwards. 'We were never worried about entertaining,' Nicol said. 'We were there to win.'

Souness was in complete control of the tempo, reducing the game to a walking pace. 'Souness did his job so professionally,' Kennedy said. 'We never gave much away.'

Falcão and Di Bartolomei were struggling to get close to the Liverpool captain, whose imperious gait matched that of any Roman emperor. Right from the start, the men in red were in control. Grobbelaar had to be sharp off his line to stop Francesco Graziani getting on the end of a Bruno Conti pass, and once a ball fizzed across the Liverpool box but otherwise there were no alarms.

Fagan had told the team to put Franco Tancredi under pressure at every opportunity. Tom Saunders's scouting reports had suggested the goalkeeper was weak on crosses and tended to push shots back out into the danger area rather than wide and away from goal. After thirteen minutes, Johnston had the chance to test the theory.

Taking possession wide on the right some eighteen yards from goal, the Australian curled in a cross that tempted the goalkeeper off his line and beyond the far post. Ronnie Whelan challenged for the ball and the Italian let it squirm free of his gloves. It was the sort of handling error that Grobbelaar was famous for but, like their Liverpool counterparts, the Roma defenders were prepared. They had swarmed around Tancredi and Sebastiano Nela pounced on the loose ball to clear. Nela panicked under pressure. His clearance hit Tancredi on the head and rebounded back into the six-yard box. Phil Neal was lurking and able to prod the ball into the Roma net. 'I can still hear Joe saying, "If you're going to join the attack, stay until it breaks down,"' Neal said. 'Well, I joined the attack and all of a sudden it continued. A ricochet falls in the six-yard box and who's in there? Me. I was as surprised as anyone to toe poke it in.'

Neal had scored a penalty at the other end of this stadium in 1977 against Borussia Mönchengladbach and now he had scored two of Liverpool's six goals in four European Cup finals. Alan Kennedy had scored another in Paris in 1981 against Bayern Munich. Anfield's full backs, whatever their critics said, clearly enjoyed the big Continental occasions.

The Stadio Olimpico was shocked into silence apart from the disembodied roar that came from the celebrating Curva Nord, where the Liverpool fans stood. Now the pressure was really on and the home side were beginning to feel it.

The Roma players flocked around Erik Fredriksson. Surely, they claimed, Whelan had fouled Tancredi when the Liverpool midfielder jumped to challenge the goalkeeper. The Swedish official had raised eyebrows when he suggested the Italian side were the favourites earlier in the week, and was a fellow countryman of the Roma coach. The lingering suspicions about the semi-final and the manner of Dundee United's defeat coloured opinions, too. Yet

Fredriksson stood firm; Liverpool were a goal up. The away victories against Athletic Bilbao and Dinamo Bucharest made it obvious they would take some shifting from the lead.

For the rest of the half, things were going to plan for Liverpool. Souness had the ball in the net almost immediately after Neal's goal but the offside flag had been raised. Then, just as the interval loomed, an increasingly troubled Roma got a lifeline.

Conti, free on the left, attempted to cross but it was blocked by Lawrenson. The ball fell favourably for the Italian and he flicked it in again. Roberto Pruzzo, who had caused Dundee United so much trouble, nipped across the front of Hansen and looped a header over Grobbelaar. Pruzzo ran towards the bench in joy and a surge of belief jolted through 60,000 Romans. Neal, who had scored at the other end, blamed himself. 'This silly bugger let him get the cross in,' he said.

'We'd been on top and then Pruzzo scored,' Kennedy said. 'You think: "Fucking hell." But it was a good goal. The next bit was simple: just don't let them get another.'

Half-time.

'Some dressing rooms would have gone into meltdown but not this one,' Johnston said. 'There was no finger-pointing. We'd been the better side. We just needed to go out and do it again.'

Fagan rammed home this message, supplemented by his chief lieutenant. 'Souness was made for times like this,' Nicol said. 'Losing was not an option. He made that point to every player, every substitute. We were going out there to get on top and win.'

There was no singing now. It was just determination. 'We felt we had their measure,' Dalglish said. 'It was ours to lose.'

Back on the pitch, the plan was executed to perfection. 'Souness was like the conductor of the orchestra,' Johnston said. 'Few men combine his toughness and elegance.' Where the Scot led, the rest followed.

'We closed down space on their leading players such as Falcão and Cerezo with not just one of our players but whoever was nearest,' Fagan said. Yet Liverpool knew this was the time the Italian side would throw everything at them. It was a period when they needed to hang on and ride out the storm.

'I had a terrible phase of play after about sixty minutes,' Kennedy said. 'I was having a really bad time. Conti was switching wings and giving me problems. I was in real trouble. Ronnie Whelan was looking at me as if to say, "Fucking hell, what are you doing? Help me out, I'm only a young lad." I had a word with him. I said, "Listen, Ronnie, I'm having a nightmare, but bear with me and I'll try to play my way out of it." So Ronnie sat in with me for a while and he helped me get over the worst of it.'

All through the season opposition teams had homed in on the Liverpool full backs, especially Kennedy. His captain was everywhere, though, stopping danger, cajoling his team-mates and denying the Roma midfield the space to create. Souness was dominant, even when the opposition were on top.

'When the Roman candle was burning at its brightest early in the second half,' Stuart Jones wrote in *The Times*, '[Souness] took the ball away from the Italians and encouraged [Liverpool] to keep it to themselves until the heat had died away.'

Then, the storm passed. Jones's colleague David Miller described the moment: 'Fifteen minutes into the second half, with Roma on a crescendo and the left back, Nela, steaming into attack past Neal, Liverpool produced a typical, anaesthetizing phase of more than twenty consecutive passes that ended with Rush caught offside. Roma were like a Ferrari confronted by endless traffic policemen.'

Cerezo summed up Roma's frustration: 'The English [sic] showed themselves to be a great team, an almost unbeatable team,' the Brazilian said after the game. 'When they passed the ball to each other, which is undoubtedly their speciality, I seemed to go mad. There was a moment when I felt like a bull in the arena. I couldn't do anything to block their style of play, their passing.'

The long hours playing one-touch games under Ronnie Moran's watchful eye were paying off in spades. The 'big-headed bastards' were holding the ball and strangling Roma's self-belief and momentum. 'They call it tiki-taka now with Barcelona,' Johnston said. 'We were doing it then. We were keeping the ball, passing to feet, probing for weaknesses.'

And now the Italians decided to park up. Pruzzo, their cutting edge, left the field after sixty-four minutes with a stomach upset and the Liverpool defence rested easier. Conviction was draining from Roma.

'They didn't challenge us,' Souness said. 'I remember the ball going out behind the Roma goal and hearing Tancredi bollock the ballboy for giving it back too fast. They were playing for penalties.'

Fear now crept into the game. No one wanted to make the error that lost his team the European Cup. Nicol came on for the exhausted Johnston. The Australian had run himself into the ground in the warm night.

At the end of normal time, Fagan took stock. 'Joe said penalties are a cruel way to decide any game and we needed to go out and make sure we didn't need them,' Kennedy said. 'But by this stage both teams were tired and frightened of making a mistake.'

'I wasn't really thinking of penalties,' Nicol said. 'There was still half an hour to go.'

In the heat – physical and psychological – of the Roman night, neither side was prepared to play risky, expansive football. 'At this stage you end up playing pretty much percentage football,' Kennedy said. 'Get it up the touchline, away from our goal.'

Then Fagan made a decision that passed off without comment in the tension of the moment but would soon have significant repercussions. Four minutes into extra time, he replaced Dalglish with Michael Robinson. 'Joe took me off because I probably wasn't as fit as I could have been after the broken cheekbone,' Dalglish said.

The big striker had little effect. Dread filled the air and a hush descended on nearly 70,000 people. The final whistle went and ended what most considered a tense and somewhat drab final but Liverpool were happy enough. 'People might not have thought it was a very exciting game but we thought we'd done well,' Kennedy said. 'We'd been good.'

But it was not quite good enough to win a fourth European Cup. Now Liverpool were about to step into the unknown and see a European Cup final decided by a penalty shoot-out for the first time.

28.

On the Spot

30 May 1984

Roma, European Cup final, Stadio Olimpico – penalty shoot-out

This was unprecedented. There was no huge roar of celebration from the crowd at the final whistle, more a worried murmur. Fagan gathered the Liverpool players and told them of his pride in them. To achieve a draw in such circumstances against one of Europe's best teams was a massive achievement. They had done all he had asked of them. Now they needed to win a contest that was little more than a coin-toss.

'The game shouldn't have been played in Rome anyway,' Dalglish said. 'It was a flaw in the competition. But we'd won anyway. In every other round of the competition, away goals count double. We were at their ground. We'd scored an away goal. Why hadn't we won? It shouldn't have needed penalties anyway.'

At Anfield, they rarely practised set pieces. The Bootroom boys trusted the talent of the players they had brought together. Who would tell the likes of Dalglish, Souness and Rush not to rely on their game intelligence and intuition? Could anyone replicate the pressure of a decisive shoot-out?

The team gathered around Fagan and began the process of picking the five penalty-takers. Phil Neal, the regular man for spot-kicks, was a definite. Souness, who would meet any challenge head on, was also an obvious choice despite missing a penalty under pressure against Leicester at Anfield in late December.

If you needed to score, from any distance, you would turn to Rush. And then Fagan looked at his talisman, Dalglish. 'I can't,' the Scot said. Fagan was outraged: of all the people, he thought he could rely on Dalglish. Why couldn't he take one?

'I got substituted, boss.'

Fagan was aghast. He blurted out, 'Who the fuck did that?'

That, at least, is the legend of Rome. Dalglish waves off the suggestion of chaos. 'Joe never asked me to take a penalty,' he said. 'Anyway, I might have missed. I might not have been one of the five.'

Souness backs him up. 'We decided who was going to take the penalties on Monday,' he said.

Others recall it differently. It is clear there was plenty of confusion in the Liverpool camp. No one had imagined that the game would reach this conclusion.

Steve Nicol volunteered to take one of the other penalties. He was young and fearless and had been on target during the practice at Melwood. 'I was confident,' Nicol said. 'Someone had to do it. I had no problem stepping up.'

There were plenty who did not want to put themselves in the line of fire. 'I was petrified about the prospect of having to take one,' Hansen said. 'If there'd been two hundred players in the team I'd still have been the last one to offer my services.'

Those who did not fancy their chances from the spot began to drift away from Fagan. 'There was lots of confusion,' Kennedy said. 'It was the first time a European Cup final had been decided this way. Everyone moved towards the centre circle and they left me and Bruce. I wasn't asked whether I wanted to take a penalty. Joe said, "Are you OK?" I said yes and next minute he was putting my name forward. I thought, "Bloody hell, I didn't mean that!"'

Johnston was feeling impotent. The Australian would have been the first to volunteer but, like Dalglish, had been substituted. 'I would have taken one, definitely,' he said. 'It was horrible standing there watching, unable to have any impact.'

The penalties were taken into the Curva Sud goal. There were no friendly faces behind the net. In fact there was an even bigger distraction than the crowd. Scores of photographers scrambled for position behind the goal, setting off their flashes as the penalty-takers addressed the ball. Ball boys in Roma tracksuits hung around making every effort to put the Liverpool players off. Tancredi took his place in the goal and, incredibly, Nicol strode up to the spot.

Neal was expecting to start the shoot-out after being told by Fagan to take the first penalty. Souness sent out the same message: 'I said, "Nealy, you go first,"' the captain said. 'Then Steve said he wanted to go first.'

The youngster's change of plan surprised Neal. 'Stevie Nicol jumped ahead,' the veteran full back said. 'He jumped the gun and Souness said, "Let him go. He's nervous, it's his first final. Let him go."'

The young Scot looked calm enough approaching the goal, rubbing the ball on his shirt. As he stood waiting for the referee to give the signal for the kick to go ahead, the noise levels went up a notch. Klaxons howled and the Curva Sud roared. Nicol took a five-step run and spooned the ball over the bar in the centre of the goal. The Stadio Olimpico erupted. Advantage Roma.

Nicol walked slowly back to the centre circle pulling at the skin on his throat close to his Adam's apple. 'I tried to look nonchalant,' he said. 'I thought maybe then the rest of the boys would forget about it.'

'Of course, we all told him they're bound to miss one,' Kennedy said. 'But we're really thinking that these Italians are pretty good at penalties, they don't normally miss them.'

The focus was suddenly on Grobbelaar. 'Just before the shoot-out began, I remember Smokin' Joe putting his arm around me,' the goalkeeper said. '"No one will blame you if you can't stop a ball from twelve yards. You've done your job, we can't blame you," he said. Then, as I walked away, he shouted: "But try and put them off!"'

Di Bartolomei faced Grobbelaar. The Roma captain stood close to the ball. He did not take a run-up. The goalkeeper's legs shook slightly as he got into position, as if he were nervous. Di Bartolomei did not notice. Instead, he took one stride and slammed the ball down the middle of the goal. Grobbelaar went to the right and watched the ball zoom into the net above his left hand. Roma were one step nearer winning the European Cup.

'So I am taking our second,' Neal said. 'If this one doesn't go in, we are two down. I am conscious of that.' The full back had scored a penalty at the other end of the stadium in 1977. His right-footed shot gave Tancredi no chance.

There was something philosophical about the smile on Grobbelaar's face as he walked back to the goal. He shook his head and was talking to the photographers. He stepped behind the goal-line and took a strand of net in his mouth. However the game turned out, the photographers got a result. It would make a great picture.

With Bruno Conti waiting, the goalkeeper stepped off his line, hands on hips, and eyeballed the Italian. Conti made a stuttering run and slammed the ball over the bar, a yard to the left of where Nicol's shot had sailed. Grobbelaar rolled out of his dive and pumped the air with his fist. The shoot-out was level again.

Souness walked up. Socks rolled down, shirt hanging over the shortest of shorts, he exuded confidence. He looked every inch a Champagne Charlie. He was the coolest man in the stadium. 'There was no pressure,' he said. 'I felt no pressure. It had to be done.

'When I put the ball down on the spot I looked up and smiled at Tancredi. I knew I was going to score. The funny thing is I normally put my penalties the other way, low to the goalkeeper's right. This one was high and to the left. I don't know what came over me.'

The shot was crisp, high and unstoppable. The advantage had switched to Liverpool.

In the centre circle, Nicol was relieved. Yet it was just what he expected. 'Someone had to step up and get me out of the shit,' he said. 'That's what they did. That's what *we* did. We stood up for each other and got each other out of the shit.'

Ubaldo Righetti could level it for Roma. He faced a curiously subdued Grobbelaar. There were no smiles, mutterings or net munching. The Italian rubbed the ball repeatedly on the penalty spot, stepped back and executed a shot as fine as Souness's. The goalkeeper went the wrong way. Now it was 2–2 and the pressure mounting.

Rush, with forty-seven goals to his name for the season, put the ball on the spot rather fussily. 'I was nervous,' the striker said. 'That walk up to the spot, with sixty thousand Italians whistling and booing, was very nerve-racking.'

Nevertheless, he sent his shot to Tancredi's left. It was not the best contact he had made that season. There was a touch of a bobble as the ball rolled into the net. Yet his placement was perfect, right in the corner. The goalkeeper went the wrong way and the lead swung back to Liverpool.

He dropped to his knees and patted his heart, misjudging its location as somewhere south of his ribcage. 'I just had an amazing sense of relief,' Rush said. 'Massive relief.'

As he walked back, he passed Francesco Graziani, who was next for Roma. Graziani had won sixty-four caps for Italy and played in the World Cup final in 1982. He thought he had seen everything. He was in for a shock.

Grobbelaar jogged to the line, loose-limbed as a marionette. As the Roma striker placed the ball, it looked like someone had cut the puppet-master's strings. The goalkeeper wobbled and shimmied. It was a fluid, rubbery movement. Nothing of the kind had been seen in a European Cup final.

Fifty yards away, Johnston was astounded. 'I thought, "What's he doing? He's lost the plot!"'

Graziani crossed himself twice but God was not going to help him. He slammed the ball over the bar. Grobbelaar ran to his right, coordination suddenly restored, clapping his hands twice in delight, and the Stadio Olimpico gave up a horrified moan.

'The way he handled the penalties tells you everything you need to know about Bruce,' Dalglish said. 'Brilliant. Extravagant. And everyone forgets. He didn't even save one!'

'When it came to Graziani, I'll never forget him putting his arm around the referee before taking it,' Grobbelaar said. 'I thought, "You can't do that, it's ungentlemanly conduct." I just started to give it spaghetti legs. I went to the right and was actually touching the floor as I looked up and saw it hit the top of the crossbar. I knew what it meant and just started running around and jumping up and down like a lunatic.'

Grobbelaar had just marked himself down in football history. For Johnston, it was awe-inspiring. 'Imagine it hadn't worked?' he asked. 'If Graziani had scored, how stupid would Bruce have looked? Would he have been the biggest clown ever to play? He was always like that: willing to take a risk for the benefit of the team.'

Ronnie Moran could not believe what he was seeing. He was glad he had no idea that the goalkeeper would act in this manner. 'If Bruce had told us beforehand that he was going to start larking about during a penalty shoot-out at the European Cup final, he would have been hit in the head,' the coach said.

The knock-kneed display was the manic encore to the singing of more than two hours earlier. Now, if Liverpool scored their fifth penalty, the cup would be theirs. 'In the centre circle, we're saying, "Score this and we win!"' Dalglish said. 'Then: "Oh Christ, it's Alan Kennedy."'

Even the coaches – for the first time – were questioning Fagan's judgement. Roy Evans groaned, 'Why Barney?'

It was a long walk to the penalty area for the left back. 'I can't remember any sensations,' Kennedy said. 'It was all a bit blank, overwhelming. I passed Bruce, who had a little bit of a grin on his face. He said, "Oh no, I didn't realize it would be fucking you to take this!" I said, "Thanks a lot, Brucie."'

Despite already having won the title and the League Cup, this was the big prize. Lose, and there would be a sour tinge of disappointment hanging over the season and the summer. Win and it would be an unparalleled achievement in English football history. And it all came down to one shot from Barney Rubble. He had won one European Cup in Paris three years earlier with a fine solo run and shot. This was a very different situation. How did he feel?

'Shitting myself,' Kennedy said. 'I was shitting myself. There was loads of whistling and booing and camera flashes.'

In the Curva Nord, the Liverpool supporters covered their eyes or prayed. In the centre circle, the team milled around, unable to do anything to help. It felt like the Stadio Olimpico had taken a deep breath and was holding it.

'I turned quickly to get my stride right,' Kennedy said. 'I was worried if I went too slowly my legs might not even get me to the ball. It was one of the most pressurized moments of my life. I didn't know which direction I was going to put it.

'At the last second I decided to open my body up and side-foot it with a bit of pace to my left, his right.'

Contact made, the ball flew from Barney's boot. Tancredi committed himself and went the wrong way. 'Everything seemed to happen very slowly now,' Kennedy said. 'But only one thing mattered to me: he went the wrong way! He went the wrong way! It was in!'

There was a dead, damp groaning hubbub across the Stadio Olimpico. Kennedy ran towards the corner of the area, pumping his arms and performing a suitably uncoordinated jig. 'I didn't know what I was doing,' the unlikely hero said. 'I'll never celebrate like that again. No one will!'

Johnston was first to the full back and hugged him before most of the team piled on top. Others peeled off and ran to Fagan on the sideline. Despite Roma's home advantage, Liverpool had snatched their fourth European Cup from under their opponents' noses.

On Curva Sud, the ultras piled their flags and scarves on the concrete and set them alight. Small fires smouldered around the emptying stadium while the Liverpool players congratulated each other, hugging and grinning. Souness went straight to Fagan. The man who had rallied the team behind the new manager the previous summer was so moved by Fagan's unprecedented achievement that he momentarily dropped his tough-guy veneer. In the smoke and joy of Rome, Champagne Charlie shed a tear.

'I cried,' Souness said. 'I get a lump in my throat thinking about it now. Joe had tears in his eyes and I was blubbing. I said something like, "We did it for you, boss." We did, too. No one believed we could win it and everyone thought Roma would beat us. But winning was no surprise to Joe and Ronnie. They knew the bunch of players they had. They knew we were good enough to have a chance against any team, anywhere. It was one of the great performances and results.'

The manager sought out the penalty hero. Alan Kennedy had now scored the decisive goal in two European Cup finals. But, as ever, the full back got the Barney Rubble treatment. 'Joe came up and said, "Did you mean it?"' Kennedy said. 'Then he winked at me.'

Souness went up the steps to the VIP box to accept the trophy from Sandro Pertini, the Italian president. If it was a painful moment for the politician, the Liverpool captain did not care. He hoisted the European Cup high into the Roman night and a Scouse roar went up from the Curva Nord, the only section of the ground that remained packed. Fagan and the men of the Bootroom stood down on the pitch and watched their boys receive their medals. The doubts of the pre-season, the defeats and the criticism, the injuries and the rows had all been worth it. It was a high-water mark for English football. Unlike Paisley, who had ended his first season without a trophy, Fagan had finished up with three.

The team took the cup to the Curva Nord – there was no need for a lap of honour in the almost empty stadium – and sang along with the Liverpool supporters. Smokin' Joe was surrounded by his team and the joy was evident. 'Look at the pictures of us after the match, the ones with Joe in the middle,' Neal said. 'You can see the sparkle in everyone's eyes. You can see it's a team.'

Nils Liedholm and his Roma side disappeared. After the semi-final they had humiliated and attacked Dundee United. Now they slunk away having confounded the hopes and expectations of the Eternal City. 'We never saw them after the game,' Dalglish said. 'They didn't hang around to watch us celebrate.'

Di Bartolomei took the defeat particularly badly. The losing captain never played for Roma again after the final. He moved to Milan and his career petered out. He was never again to experience the success or adulation he had earned in the Stadio Olimpico.

He suffered from financial and family problems and depression. On the tenth anniversary of this crushing defeat, he shot himself through the heart.

There is nothing to prove that his suicide, at the age of thirty-nine, had anything to do with that penalty shoot-out in front of the Curva Sud, but it seems unlikely that the date was coincidental.

'He never looked me in the eye,' Souness said. 'Not before kick-off, nor when we tossed for penalties. Not once.' The Liverpool captain, for whom eye contact was a significant part of establishing presence on the pitch, was bemused by his Roma counterpart's behaviour. 'It was shocking what happened to him.'

Had Roma won, it is likely that Fagan's team would have got the same treatment as Dundee United. But there was no gloating from the winning side. Liverpool's triumphalism came before the game. They would sing again in their own dressing room but it would not be the same. There would be no banging on Roma's door now. 'The club had an attitude from top to bottom,' Dalglish said. 'We hated losing but we were magnanimous losers. We were humble winners, too.'

Rome was not a good loser. The city was angry. As the Liverpool supporters filed out of the Curva Nord, Roma fans waited on the elevated road above the stadium and hurled down missiles at the cowering Scousers. Metal bins were set alight and rolled down the slope and huge mobs of furious ultras attacked any rival fans they could find. Walking back towards the centre of town became a dangerous proposition and the Ponte Duca d'Aosta turned into a stabbing zone.

A blinding explosion of rage took hold of the city and the police stood by and watched the frenzy play itself out in the dark, lobbing the odd canister of tear gas into the Liverpool supporters to add to the terror and confusion. *Puncicate* had been a mere taster of the violence to come. 'Hundreds of young thugs chased Liverpool supporters through the streets beating, stabbing and kicking,' Brian Glanville wrote. 'One saw why Roma's wilder fans are among the most feared in Italy.'

In the midst of the savagery, a large group of Lazio fans – Roma's city rivals – turned out to gloat and took some of the pressure off Liverpool supporters. The Italians fought among themselves throughout a fractious night. The casualty figures were sketchy but more than forty people were reported stabbed. Anecdotal evidence and eyewitnesses suggest that the numbers could easily be double that. Many Liverpool fans characterized knife cuts as deep scratches rather than slashes and headed back to their transport in their eagerness to get out of Rome.

There was one death: a Roma fan who fell from a moving vehicle after the match. A Liverpool supporter, George Sharp, was left in a critical condition when he was stabbed in the liver and lung. He had been at the match with his sixteen-year-old son and fell victim to the ultras when he stopped to help a youth in a red shirt who was being beaten up by a mob. The young man he saved was an Italian, mistaken by the ultras for a Liverpool fan for picking the wrong colour top. When Ian Sharp attempted to get a policeman to help his stricken father, the carabiniere broke the teenager's nose with his truncheon.

The incidents went largely unreported in the British press. At a time when even minor occurrences of hooliganism would be splashed across the front pages of the tabloids as 'the English disease' there was a disturbing lack of reaction from most of the domestic media. The British Embassy issued a statement: 'Liverpool supporters behaved as everyone expected them to and maintained their good reputation. It appears they were subject to unprovoked attacks by a small minority of Roma fans.' The only thing most Liverpool fans who were there that night would take issue with is the use of the phrase 'small minority'.

Uefa said it would take steps to ensure that no European Cup finalist would have a 'home' fixture again. European football's governing body also said it would reassess whether penalties were a reasonable way of ending such an important match. A replay, Uefa said, would be fairer. Both notions were forgotten as soon as the tear gas of Rome cleared. Eventually, the ruling body decided both clubs shared the blame for the disturbances and fined each £1,270.

A year later, Liverpool reached another European Cup final, against Juventus in Brussels. Uefa's incompetence set up a dangerous situation. The game took place at a decrepit Heysel Stadium, where it was possible to kick holes in the outer wall to enter the ground. They made part of the Liverpool end a 'neutral' section and the tickets were swept up by the Belgian capital's large Italian community. The atmosphere was volatile and too many Liverpool supporters had hair-trigger tempers after the events in Rome. Before the match there was an exchange of missiles and the police were unable to prevent groups of Liverpool fans from swarming over the fences into the neutral section. A charge took place, the predominantly Italian crowd backed away and a wall collapsed. When the chaos subsided, thirty-nine people were dead.

The finger was rightly pointed at Liverpool supporters: fourteen fans were convicted of involuntary manslaughter and sentenced to three-year jail terms. Yet it was more complex than simple hooliganism. 'Heysel had its roots in Rome,' Kenny Dalglish said. 'Without the violence in Rome, Heysel would have been different.'

Back in the Stadio Olimpico the players were oblivious to what was happening in the streets outside. They could feel the anger while they waited for the drug-testers to complete their work but it was expressed in sullenness. 'Me and Sammy Lee had to stay behind for the urine test,' Johnston said. 'He couldn't pee. They were hostile. Not very nice.'

Things got better quickly. The team were taken on a coach up to a villa on one of the Italian capital's hills to begin a night of celebration with the staff, team-mates and families. By now, Nicol had come to think his nonchalant walk back from the penalty spot had worked. In all the mayhem and excitement, everyone seemed to have forgotten he had missed his first kick. 'On the bus, Hansen sat behind me,' Nicol said. 'He put his hand on my shoulder. I thought he was going to tell me it was OK, we'd won the cup, after all, and console me. But Big Al said, "What the fuck was that? It was miles over!" You got away with nothing in this dressing room.'

'Steve was the only one who scored when we practised at Melwood,' Souness said. 'It was the opposite in the shoot-out.'

It was a big night that ranks high among the squad's drinking sessions.

'We went to a hotel up in the hills,' Johnston said. 'It turned into a giant sing-song. Ronnie Whelan wound me up to sing "Waltzing Matilda" and I belted it out.'

The entire group joined in. In victory, it was not important whether you had played or not. Everyone's contribution across the season was recognized and celebrated. 'It didn't matter who you were, how talented you were,' Dalglish said. 'Every one of the players treated each other with respect. We would not let anyone come between us.'

From the man who scored the winning goal to Bob Bolder, the substitute goalkeeper, Liverpool enjoyed the fruits of victory. 'It was a beautiful place in the hills,' Kennedy said. 'We were all together. The team spirit was superb. Everybody was part of it. People like Bob contributed even though he didn't play a game. He worked as hard for it as any of us and we appreciated it.'

This was the culmination of the year. All the beery bonding sessions and madcap days on the ale had created this special feeling that, added to brilliance on the pitch, produced a special alchemy. Even Johnston, who had felt the frustration gnawing at him all through the season, had always understood the importance of togetherness.

'Everybody secretly loved everyone else,' he said. 'Everybody liked each other. We were all culturally connected. We all wanted each other to look good. That was why we were a brilliant team.'

The captain believes the players he led were exceptional. 'I've been a manager,' Souness said. 'Sometimes you stand in a dressing room and think, "What the fuck am I going to get today?" Joe and Ronnie must never have felt like that. They knew what they were getting. It was a cute bunch of players. A special bunch.'

As the dawn broke over Rome's seven hills, Fagan and his boys enjoyed the moment. Smokin' Joe lounged by the pool with the

European Cup, looking as unperturbed as ever. 'It probably won't sink in until the middle of next week when I shout "whoopee" and punch the air,' he said. Everyone listening knew the whoopee moment would probably never arrive.

'Drinking and singing all night, about two hours' sleep and then back to the airport for the flight home,' Kennedy said. 'More ale and the open-top bus parade. What a night! What a day!'

Postscript

The reaction in Britain to Liverpool's feat was underwhelming. Outside the local media, who understood the scale of the achievement, many focused on what they saw as a drab game and bemoaned the lack of adventure rather than the extraordinary exploits in overturning Roma's advantage to win a treble. Only Frank McGhee, in the *Daily Mirror*, understood the magnitude of the victory. 'No English team will ever match what Liverpool achieved in the Olympic Stadium,' he wrote.

There was a disturbing story in the newspapers, too. Speculation that Souness would be leaving the club to sign for Sampdoria. There had been unofficial inquiries from the Genoa-based club as well as from Verona and Barcelona.

Rush was also in demand. The striker had to deny that Barcelona had made a £5.7 million offer for his services. Even at the greatest moment of triumph, the winds of change were blowing through Anfield.

None of this was discussed on the plane coming back. The players were too busy enjoying themselves. Waiting for them at Speke Airport were two open-topped buses, the League Championship trophy and the League Cup. Waiting along Queens Drive and in the city centre were an estimated 300,000 people to welcome them home. It was a magnificent culmination to an incredible year.

'I looked at all those faces cheering us and it was wonderful,' Johnston said. 'Me and Bruce were outsiders but we understood what it meant to be Scouse. You could see the joy on the streets.'

For Sammy Lee, it truly was a homecoming. 'I'd seen so many parades like this when I was a kid,' he said. 'You want to play for Liverpool and dream of scoring in front of the Kop but you never think you'll be up there on the top deck of the bus. When it happens, it's something else.'

Downstairs, hidden from prying eyes, was Fagan. Smokin' Joe never craved attention. Now, he spent the first hour of the drive into town having a drink with his staff, letting his players have a party on the top deck. The bus had arrived at the city centre before the players cajoled him up the stairs to take the plaudits of the crowd.

'Only when you look back do you realize how good, how special it was,' Nicol said. He was talking about more than the parade and the winning. He meant the mentality, the sense of purpose and the kinship that came from being involved with this special group of men. 'The attitude was clear,' he said. 'Win. When you do, enjoy it today. Start working again tomorrow.'

The veteran Neal understood he was part of something unique, too. From Wembley in August to Rome on the last day of May, the campaign had been a long and at times arduous slog, but the momentum had rarely stalled. 'I wrote to Joe and all the staff afterwards thanking them each individually,' the right back said. 'They motivated us through sixty-seven games that season. That is not easy. It was a magnificent feat.'

The season was not quite over. The team were back together the next day to fly to Swaziland, where two friendly matches against Tottenham Hotspur had been scheduled.

The timing might have seemed poor but it allowed the party atmosphere to continue. Once in Africa, Liverpool met their White Hart Lane counterparts and together the teams drank long and hard into the night.

Steve Perryman, the Tottenham captain, was impressed. 'We were big drinkers at Tottenham,' he said. 'But they were impressive. The night before the match, we were having a drink. In the early hours, I was the only one of our lot left. There were four or five of them still hammering it. Everyone had hangovers the next day. We could hardly run.'

Perryman grasped Liverpool's secret as they inflicted a 5–2 defeat on his side. 'They passed the ball so well,' he said. 'They didn't need to run. We were chasing the ball everywhere. You don't want to do that much running with a hangover. They hardly moved.'

Souness was ready to move. It became clear he was going to leave. The whispers about a transfer to Sampdoria were true. 'There had been rumours but no contact. In Swaziland I got a call from Peter Robinson to say they'd been in touch,' Souness said. The move was a surprise even for Dalglish. 'When did I know Charlie was going to leave?' his room-mate said. 'When he didn't get out of bed to play Tottenham in Swaziland.'

'I was too pissed to play in the first game,' Souness said. 'I wasn't around for the second one. I came back early.' His Liverpool career was over.

'You never stand still,' Dalglish said. 'In football, you're either going forward or you're going backward.'

The 1983–84 season officially ended on 9 June in Africa. The second game against Spurs finished in a 1–1 draw and, appropriately, Rush scored in the final minute. Now, the heroes of Rome could finally go on holiday or, in Souness's case, plan for a future away from Anfield.

The same day, Souness confirmed that he was looking to move to a new club. 'If they match my personal needs,' he said, 'I will sign with them.' Two days later, the man who had done so much to determine the direction of Liverpool's season signed for the Serie A club. This time his reception in Italy was more welcoming. More than 2,000 fans were there to greet the Scot. 'It's fantastic,' he said. 'I had never received such a welcome in England, not even when Liverpool won three cups in a single season.'

Back on Merseyside, George Sharp was recovering in hospital from the wounds he had sustained in Rome. He was visited by Fagan and Paisley. The patient told his visitors that the sale of Souness had not helped his recuperation. The men from the Bootroom shrugged. Their former captain's legs were going, they said. At thirty-one, he was past his best and £650,000 was good value. It made Sharp wonder just exactly who was suffering the effects of medication.

Still, football moves on. The rest of the team returned to Speke. When the coach from the airport reached Anfield, the squad disembarked to go their separate ways. Ronnie Moran stood by the vehicle's door watching his 'big-headed bastards' make for their cars. He called out after them as they walked away, a combination of threat and relish infusing his voice. 'He was smiling and rubbing his hands together,' Kennedy said. '"Twenty-six days," he was saying. "Twenty-six days. Then you're back in pre-season training. Do what you like until then, but in twenty-six days you're mine." It was his way of saying forget the treble, forget the glory. We had to start again.'

The Bootroom had spoken: 1983–84 was over. The new season had just begun.

Appendix: Liverpool FC statistics, competitive matches, 1983–84

The Players

Name	Appearances	Subbed	Sub (played)	Sub (unused)	Goals
Bruce Grobbelaar	67	–	–	–	–
Alan Kennedy	67	–	–	–	2
Sammy Lee	67	1	–	–	3
Alan Hansen	67	–	–	–	1
Mark Lawrenson	66	1	–	–	–
Ian Rush	65	1	–	–	47
Phil Neal	64	1	–	–	3
Graeme Souness	61	2	–	–	12
Craig Johnston	52	4	3	10	4
Kenny Dalglish	51	6	1	–	12
Michael Robinson	42	7	3	3	12
Steve Nicol	38	3	6	11	7
Ronnie Whelan	34	–	5	6	9
David Hodgson	12	–	9	19	1
John Wark	9	–	–	–	2
Gary Gillespie	1	–	–	9	–
Phil Thompson	1	1	–	1	–

The Games

Division One

27/08/1983 Wolverhampton Wanderers 1 (Palmer 2 pen) Liverpool 1 (Rush 46)

Grobbelaar, Neal, Kennedy, Lawrenson, Johnston, Hansen, Dalglish, Lee, Rush, Robinson, Souness

Unused substitute: Nicol

31/08/1983 Norwich City 0 Liverpool 1 (Souness 29)
Grobbelaar, Neal, Kennedy, Lawrenson, Johnston, Hansen, Dalglish, Lee,
  Rush, Robinson, Souness
Unused substitute: Nicol

03/09/1983 Liverpool 1 (Rush 84) Nottingham Forest 0
Grobbelaar, Neal, Kennedy, Lawrenson, Johnston, Hansen, Dalglish, Lee,
  Rush, Robinson (Hodgson 79), Souness

06/09/1983 Liverpool 1 (Rush 60) Southampton 1 (Mills 84)
Grobbelaar, Neal, Kennedy, Lawrenson, Johnston, Hansen, Dalglish, Lee,
  Rush, Robinson, Souness
Unused substitute: Hodgson

10/09/1983 Arsenal 0 Liverpool 2 (Johnston 17, Dalglish 67)
Grobbelaar, Neal, Kennedy, Lawrenson, Johnston, Hansen, Dalglish, Lee,
  Rush, Robinson, Souness
Unused substitute: Nicol

17/09/1983 Liverpool 2 (Dalglish 73, Rush 79) Aston Villa 1 (Gibson 85)
Grobbelaar, Neal, Kennedy, Lawrenson, Johnston, Hansen, Dalglish, Lee,
  Rush, Robinson, Souness
Unused substitute: Hodgson

24/09/1983 Manchester Utd 1 (Stapleton 52) Liverpool 0
Grobbelaar, Neal (Nicol 78), Kennedy, Lawrenson, Johnston, Hansen,
  Dalglish, Lee, Rush, Robinson, Souness

01/10/1983 Liverpool 0 Sunderland 1 (Rowell 29 pen)
Grobbelaar, Nicol, Kennedy, Lawrenson, Johnston, Hansen, Dalglish,
  Lee, Rush, Robinson, Souness
Unused substitute: Hodgson

15/10/1983 West Ham Utd 1 (Devonshire 86) Liverpool 3 (Robinson 15, 24, 74)
Grobbelaar, Neal, Kennedy, Lawrenson, Johnston (sent off 64), Hansen,
  Dalglish, Lee, Rush (Hodgson 57), Robinson, Souness

22/10/1983 Queens Park Rangers 0 Liverpool 1 (Nicol 83)

Grobbelaar, Neal, Kennedy, Lawrenson, Johnston (Nicol 69), Hansen, Dalglish, Lee, Rush, Robinson, Souness

29/10/1983 Liverpool 6 (Rush 2, 5, 36, 55, 88, Dalglish 38) Luton Town 0

Grobbelaar, Neal, Kennedy, Lawrenson, Nicol, Hansen, Dalglish, Lee, Rush, Robinson, Souness

Unused substitute: Hodgson

06/11/1983 Liverpool 3 (Rush 16, Robinson 60, Nicol 85) Everton 0

Grobbelaar, Neal, Kennedy, Lawrenson, Nicol, Hansen, Dalglish, Lee, Rush, Robinson, Souness

Unused substitute: Johnston

12/11/1983 Tottenham Hotspur 2 (Archibald 24, Hoddle 72 pen) Liverpool 2 (Robinson 6, Rush 65)

Grobbelaar, Neal, Kennedy, Lawrenson, Nicol, Hansen, Dalglish, Lee, Rush, Robinson, Souness

Unused substitute: Hodgson

19/11/1983 Liverpool 1 (Rush 67) Stoke City 0

Grobbelaar, Neal, Kennedy, Lawrenson, Nicol, Hansen, Dalglish, Lee, Rush, Robinson, Souness

Unused substitute: Whelan

26/11/1983 Ipswich Town 1 (Wark 60) Liverpool 1 (Dalglish 62)

Grobbelaar, Neal, Kennedy, Lawrenson, Nicol, Hansen, Dalglish, Lee, Rush, Whelan, Souness

Unused substitute: Hodgson

03/12/1983 Liverpool 1 (Rush 86) Birmingham City 0

Grobbelaar, Neal, Kennedy, Lawrenson, Nicol, Hansen, Johnston, Lee, Rush, Robinson (Whelan 48), Souness

10/12/1983 Coventry City 4 (Platnauer 1, Gibson 19, 44, 84) Liverpool 0
Grobbelaar, Neal, Kennedy, Lawrenson, Nicol, Hansen, Dalglish, Lee,
   Rush, Whelan, Souness
Unused substitute: Johnston

17/12/1983 Liverpool 5 (Nicol 12, Souness 22 pen, 83, Hunt og 35, Rush 50)
   Notts County 0
Grobbelaar, Neal, Kennedy, Lawrenson, Nicol, Hansen, Dalglish, Lee,
   Rush, Johnston, Souness
Unused substitute: Hodgson

26/12/1983 West Bromwich Albion 1 (Morley 61) Liverpool 2 (Nicol 16,
   Souness 62)
Grobbelaar, Neal, Kennedy, Lawrenson, Nicol, Hansen, Dalglish, Lee,
   Rush, Johnston, Souness
Unused substitute: Hodgson

27/12/1983 Liverpool 2 (Lee 74, Rush 83) Leicester City 2 (Smith 7, Banks
   70)
Grobbelaar, Neal, Kennedy, Lawrenson, Nicol, Hansen, Dalglish, Lee,
   Rush, Johnston (Hodgson 62), Souness

31/12/1983 Nottingham Forest 0 Liverpool 1 (Rush 28)
Grobbelaar, Neal, Kennedy, Lawrenson, Nicol, Hansen, Dalglish (Whelan
   87), Lee, Rush, Johnston, Souness

02/01/1984 Liverpool 1 (Johnston 32) Manchester Utd 1 (Whiteside 89)
Grobbelaar, Neal, Kennedy, Lawrenson, Nicol, Hansen, Dalglish
   (Hodgson 48), Lee, Rush, Johnston, Souness

14/01/1984 Liverpool 0 Wolverhampton Wanderers 1 (Mardenborough 8)
Grobbelaar, Neal, Kennedy, Lawrenson, Nicol (Whelan 76), Hansen,
   Robinson, Lee, Rush, Johnston, Souness

20/01/1984 Aston Villa 1 (Mortimer 15) Liverpool 3 Rush (46, 70, 80)
Grobbelaar, Neal, Kennedy, Lawrenson, Nicol, Hansen, Robinson, Lee,
  Rush, Johnston, Souness
Unused substitute: Whelan

01/02/1984 Liverpool 3 (Rush 10, Nicol 41, Whelan 45) Watford 0
Grobbelaar, Neal, Kennedy, Lawrenson, Nicol, Hansen, Robinson, Lee,
  Rush, Johnston, Whelan
Unused substitute: Hodgson

04/02/1984 Sunderland 0 Liverpool 0
Grobbelaar, Neal, Kennedy, Lawrenson, Nicol, Hansen, Robinson, Lee,
  Rush, Johnston, Whelan
Unused substitute: McGregor

11/02/1984 Liverpool 2 (Kennedy 12, Neal 78) Arsenal 1 (Rix 45)
Grobbelaar, Neal, Kennedy, Lawrenson, Nicol, Hansen, Robinson, Lee,
  Rush, Johnston, Whelan
Unused substitute: Hodgson

18/02/1984 Luton Town 0 Liverpool 0
Grobbelaar, Neal, Kennedy, Lawrenson, Whelan, Hansen, Hodgson, Lee,
  Rush, Johnston, Souness
Unused substitute: Nicol

25/02/1984 Liverpool 2 (Robinson 55, Rush 80) Queens Park Rangers 0
Grobbelaar, Neal, Kennedy, Lawrenson, Whelan, Hansen, Robinson, Lee,
  Rush, Johnston, Souness
Unused substitute: Nicol

03/03/1984 Everton 1 (Harper 84) Liverpool 1 (Rush 17)
Grobbelaar, Neal, Kennedy, Lawrenson, Whelan, Hansen, Robinson, Lee
  (Nicol 19), Rush, Johnston, Souness

10/03/1984 Liverpool 3 (Dalglish 41, Whelan 43, Lee 88) Tottenham
Hotspur 1 (Stevens 2)

Grobbelaar, Neal, Kennedy, Lawrenson, Whelan, Hansen, Dalglish, Lee,
Robinson, Johnston, Souness

Unused substitute: Hodgson

16/03/1984 Southampton 2 (Wallace 44, 85) Liverpool 0

Grobbelaar, Neal, Kennedy, Lawrenson, Whelan, Hansen, Dalglish, Lee,
Rush, Johnston, Nicol (Robinson 53)

31/03/1984 Watford 0 Liverpool 2 (Wark 58, Rush 80)

Grobbelaar, Neal, Kennedy, Lawrenson, Whelan, Hansen, Dalglish, Lee,
Rush, Wark, Souness

Unused substitute: Johnston

07/04/1984 Liverpool 6 (Rush 6, 18, Dalglish 12, Whelan 28, Souness 62,
70) West Ham Utd 0

Grobbelaar, Neal, Kennedy, Lawrenson, Whelan, Hansen, Dalglish, Lee,
Rush, Wark, Souness

Unused substitute: Johnston

14/04/1984 Stoke City 2 (Painter 21, Russell 51) Liverpool 0

Grobbelaar, Neal, Kennedy, Lawrenson, Whelan, Hansen, Dalglish
(Johnston 72), Lee, Rush, Wark, Souness

18/04/1984 Leicester City 3 (Peake 30, Lynex 44, Lineker 75) Liverpool 3
(Whelan 14, Rush 59, Wark 81)

Grobbelaar, Neal, Kennedy, Lawrenson, Whelan, Hansen, Dalglish, Lee,
Rush, Wark, Souness

Unused substitute: Johnston

21/04/1984 Liverpool 3 (McNaught og 20, Souness 25, Dalglish 29) West
Bromwich Albion 0

Grobbelaar, Neal, Kennedy, Lawrenson, Whelan, Hansen, Dalglish, Lee, Rush, Wark, Souness
Unused substitute: Johnston

28/04/1984 Liverpool 2 (Kennedy 31, Rush 37) Ipswich Town 2 (Gates 19, 57)
Grobbelaar, Neal, Kennedy, Lawrenson (Nicol 75), Whelan, Hansen, Dalglish, Lee, Rush, Wark, Johnston

05/05/1984 Birmingham City 0 Liverpool 0
Grobbelaar, Neal, Kennedy, Lawrenson, Whelan, Hansen, Dalglish, Lee, Rush, Wark, Souness
Unused substitute: Johnston

07/05/1984 Liverpool 5 (Rush 43, 45, 57 pen, 81, Hansen 71) Coventry City 0
Grobbelaar, Neal, Kennedy, Lawrenson, Whelan, Hansen, Dalglish, Lee, Rush, Wark, Souness
Unused substitute: Johnston

12/05/1984 Notts County 0 Liverpool 0
Grobbelaar, Neal, Kennedy, Lawrenson, Whelan, Hansen, Dalglish, Lee, Rush, Wark, Souness
Unused substitute: Johnston

15/05/1984 Liverpool 1 (Rush 30) Norwich City 1 (Devine 23)
Grobbelaar, Neal, Kennedy, Lawrenson, Whelan, Hansen, Dalglish, Lee, Rush, Johnston, Souness
Unused substitute: Nicol

Charity Shield

20/08/1983 Liverpool 0 Manchester Utd 2 (Robson 23, 60)
Grobbelaar, Neal, Kennedy, Lawrenson, Thompson (Johnston 61), Hansen, Dalglish, Lee, Rush, Robinson (Hodgson 61), Souness*
*Two substitutes allowed

FA Cup

06/01/1984 3rd round Liverpool 4 (Robinson 8, Rush 28, 86, Johnston 63)
   Newcastle Utd 0
Grobbelaar, Neal, Kennedy, Lawrenson, Nicol, Hansen, Robinson, Lee,
   Rush, Johnston, Souness
Unused substitute: Whelan

29/01/1984 4th round Brighton and Hove Albion 2 (Ryan 57, Connor 58)
   Liverpool 0
Grobbelaar, Neal, Kennedy, Lawrenson, Nicol, Hansen, Robinson, Lee,
   Rush, Johnston, Souness (Whelan 34)

League Cup

05/10/1983 2nd round, 1st leg Brentford 1 (Roberts 24) Liverpool 4 (Rush
   23, 70, Robinson 51, Souness 57)
Grobbelaar, Nicol, Kennedy, Lawrenson, Johnston, Hansen, Dalglish,
   Lee, Rush, Robinson, Souness
Unused substitute: Hodgson

25/10/1983 2nd round, 2nd leg Liverpool 4 (Souness 38 pen, Hodgson 65,
   Dalglish 69, Robinson 87) Brentford 0
Grobbelaar, Neal, Kennedy, Lawrenson, Johnston, Hansen, Dalglish, Lee,
   Hodgson, Robinson, Souness
Unused substitute: Nicol

08/11/1983 3rd round Fulham 1 (Lock 63 pen) Liverpool 1 (Rush 64)
Grobbelaar, Neal, Kennedy, Lawrenson, Nicol, Hansen, Dalglish, Lee,
   Rush, Robinson, Souness
Unused substitute: Johnston

22/11/1983 3rd round replay (after extra time) Liverpool 1 (Dalglish 50)
   Fulham 1 (Lock 85 pen)

Grobbelaar, Neal, Kennedy, Lawrenson, Nicol, Hansen, Dalglish, Lee, Rush, Robinson (Johnston 55), Souness

29/11/1983 3rd round 2nd replay (after extra time) Fulham 0 Liverpool 1 (Souness 116)

Grobbelaar, Neal, Kennedy, Lawrenson, Nicol (Whelan 91), Hansen, Johnston, Lee, Rush, Robinson, Souness

20/12/1983 4th round Birmingham City 1 (Harford 75) Liverpool 1 (Souness 26)

Grobbelaar, Neal, Kennedy, Lawrenson, Nicol, Hansen, Dalglish, Lee, Rush, Johnston, Souness

Unused substitute: Hodgson

22/12/1983 4th round replay Liverpool 3 (Nicol 39, Rush 53, 74 pen) Birmingham City 0

Grobbelaar, Neal, Kennedy, Lawrenson, Nicol, Hansen, Dalglish (Hodgson 53), Lee, Rush, Johnston, Souness

17/01/1984 5th round Sheffield Wednesday 2 (Megson 30, Lawrenson og 52) Liverpool 2 (Nicol 20, Neal 60 pen)

Grobbelaar, Neal, Kennedy, Lawrenson, Nicol, Hansen, Robinson, Lee, Rush, Johnston, Souness

Unused substitute: Whelan

25/01/1984 5th round replay Liverpool 3 (Rush 37, 85, Robinson 71) Sheffield Wednesday 0

Grobbelaar, Neal, Kennedy, Lawrenson, Nicol, Hansen, Robinson, Lee, Rush, Johnston, Souness

Unused substitute: Whelan

07/02/1984 Semi-final, 1st leg Liverpool 2 (Whelan 14, 73) Walsall 2 (Neal og 42, Summerfield 74)

Grobbelaar, Neal, Kennedy, Gillespie, Nicol, Hansen, Robinson (Hodgson 61), Lee, Rush, Johnston, Whelan

Appendix

14/02/1984 Semi-final, 2nd leg Walsall 0 Liverpool 2 (Rush 13, Whelan 49)
Grobbelaar, Neal, Kennedy, Lawrenson, Whelan, Hansen, Hodgson, Lee, Rush, Johnston, Souness
Unused substitute: Nicol

25/03/1984 Final, Wembley Stadium (after extra time) Liverpool 0 Everton 0
Grobbelaar, Neal, Kennedy, Lawrenson, Whelan, Hansen, Dalglish, Lee, Rush, Johnston (Robinson 91), Souness

28/03/1984 Final replay, Maine Road Liverpool 1 (Souness 21) Everton 0
Grobbelaar, Neal, Kennedy, Lawrenson, Whelan, Hansen, Dalglish, Lee, Rush, Johnston, Souness
Unused substitute: Robinson

European Cup

14/09/1983 1st round, 1st leg Odense 0 Liverpool 1 (Dalglish 14)
Grobbelaar, Neal, Kennedy, Lawrenson, Johnston, Hansen, Dalglish, Lee, Rush, Robinson, Souness
Unused substitutes: Bolder, Gillespie, McGregor, Hodgson, West

28/09/1983 1st round, 2nd leg Liverpool 5 (Robinson 14, 72, Dalglish 32, 40, Clausen og 65) Odense 0
Grobbelaar, Nicol, Kennedy, Lawrenson, Johnston, Hansen, Dalglish, Lee, Rush, Robinson, Souness (Hodgson 85)
Unused substitutes: Bolder, Gillespie, McGregor, West

19/10/1983 2nd round, 1st leg Liverpool 0 Athletic Bilbao 0
Grobbelaar, Neal, Kennedy, Lawrenson, Johnston, Hansen, Dalglish, Lee, Rush, Robinson, Souness
Unused substitutes: Bolder, Gillespie, McGregor, Nicol, Hodgson

02/11/1983 2nd round, 2nd leg Athletic Bilbao 0 Liverpool 1 (Rush 66)
Grobbelaar, Neal, Kennedy, Lawrenson, Nicol, Hansen, Dalglish, Lee, Rush, Robinson (Hodgson 83), Souness
Unused substitutes: Bolder, Gillespie, Johnston, Whelan

07/03/1984 Quarter-final, 1st leg Liverpool 1 (Rush 66) Benfica 0
Grobbelaar, Neal, Lawrenson, Hansen, Kennedy, Whelan, Robinson (Dalglish 46), Lee, Souness, Rush, Johnston
Unused substitutes: Bolder, Gillespie, Nicol, Hodgson

21/03/1984 Quarter-final, 2nd leg Benfica 1 (Nené 74) Liverpool 4 (Whelan 9, 87, Johnston 33, Rush 79)
Grobbelaar, Neal, Kennedy, Lawrenson, Whelan, Hansen, Dalglish, Lee, Rush, Johnston, Souness
Unused substitutes: Beglin, Bolder, Gillespie, McGregor, Robinson

11/04/1984 Semi-final, 1st leg Liverpool 1 (Lee 25) Dinamo Bucharest 0
Grobbelaar, Neal, Kennedy, Lawrenson, Whelan, Hansen, Dalglish, Lee, Rush, Johnston, Souness
Unused substitutes: Bolder, Nicol, Gillespie, Robinson, Hodgson

25/04/1984 Semi-final, 2nd leg Dinamo Bucharest 1 (Orac 39) Liverpool 2 (Rush 11, 84)
Grobbelaar, Neal, Kennedy, Lawrenson, Whelan, Hansen, Dalglish (Nicol 76), Lee, Rush, Johnston, Souness
Unused substitutes: Bolder, Gillespie, Thompson, Hodgson

30/05/1984 Final, Stadio Olimpico, Rome (after extra time) Liverpool 1 (Neal 14) Roma 1 (Pruzzo 44) Liverpool win 4–2 on penalties
Grobbelaar, Neal, Kennedy, Lawrenson, Whelan, Hansen, Dalglish (Robinson 95), Lee, Rush, Johnston (Nicol 73), Souness
Unused substitutes: Bolder, Gillespie, Hodgson
Penalties Nicol (miss 0–0); Di Bartolomei (goal 0–1); Neal (goal 1–1); Conti (miss 1–1); Souness (goal 2–1); Righetti (goal 2–2); Rush (goal 3–2); Graziani (miss 3–2); Kennedy (goal 4–2)

Essential Reading

Joe Fagan: Reluctant Champion by Andrew Fagan and Mark Platt, Aurum Press, 2011

Red Machine: Liverpool FC in the 1980s by Simon Hughes, Mainstream Publishing, 2013

Secret Diary of a Liverpool Scout by Simon Hughes, Trinity Mirror Sport Media, 2009

Three Sides of the Mersey: Oral History of Everton, Liverpool and Tranmere Rovers by Rogan Taylor and Andrew Ward, Robson Books, 1998

Acknowledgements

This book could not have happened without a number of people. Joel Rickett and Kevin Pocklington deserve most credit, Joel for his idea and Kevin for deciding I was the man for the job. Thanks to John Aizlewood for pointing Kevin in my direction. The players were magnificent in giving me time and insight. Talking to them gave me almost as much pleasure as watching them thirty years ago.

Finally, thanks to Alisa and Grace, who spent many Saturdays and holidays patiently putting family life on hold, allowing me to sit at a computer and write these words.

Index

He just wanted a decent book to read ...

Not too much to ask, is it? It was in 1935 when Allen Lane, Managing Director of Bodley Head Publishers, stood on a platform at Exeter railway station looking for something good to read on his journey back to London. His choice was limited to popular magazines and poor-quality paperbacks – the same choice faced every day by the vast majority of readers, few of whom could afford hardbacks. Lane's disappointment and subsequent anger at the range of books generally available led him to found a company – and change the world.

'We believed in the existence in this country of a vast reading public for intelligent books at a low price, and staked everything on it'
Sir Allen Lane, 1902–1970, founder of Penguin Books

The quality paperback had arrived – and not just in bookshops. Lane was adamant that his Penguins should appear in chain stores and tobacconists, and should cost no more than a packet of cigarettes.

Reading habits (and cigarette prices) have changed since 1935, but Penguin still believes in publishing the best books for everybody to enjoy. We still believe that good design costs no more than bad design, and we still believe that quality books published passionately and responsibly make the world a better place.

So wherever you see the little bird – whether it's on a piece of prize-winning literary fiction or a celebrity autobiography, political tour de force or historical masterpiece, a serial-killer thriller, reference book, world classic or a piece of pure escapism – you can bet that it represents the very best that the genre has to offer.

Whatever you like to read – trust Penguin.